Lives of Houses

Lives of Houses

Edited by

Kate Kennedy and Hermione Lee

PRINCETON UNIVERSITY PRESS

Princeton and Oxford

Copyright © 2020 by Kate Kennedy and Hermione Lee

Requests for permission to reproduce material from this work
should be sent to permissions@press.princeton.edu

Published by Princeton University Press
41 William Street, Princeton, New Jersey 08540
6 Oxford Street, Woodstock, Oxfordshire OX20 1TR

press.princeton.edu

All Rights Reserved

Library of Congress Control Number 2019955826

ISBN 978-0-691-19366-3
ISBN (e-book) 978-0-691-20194-8

British Library Cataloging-in-Publication Data is available

Editorial: Ben Tate and Charlie Allen
Production Editorial: Jill Harris
Text Design: Carmina Alvarez
Production: Jacqueline Poirier
Publicity: Jodi Price and Katie Lewis

Jacket art and design by Jason Anscomb / Rawshock Design

This book has been composed in Perpetua Std

Printed on acid-free paper. ∞

Printed and bound in Great Britain by Clays Ltd, Elcograf S.p.A.

1 3 5 7 9 10 8 6 4 2

This book is dedicated to the philanthropist

HARRY WEINREBE (1914–2000)

whose Dorset Foundation enabled the creation of the
Oxford Centre for Life-Writing at Wolfson College

Contents

Dream Houses

Creative Houses

House-Proud

Unhoused

The Afterlives of Houses

Illustrations

Preface

HERMIONE LEE

The writing of lives often involves writing about houses. Bringing a house to life through observation, familiarity, memory, or excavation can be a vital part of narrating the life of an individual, a family, or a group: life-writing as housework. A house can embody a person's childhood, the story of a marriage, an inherited way of life, or a national history. The constructing of a house can be the fulcrum of dreams, ambitions, illusions, and pretensions. How a house is lived in can tell you everything you need to know about people, whether it's the choice of wallpaper, the mess in the kitchen, the silence or shouting over meals, doors left open or closed, a fire burning in the hearth. The loss of a house can be a turning point that shapes the rest of a life.

Memoirs or autobiographies often start with the memory of a house. One of Virginia Woolf's first memories was of waking up as a child in the nursery of Talland House in Cornwall, her family's summer home. From that first memory she reconstructs, through colours and sounds and rhythms and fragments, the life they lived in that house, inseparable from her emotions about it. Henry James, setting out on his minutely recalled, fine-tuned, late-life autobiography, opens the book of his life with his faint, glimmering memory of his grandmother's house in Albany, and her reading in it, holding her book out at a distance by the light of a single candle. Eudora Welty, telling the story of what made her a writer, begins with her description of her family house, where, at the time of writing, she still lived, eighty years on: "In our house on North Congress Street in Jackson, Mississippi, where I was born, the oldest of three children, in 1909, we grew up to the striking of clocks." The life of a house is, also, a story of time.

Some life-stories—and these can be told in poems, plays, and novels, as well as autobiographies and biographies—are fixed inside one overpowering house, a house that can't be escaped from. Some make their story turn on the moment that a beloved old house has to be left. Some build their life-story on memories, which often include memories of houses, or they imagine the house of troubled inhabitants as a kind of haunted house. Hilary Mantel starts her autobiography, *Giving Up the Ghost*, on the day she and her husband have decided to sell their second home, a Norfolk cottage where her mother and her late stepfather often came to stay. Looking up, she sees the air move, and she knows it is her stepfather's ghost coming down the staircase. This does not "perturb" her. She often thinks in terms of haunted houses. Every house you live in involves other, abandoned choices, roads not taken, ghosts from the past. "All your houses are haunted by the person you might have been."

That tremor in the air, which reminds you that solid bricks-and-mortar can also be unstable, and that the lives of houses, like everything we know, must pass, is often built into the narratives of houses. Long after the family had left it, Woolf turned Talland House into fiction in *To the Lighthouse*, and imagines the moment when the long-deserted house might just tip over into becoming a ruin, as houses easily can:

> The house was left, the house was deserted. It was left like a shell on a sandhill to fill with dry salt grains now that life had left it. . . . One feather, and the house, sinking, falling, would have turned and pitched downwards to the depths of darkness.

Robert Frost's haunting poem "Directive" takes you on a journey looking for traces of a house that disappeared long ago and has fallen back into a remote, neglected New England landscape. It is now "a house that is no more a house." Yet it might be a place where, in your imagination, you could "make yourself at home."

"House" and "home" notoriously make awkward neighbours. Sometimes the words invite each other in; sometimes they won't give each other the time of day. Dictionaries and books of proverbs and old sayings tell you different things. We all know that "a house is not a home" (was it Benjamin Franklin who first coined this useful cliché?), and we are often told so, whether in hokey popular sayings ("It takes a heap of living to make a house a home") or lifestyle instructions in the pages of *House* (not *Home*) & *Garden*: "Wallpaper emits a warmth, a cheer, that makes a house a home." But definitions, of either word, tend to overlap as well as distinguish, as in the *Oxford English Dictionary*:

> *Home*: a person's house . . . fixed residence of a family or household . . . a private house or residence considered merely as a building. . . . The place where one lives or was brought up, with reference to the feelings of belonging, comfort, etc., associated with it. . . . A refuge, a sanctuary.

> *House*: a building for habitation, typically and historically one that is the ordinary residence of a family . . . a person's home.

Sometimes the words are set firmly apart. Wikipedia will tell you with confidence that "a house is just a physical structure, while a home is lived in (often by a family) and full of memories." Asked to sum up the distinction, one friend told me: "A house is a building; a home is a concept." And there are of course many usages of the word "house" that have nothing to do with "home." That would be house as lineage, as in the House of Atreus or the House of Windsor; house as institution, as in the House of Lords or an Oxford College; publishing house, playhouse, or House of God; house of infamy or shame, like a brothel or a gambling den, and god help you if that is also your home. But other usages run both words together. There are hundreds of magazines and websites for anything from fridges to beds or stoves called "House and Home." Being driven out of "house and home" doesn't distinguish, though Johnson tried to, in his *Dictionary*: "He harried me out of house and home": that is, "he robbed me of my goods and turned me out of doors."

But it's after that moment of being turned out of doors when the two words may turn on each other most fiercely. Many people don't have houses to live in, though they may live in households. Many people must live where they can, or are forced to live in places not of their choice, or have had to leave their houses, or have nowhere to live. King Lear's anguished cry in the storm on the heath must be heard:

> Poor naked wretches, wheresoe'er you are
> That bide the pelting of this pitiless storm,
> How shall your houseless heads and unfed sides,
> Your looped and windowed raggedness, defend you
> From seasons such as these?

Most of the contributors to this book use "house" and "home" interchangeably; some prefer "household"; one, writing about moving house, asks how a new house is to be made a home. But the distinction between "house" and "home" is most noticeable in the essays here about homelessness. Having a "home" and being "unhoused" are in sharp contrast here.

~⁓

This collection originally came out of a conference titled "The Lives of Houses," held in 2017 at the Oxford Centre for Life-Writing at Wolfson College, Oxford. The emphasis of the conference was on Western houses (British, Irish, American, European) and that has been mainly retained. The event brought together, as "life-writing" tends to do, a great many disciplines and professions, and that mixture is reflected in this book. It looks at the lives of houses from the point of view of archaeologists, museum curators, fiction writers, poets, illustrators, biographers, autobiographers, historians, and literary critics. It roams around the lives of houses of writers, politicians, composers, collectors, artists—men and women who have shaped and recorded the history of their houses through their own work—and the unknown and obscure. It goes far back in time and travels to vanished or much-altered houses as well as still visitable houses. It tells the story of house-moves, of houses lost and found, of the traces of houses and of their contents.[1]

Lives of Houses is interdisciplinary, pluralist, eclectic, and open-ended. It asks and provokes questions, rather than coming to conclusions, about the relationship between houses and their inhabitants and inheritors. It is arranged with an underlying narrative, beginning with quests for houses (some left, some lost, some buried in time) and ending with their reconstruction or re-finding or becoming public sites. In between it explores the family life that goes on in houses, the dreams and fantasies and hopes that attach to them, the creative life that goes on within them, the way they reflect aspirations, social gradations, and pretensions, and, by contrast, the lives of those who fear, or miss, or reject life lived in a house. Overlapping questions run through all the pieces in the collection. What kind of life choices does the making of a house reveal? What does it feel like to long for a lost house, to have to move house unwillingly, to be unhoused, or to be afraid of living under a roof? What presence do the ghosts of vanished houses play in our lives? What is the cost of keeping up appearances or living in a house beyond one's means? How does the personality of the inhabitants shape, or become shaped by, the house they live in? The book looks, too, at tourism, house visiting, and the relationship between biography and houses. Why do we love to visit the houses of the famous, and what do we get from those visits? How should houses best be preserved, and what is the relation between a living house and its afterlife as a museum? What are the financial and political demands at work when a house is maintained by organisations such as the National Trust, or by private owners and inheritors? *Lives of Houses* opens doors onto what went on between the walls of a house, what secrets a house might contain, how it has been remembered and written about, and what remains of it, in the real world, and in the mind's eye.

Houses Lost
and Found

1
Moving House

ALEXANDRA HARRIS

I sit me in my corner chair / That seems to feel
itself from home.
—John Clare, "The Flitting"

The clock ticks on Hardy's mantelpiece; Woolf's reading chair is next to
the fire; Erasmus Darwin's geological specimens are laid out under the
window at Lichfield. House museums go to great lengths to make things
look settled and accustomed. There are curtains at the windows and
shades on the lamps, and no reason to question the position of the bedroom chest that fits, just so, in the alcove. When I think of the homes
of friends and family, too, they come to mind fully formed; it's obvious
where the coats live and the hallway has never been other than green.

Or at least so it was until I moved house and found myself shaken in
previously unsuspected ways by the strangeness of objects pulled out
from their habitual moorings, the physical effort and logistical cunning
required to collapse rooms into taped cartons and reassemble them in
new combinations, and most of all the imaginative effort, the sheer invention, involved in making up the life of a new home. I realised then
that feelings about homeliness are liable to assert themselves most acutely
when the furniture is upended and the books stacked in crates. I wanted
to ask some of those who have thought most intensely about belonging,
and belongings, how they responded to these episodes of upheaval when
the still point goes spinning.

"O what a dislocation of comfort is contained in that word moving," Charles Lamb lamented: not only the lamps but comfort itself turned out from its usual home.[1] William Cowper could get nothing written: "The confusion which attends a transmigration of this kind is infinite, and has a terrible effect in deranging the intellects."[2] As I packed and sorted, phantasmagorias of combined removing seemed to appear: long caravans of borrowed waggons and laden people, tallboys with the drawers out, half-wrapped mirrors, and confused pets. I started to see the lampshades of the past dislodged and waiting vulnerably on top of boxes into which they would not fit. I began to be aware of movers of many kinds and from several centuries, each making their way from one life to another with a different combination of anxiety, exhaustion, loss, and hope.[3]

The processions I conjured were in reality a common annual or bi-annual spectacle across Europe and America from the Middle Ages to the early twentieth century. Leases ran from one quarter-day to another and expired in tandem, so that almost every tenant intending to move house that season would do so at the same time. The spring quarter-day was generally the one for moving: Whitsun in Scotland (25 May) and Lady Day in England (25 March or, after the calendar reforms of 1752, "Old Lady Day": 6 April). There might be another round of removals at Michaelmas, and Martinmas (11 November) was the traditional date in large parts of continental Europe, but in Britain the spring Flitting Days were firmly established.

The timing suited the agricultural year, with the winter crops gathered and the ground open again for sowing. But it only suited at a stretch: outgoing tenants wrangled over rights to a "flitting crop," to be squeezed in before departure, and new arrivals were hard-pressed in April, and certainly in May, to plant in time for summer harvest. Farmers asked themselves each year whether they would sow again in the same ground, or try a change. These decisions were generally made at Candlemas (2 February), the time when deals were done at hiring fairs and land agents knocked at doors to ask tenants whether they intended to "sit or flit." By association with holy days, moving acquired forms of transferred liturgical significance. Candlemas, the feast of the Purification, came with questions about how to start afresh, whether to clear out, to white-wash the walls for a newcomer and take on newly washed walls of one's own. Robert Chambers described in his *Book of Days* the practice in nineteenth-century Scotland: "The two or three days following upon the Purification become distinguished by a feathering of the streets with boards projected from the windows, intimating A House to Let. Then comes on a most lively excitement for individuals propos-ing to remove."[4]

Moving was part of the shared annual cycle. The Flemish artist Abel Grimmer (compared with Brueghel the Younger in his time but not now much remembered) painted a series of season pictures in 1599 and chose to fill his *Spring* panel with a combination of garden planting and house-moving. A horse-and-cart in the foreground is so laden with belong-ings that it needs a push.[5] The iconography makes clear that the sowing season was also the time of new beginnings in new homes.

The practice of regular, and synchronised, moving became more and more common amongst farming families in the eighteenth and nineteenth centuries. Thomas Hardy in *Tess of the D'Urbervilles* de-scribed the annual moment of flux: "At length it was the eve of Old Lady-Day, and the agricultural world was in a fever of mobility." Exo-dus recurred, each family's cart filled with anticipation of something better: "The Egypt of one family was the Land of Promise to the family who saw it from a distance, till by residence there it became in turn their Egypt also; and so they changed and changed."[6] Flitting Day was still such a fever of mobility in Edwardian rural England that the traffic ground to a halt. Ford Madox Ford observed the "tall waggons with tarpaulins" to be seen in the lanes of Kent and Sussex each spring. They were liable to become stuck in the "elbow-like angles of sunken lanes," with long queues building up behind them.[7] An inveterate mover himself, Ford sensed excitement in these covered waggons that lumbered, however slowly, towards new prospects. He knew the hard and hopeful work that would await them in the planting season; sev-eral times in his life he joined the Lady Day migrations and took on the ancient challenge of rapidly digging his new ground in time for summer crops.

Town and city moving days were another kind of spectacle. In New York, through the eighteenth and nineteenth centuries, 1 May was notorious for its chaos of furniture in the streets. Businesses stopped trading for the day to allow the great reshuffling of people and their things. The furniture itself, from those times when even prosperous families were more likely to rent than to own property, seems to speak of moving. Rugs could be rolled and trimmed (no one thought of fitted carpet). The tables of choice were gate-legged, or snap-topped, or—like the ubiquitous Pembroke tables—ready to lower their flaps for transit. The most sought-after moving men were carpenters, who would alter cabinetry to fit through doors and repair it again once in place. Often, too, they had furniture ready to hire out by the year: tables to be leased like the house.[8] Much more so than it is today, moving on was an expectation from the start. And more than today, when moving is the private fate of individual households, there was about it the sense of a common enterprise.

Tables may fold and rugs may roll, but moving has always been a heavy-laden business. "Flitting," the Scottish and northern English term (used across Britain in the nineteenth century and well into the twentieth), sounds so quick and weightless. Bats flit in the dark: blink and you miss them. A mercurial hostess might flit about her party; Bathsheba Everdene's heart flits with excitement. Was a flitting between houses ever so light as its name? In some circumstances it was best to depart unnoticed; "moonlight flitting" was long synonymous with the rapid departure of those in debt or disgrace. Victorian cartoonists had cruel fun with images of families trying to melt into the night. The children are always lugging things too large for them while dogs and chickens circle at their feet. No degree of light-footedness can silence the clunk and clatter of removal. Though the term "flitting" has come down to us from the Old Norse "fleet" and "float," so that one thinks fancifully of Viking ships moving fast and soundlessly through water, domestic removals are more likely to evoke sensations of sinking.

Vincenzo Campi's *San Martino* (or *Trasloco*) is one of a series of large paintings showing scenes from rural life in the 1580s.[9] St. Martin's Day was Moving Day in Italy (in wine-growing areas, especially, it made sense that removals should follow the grape harvest), and here is a farming family all packed to go. The picture suggests horror if not outright disaster. A high wind is whipping through trees that struggle against a thunderously dark sky. The open door of the house is a black depth from which the whole paraphernalia of a household have spilled into the lurid light of the stormy day. Women sort linens and carry trays while a horse is being loaded in the courtyard, and the immediately striking fact is that we have a close-up view of the horse's backside. This is the opposite of an idealised composition; its very subject is life discomposed.

Campi was one of the first painters of still life, inventing the new genre as he went, packing his canvases with the whole contents of kitchens and fishmongers' stalls, painting teeming material worlds with all the greedy urgency that came of his realisation that tangible daily things—these infinitely various fishy, fleshy, rotting, wooden, ceramic, dirty, shiny, ordinary, and utterly compelling things—might now be the subjects of art. His attention was not drawn to the beauty of a single peach or the glint of a well-cleaned copper pan but to unsuitable combinations and upendings. At the birth of still life, then, he painted the turmoil of moving. *Trasloco* sets up a game in which we try to identify the objects piled onto the horse and stacked on the ground. One by one they become clear—colander, sieve, andirons, basket, rush-stool, wooden ladles—and there's a touching specificity about each. But as a whole they are hideous. It's hard to believe that this chaos of sticks and legs and levers might be the ingredients of orderly life.

Campi was interested in the coarse rusticity of his subjects; he was painting for his time and place, sharing with his patrons his laughing disgust at the peasants as well as his rapt attention. But he caught and held ideas that concern movers everywhere. He saw that private possessions come into the outdoor light where they were never meant to be seen. He saw the absurd, comical, ugly conglomerations that are also intimate and eloquent. He saw, most simply and enduringly, that moving involves the making strange of familiar things in ways that are both disturbing and charged with possibility. The contraptions piled onto the horse might have been put there by Duchamp. In fact Duchamp hung a bottle rack from a gallery ceiling in 1914, which was only slightly more alarming. Displaced from its work of drying bottles, it looked a gruesome thing, its prongs designed for some uncertain form of torture. In 1920 Man Ray wrapped up a sewing machine in a blanket and tied it with string. The resulting package, called *L'Enigme d'Isidore Ducasse*, was both sinister and banal. It sat there quiescent; why then wouldn't one want to touch it? It was threatening: if you didn't know the contents the imagination would supply horrible possibilities; if you did, the machine seemed to loom with its glistening needle poised. It was also pitiful: the string confined the sewing machine in its muffling blanket like a victim gagged and bound.

The house-mover is forced to confront the peculiar liveliness and deadness of objects. "It belongs to furniture of all kinds," remarked Cowper, "however convenient it may be in its place, to be a nuisance out of it."[10] It will trip you up or crowd you out. Some things, released from their usual places and functions, look grotesquely misshapen or unwieldy; others settle obligingly into new corners. Some harbour associations in every scratch; others seem barely to know you. Packing requires the appraisal of each and every item: should it be kept, what can it be grouped with, where will it end up? Taxonomy is the mover's special branch of learning, and lists become an art form. Some writers on the process have relished the mounting gallimaufry. Walter Scott enjoyed reporting (if not supervising) the progress of his belongings across the Tweed from Ashestiel to Abbotsford in 1812. "Old swords, bows, targets and lances, made a very conspicuous show," he told his friends, trundled along in twenty-five carts, accompanied by dogs, pigs, ponies, a herd of cattle, and "a family of turkeys accommodated within the helmet of some *preux* chevalier of ancient border fame."[11] But even Scott, with his taste for bizarre collections, said his flitting "baffled all description."[12]

Charles Lamb, who loved the familiar presence of his books and objects, looked in horror at those same things strangely massed and tumbled. Worst of all was the "heap of little nasty things" left over once the main items were in the cart: "worn-out brushes, gallipots, vials." And then for ages afterwards he couldn't find what he wanted. "You must comb your hair with your fingers, wash your hands without soap."[13] In his later life it was his maid Becky who took charge of the operation ("O the moving Becky!") so that when Lamb eventually sat down in his new room in Enfield at Michaelmas 1827 it was as if he had been transported in the night, like Gulliver in his flying house. But he knew what dust and labour went on beneath that magic. Even the process of relocating his beloved library had roused a sense of shame. "I am a drayhorse if I was not asham'd of the indigested dirty lumber as I toppled 'em [the books] out of the cart."[14] These books are thrown up in a bout of nausea, or have they not yet been swallowed down?

Lamb's language is extraordinarily raw and bodily. "'Twas with some pain we were evuls'd from Colebrook," he continued in this same letter to his friend Thomas Hood, straining for language adequate to the experience and alighting on that word "evuls'd," of which this is the first recorded use. It's as if "convulsed" and "ejected" have been smashed together, perhaps with "pulverized" as well. Evulsed was already extant as an adjective, from *vellere*, to pluck. A chicken might be evulsed: left naked, pink, and goose-bumped. Lamb seems to have felt himself left equally bare. "You may find some of our flesh sticking to the doorposts," he went on, suggesting an attachment to the old house so bodily and strong that to sever it was a kind of flaying.[15]

⁓

John Clare walked with his family to a new home in Northborough on the last day of April 1832. Three hundred books and a large bookcase had gone on ahead; now Clare, his wife, and six children, one a baby, set out from their cramped cottage in Helpston towards a larger, brighter house about three miles away that had just been refurbished for them. There were three bedrooms, a large kitchen, and most importantly a plot of land on which they could be at least partly self-sufficient. Clare had been disablingly ill all through the last year at Helpston, seeing little ahead of him except "stupid and stunning apathy, or lingering madness and death."[16] The unpaid rent and doctor's bills were "millstones" pulling him down.

FIGURE 1.1. A moonlight flitting illustrated by George Cruikshank in *The Comic Almanac*, 1836. (Credit: Spitalfields Life)

The move now offered a "promised land," a "sunny prospect" of solvency and independence: he could see that he must do it and do it well.[17]

None of which made the leaving of Helpston any easier. For months Clare had been trying to prepare himself, paying his respects to birds and plants and "favourite spots that have known me so long," working out his emotions in letters (some of which he could not bring himself to send). "The very molehills on the heath & the old trees in the hedges," he thought, "seem bidding me farewell."[18] Like many movers who have witnessed great changes in their habitual surroundings, he reminded himself that Helpston itself had changed irreparably. Even at home he had felt an exile since the enclosure of lands and the felling of trees eradicated some of his most loved corners. "All the associations are going before me," he wrote sadly when a favourite elm was felled and a plum tree blew down: he was losing the old place whether he moved or not.[19]

He moved. By the summer, after several months at Northborough, he was still missing terribly his familiar spots. He needed to imagine his way back to them and in his poem "Remembrances" he inhabited again the country of his boyhood. He wrote the names of fields and paths

FIGURE 1.2. *Cowper's Summer House.* (From *The Rural Walks of Cowper*, James Storer, 1825. Copyright © the British Library Board 11643.k.1)

as if his sanity might depend upon it, and it may well have done. He conjured the sounds of boys playing on the grassy bank of Langley Bush and skipping on the "roly-poly up and downs of pleasant Swordy Well," but the banks were silent and flattened now, and "words are poor receipts for what time hath stole away." He sorrowed for the moles, "little homeless miners," feeling that he shared their fate.[20]

Yet he had a house: a good one. He reproached himself for attachments that felt childish and worked with all the power of his mature mind to establish a homely relationship between himself and his new place. He planted energetically in the garden; he studied the flowers and Northborough village trees as another person might go round to meet the neighbours. Out on the fens, he watched the snipe, that "lover of swamps," which made its nest in places that looked to Clare devoid of comfort. The snipe's home, he wrote, "teaches me / Right feelings to employ / That in the dreariest places peace will be / A dweller and a joy."[21] But that effort of "right feeling" involved an almost mystical concentration, a willed lifting of himself away from the love of particular things. What lay beneath was bafflement and mourning. "Ive left my own old home of homes," he wrote, "Green fields and every pleasant place / The summer like a stranger comes / I pause and hardly know her face." This was to be one of the great poems of dislocation: "The Flitting."[22]

He had been used to the particular expression of the seasons in fields close to home, but summer was not now to be found in certain clumps of hedgerow flowers and well-known patterns of heat and shade. Light, sounds, scale, colour—all were different. Nightingales sang in his new orchard, and he knew they should give him delight; why then did they sound so strange? "A nightingale is singing now / But like to me she seems at loss / For royce wood and its shielding bough." Clare himself was at a loss and heard loss in every voice. The house itself offered little sanctuary in these alien surroundings. To sit in a familiar seat, especially a corner chair with its associations of tucked containment, should have been some relief at least in a time of disturbance, but it was not so: "I sit me in my corner chair / That seems to feel itself from home."

In November 1786, William Cowper took his last look round Orchardside on moving day. He had lived there eighteen years and had written *The Task* there: a poem rich in appreciation for quiet contentment in a secluded home. Yet he had never liked the structure of the house, or its awkward, gloomy rooms, or its windows fronting onto Olney marketplace. It was his "old prison," he was "weary of every object," he had "long wished for a change." He had thought the house ugly when he first moved there and it was still ugly. All the same, he said farewell to it with a fondness that surprised him, even "something like a heartache." The scene "certainly in itself had nothing to engage affection." "But I recollected that I had once been happy there, and could not without tears in my eyes bid adieu to a place in which God had so often found me."[23]

For Cowper a home was, first and foremost, a home for God. Comfort was where God entered, and a place from which he was absent was a void, no matter what pleasant surroundings might be contrived in the arrangement of books and rugs. For Evangelical Christians of many kinds, the home was a place in which to be discovered; one must always be ready to be seen and known. Though the front door may be closed, the house must be conceived as always open, to be entered at any moment by the longed-for visitor. "Amazing Grace," one of the songs of praise written by Cowper and his friend John Newton for their *Olney Hymns*, sung out again and again the joy of that finding: "I was lost, but now am found."

For long stretches of his life in Olney, however, Cowper had believed himself abandoned. When God refused to come, Cowper held on as tight as he could to small domestic supports that might help him across the gulfs of emptiness. The presence of familiar items like cups and trays were to him the handrails of a narrow bridge or the bannisters of an agonisingly steep and long staircase. He knew that he was clutching ephemeral things: any Christian's house, like his body, is merely on temporary loan. Cowper would go into his garden, water the plants lovingly, and turn away saying, "This is not mine; 'tis a plaything lent me for the present; I must leave it soon."[24] Yet where many devout householders left their rooms plain and permitted little talk of these trifles, Cowper gave his utmost attention to his material surroundings. Their temporariness deepened his feeling for them.

This is partly what mattered so much to the late eighteenth-century and Victorian readers who responded to him as if he were a personal friend. He sang the sofa with all the conviction Virgil had reserved for singing "arms and the man," insisting that the sofa mattered. The set-piece celebrations of home life in *The Task* were purposely charming in their conversational ease, but layers of feeling were at work in them. If God were to visit the lonely soul of William Cowper, it would be amongst tables and chairs that in their very design seemed to speak of peaceful life. So he expressed his attachment to his fireside and writing desk, and the Turkish carpet that became an indoor lawn for his tame hares, while unashamedly hoping he might one day find a better house with less rot and brighter rooms. The move was in November (the lease taken from Michaelmas), but the new place felt "verdant" to him, like

FIGURE 1.3. Cowper's sofa. (Reproduced courtesy of the Trustees of the Cowper & Newton Museum)

a late spring in his middle age. He hardly dared believe that after deepest glooms the evening of his life might "open clear."[25]

A few weeks after leaving, Cowper went back. "Once since we left Olney I had occasion to call at our old dwelling, and never did I see so forlorn and woeful a spectacle." The emptiness he saw was the absence of God, as he told Newton. "The coldness of it, the dreariness and the dirt, made me think in no unapt resemblance of a soul that God has forsaken. While he dwelt in it and manifested himself there, he could create his own accommodations and give it occasionally the appearance of a palace, but the moment he withdraws and takes with him all the furniture and embellishment of his graces, it becomes what it was before he enter'd it, the habitation of vermin and the image of desolation."[26] Cowper was used to thinking of his own soul as one deserted by God; in an extraordinary turn here the old house became a self-portrait. The building before him was an external version of the desolate ruin he had often imagined to be deep within him. Might a soul be like a house,

FIGURE 1.4. The cottage in Helpston that Clare left behind. (Illustration: R. K. R. Thornton)

with echoing corridors and dank corners, and might a house look like one's soul? There was a note of terror, as often in Cowper, but his letter was one of praise—for a God who, where it pleased him, furnished rooms more finely than could ever be achieved with joint stools and linens.

⁓

What is an empty house? A mould, a negative impress, a hollowed shell. Room by room it is revealed. The hefty furniture goes first onto the van outside, followed by chairs and side tables, and then boxes. Inside, the sound of voices changes and the echoes take hold. No longer are words caught between sofa cushions and curtain folds; they bounce about itinerantly from floor tiles to ceilings. A restless optical illusion starts up as the walls draw towards each other and out again: are these bare rooms larger or smaller than they always seemed? The quality of light is grainier and flattening. The bulb blazes out, but the hallway feels dim, as if light slipped from plain walls, finding nothing to refract it.

The empty house is an immediate to-do list presented in the form of filthy skirtings and undusted corners. It is accusatory: there, revealed, is the long-ago stain. Bare cupboards stand with their doors open ready for inspection. Nothing now may be swept under the carpet. Here is the creased envelope of an escaped letter never answered. An imaginary Hogarth, fresh from *The Rake's Progress*, surveys the scene with a knowing eye. Even the most virtuous householder is at risk of feeling their guilt exposed.

The mover from one house to another is likely to face two empty buildings on a single day. How is the new one to be made a home? Relations with the relics of previous occupants must be rapidly negotiated. Should one attempt an all-out conquest or play guest amongst the fixtures and fittings of an absent host? A home with no resident spirits can be the strangest of all, emptiness more frightening than a supernumerary presence. Some movers will feel a house to be theirs as soon as they take hold of the keys. For others there will be a realisation, months later, in some unexpected moment, turning on the lights perhaps, or taking a saucepan quite routinely off the heat, that home is no longer somewhere else but here.

The ghosts most commonly seen by movers are those of past and future selves. Lives can be counted out in house-moves, and biographers will often begin a new chapter when their subject changes homes. Like birthdays and new years, but generally more so, flittings are occasions for taking stock. When a home is to be yours for the whole foreseeable future, all life is suddenly unfolding before you. Here you are; this is it. Painting his newly acquired London flat in 2014, happily occupied with brushes and masking tape, Laurence Scott and his partner felt themselves shadowed by a domestic future indecently speeded up. The idea came to them that "this was all part of a montage in a commercial for a department store, or life insurance. 'Whatever stage you're at, we have you covered!'" It was hard to banish the time-lapse advert once it had taken hold: "cut to us in middle age with talcum-powder temples, waving some young scamp off to university. Then onwards still, stage after stage, until we're two dandelion clocks cuddled on a park bench, shot from behind." Then the logical end not featured in the soft-lit brochures: "the pair of us dropping to dust beside a pot of Vanilla Mist Number 4."[27]

People with firm ambitions to belong in a single place have been known to recoil in panic from the fixity of the long-term homes to which, after all the myopic attention to contracts and deposits, lists and boxes, they find they are unalterably locked. To take possession of one front door requires, after all, the closure of all other doors. Not only the past houses but the dream houses rise up: the brass handles that will never now turn in your hand, the windows through which you will never watch a dusk draw in until the room is reflected in the pane. These are the ghost houses that will take their places, more or less quietly, more or less contentedly, in the rooms where you are now to sit.

2
Built on Memory

Notes on the Later Life of a Roman House at the Edge of Empire

SUSAN WALKER

On the fertile northern foothills of the Atlas Mountains in modern Morocco lie the evocative ruins of the ancient city of Volubilis. About the time of the birth of Christ, Volubilis was the inland capital of Juba II, king of Mauretania. After Juba's son Ptolemy died in AD 43, Mauretania became a province of the Roman Empire, and Volubilis became the empire's southernmost city. Much was invested in the former capital, a remote display space for urban Roman life whose people prospered from the local production of olive oil. We know little of the individual inhabitants of Volubilis, but one, at least, enjoyed life in a remarkable house, known today as the House of Venus after the subject of its finest mosaic, moved some sixty years ago to the Kasbah Museum in Tangier.[1] The following impressions are drawn from what the ruins at the site of Volubilis and some of the finds in the museum at Rabat can tell us now; however, there has been no recent excavation of the House of Venus, nor has it been possible to locate any unpublished excavation notebooks compiled in the 1940s and 1950s by the French archaeologist Raymond Thouvenot.[2] Inevitably we see on site the latest stages of life in the House of Venus, but such limited vision is compensated by the unusual preservation, at the time of excavation, of the relationship between the decorated floors and some of the sculptures displayed there.

FIGURE 2.1. The House of Venus seen from the street. (Photo: Niccolò Mugnai, 2016)

From these impressive, albeit fragmentary, survivors of an unexpect-edly ambitious lifestyle we can reconstruct the taste and some of the sensibility of the owner of the House of Venus at the end of the Roman city's life.

A Roman Guest Visits the House of
Venus, Volubilis, Morocco

Entering the house by a ramp leading into a paved vestibule, a Roman visitor might then dismount from horse or carriage to be name-checked by a porter. Beyond the lodge lay an enclosed garden, with water flow-ing through a channel built into the centre of it (figure 2.1). If on busi-ness, the visitor would be most likely escorted to an office set to the right of the garden. This was furnished with a mosaic pavement featur-ing at its centre two cupids feeding birds, the image framed, indeed somewhat eclipsed, by a series of complex, coloured mosaic geometric panels. An antique bronze statue of a fisherman (figure 2.2) was displayed here, or was possibly set just outside the room, as if seen to fish from the water flowing through the garden.[3]

FIGURE 2.2. Bronze statue of a fisherman from the House of Venus. (Credit: akg-images / De Agostini Picture Lib./G. Dagli Orti)

Between the office and the vestibule was a large private bath suite, itself furnished with hot and cold rooms and a portable bronze water heater, from which hot water could be drawn in cups to splash the bather. The suite could be accessed from the courtyard garden or, via a second vestibule leading into a changing room, from the street, which suggests that this quintessentially urban Roman facility was used by a wider society than the household and invited guests.

A dinner guest of the host would see at the far end of the garden the dining room, furnished with antique couches and a splendid pictorial mosaic of Venus riding in triumph through the Mediterranean Sea, accompanied by water nymphs and an entourage of sea giants, the flotilla sailing through waters teeming with dolphins and fish.[4] The vestibule to this room was paved with a lively parody of the favoured Roman sport of chariot racing in the circus; in this version the chariots are drawn not by horses but by geese.[5] Some jokey smaller panels elaborated the theme of Roman urban entertainment inside the entrance to the dining room: one portrayed a rat named after a gladiator famed in the provinces of North Africa, who is soundly defeated by a similarly named cat.[6]

FIGURE 2.3. Detail of the mosaic of Hylas's abduction by the nymphs, House of Venus. (Photo: Ruth Pelling and Elizabeth Fentress, 2018)

A favoured male guest might be invited to a pair of rooms at the back of the house, to the right of the dining room. To reach them the party passed through a second courtyard equipped with a fountain, like the reception room decorated with an antique bronze statue, in this case representing a lion, itself worked in a style of an even earlier time, and now performing as a water spout. Like the dining room, the pair of rooms were decorated with two large pictorial mosaics, evidently the work of the same team of mosaicists, who here portrayed Diana at her bath, attended by water nymphs and once spied upon by the shepherd Actaeon (who suffered a brutal death for such voyeuristic impertinence, the goddess changing him into a stag to be devoured by his own hounds). In the adjoining room the beautiful youth Hylas, another shepherd who stopped at a pool to fill his water jar, is shown seized by water nymphs, the sexual nature of the dramatic rape explicitly captured as Hylas ejaculates onto his thigh (figure 2.3).[7] This panel was edged with scenes of the punishment of Venus's wayward

FIGURE 2.4. Rectified aerial view of the room with the mosaic of Diana, showing (below, with shadow) the position of the pedestal for the portrait of Juba. (Photo credit: Alasia Vicarelli di Saluzzo and Gaetano Palumbo, 2002)

son Cupid; here too the house owner's taste for parody was indulged, with animals acting as prison guards.

Taking that taste for parody to extremes, an antique bronze portrait bust of Juba II of Mauretania, the former king of Volubilis and its surrounding territory, was set on a carefully aligned pedestal facing the first mosaic as if to act as Actaeon and spy on Diana, who is alluringly shown from the rear (figure 2.4), while next door an antique bronze portrait bust of the Roman Stoic philosopher and politician the younger Cato admired the full-frontal Hylas in mid-ejaculation. Cato had taken his own life in Utica (near Carthage, in modern Tunisia) in 46 BC rather than submit to Julius Caesar, then dictator of Rome, and was regarded as a hero by those seeking independence or a republican system of government.

In both rooms priority was given to the enlisting of the historic sculptures as actors in the narrative of the mosaic panels. The need for Juba to gaze directly at Diana, who is shown off-centre in her panel, meant that his pedestal was displaced from the normal central position. Such a move caused a problem for the mosaicist, who could devise no overall floor plan, so the monochrome geometric panels surrounding the scene of Diana were laid in sections, each of which may have been designed to fit beneath a couch. These two rooms were probably used for sexual encounters and other post-prandial entertainments, perhaps involving music or dancing.

The rooms to the other side of the principal courtyard garden were probably not open to our visitor, whatever his purpose. At the back of the house, to the left of the dining room, was a room approached by a passageway, which opened onto a generous, square space, its floor more soberly decorated with a mosaic probably representing Annus, a personification of the year, surrounded by the four seasons.[8] Between this chamber, which may well have served as the owner's private bedroom, and the vestibule at the main entrance to the house was a series of small rooms, two of them knocked into one with the former dividing wall converted to an arcade. At the far end of the suite was a larger room. Nearly all of these spaces were decorated with highly coloured mosaic pavements designed as simple geometric grids. The image of Annus and probably the gridded floors were the work of the same team of mosaicists who had decorated the office floor.

The House of Venus in Time and Place

The House of Venus, with its saucy and irreverent parodies of life in a Roman city and references to the city's pre-imperial past, conspicuously lacked any visible sign of economic and logistical support. In this respect it is very atypical of houses in Volubilis.[9] There are no kitchens or lavatories to serve the diners and bathers, and, though the house was located on a major artery within the city's northeast quarter, it was not equipped with street-front shops for the sale of agricultural produce. There are no spaces to install presses for making olive oil, the staple of the local economy. However, such installations could well have been located next door in the House of the Bronze Bust, named after the bust of Juba whose remarkable installation in the House of Venus is described above. The bust was found in a small storeroom at the back of the house, close to the pair of rooms at the back of the House of Venus. In all other respects the House of the Bronze Bust supplies the support required to maintain the extravagant lifestyle of the owner of the House of Venus, to which it was connected by a trapezoidal space often described as a side street but is better understood as an open court, walled off at the narrow end. From this area it was also possible to access the complex network of service rooms supplying the bath suite with water and heat.

The hypothetical visit outlined above would have taken place in the fourth century AD, a time when the city of Volubilis is widely considered by modern archaeologists to have been abandoned. In 285 the Roman governor of Mauretania Tingitana, as the provincial region was known, was ordered by Emperor Diocletian to withdraw from the interior to Tangiers, as part of a complex restructuring and subdivision of the Roman Empire devised by Diocletian to overcome decades of administrative chaos and military weakness. Yet, far from causing the abandonment of the city, the move simply appears to have encouraged the privatisation of public space and the concentration of wealth amongst a few surviving individuals who were no longer accountable to the formerly ubiquitous Roman taxman. The House of Venus is typical of the era in accommodating a large bath suite in a private house, since the public baths were no longer reliably functioning. Sculptures such as the portraits of Juba and Cato would surely not have been available for private erotic display before the abandonment of government; they must have come from a public building that had fallen out of use. Also characteristic of the age, indeed seen elsewhere in Volubilis and in many other late antique cities, is the tendency of wealthy householders to acquire adjacent properties and turn formerly multiple, often subdivided residences into a single, grand establishment, thereby allowing the separation of commerce, agriculture, and domestic service from the pleasures of socialising at the bath and entertaining at and after dinner.[10]

Focusing on the interior arrangements, the installation of a couple of rooms for entertainment and sexual encounters, linked to a large dining room by a courtyard with washing facilities, is also found in other late Roman cities of North Africa and Spain. A very similar complex of rooms in a house at Neapolis (Nablus), Tunisia, is dated to the early decades of the fourth century AD by the helpful find of a coin bedded in the support for the mosaics.[11] This suite was furnished with a strikingly similar set of mosaics to those of the House of Venus, their narratives centred on themes of the sea and seduction. A suite of rooms in a villa at Carranques in central Spain includes portrayals of Venus, Diana, and Hylas.[12] The depiction of the rape of Hylas is repeated, albeit without the dramatic sexual charge of the mosaic in the House of Venus, in pavements from private houses in various Mediterranean locations, from the very grand townhouse of the fourth-century consul Junius Bassus in central Rome to a country villa near Amphipolis in northern Greece.[13] Several fourth-century houses are known to have held collections of antique sculpture, most notably at Chiragan in southern France; but, of especial significance for the House of Venus, no fewer than three excavated houses at Cherchel, Juba II's coastal capital in modern Algeria, each included a marble portrait of the Mauretanian king within the collection.[14]

Volubilis and Cherchel

Cherchel was a particular focus of interest for the owner of the House of Venus in Volubilis. Juba II's principal capital was named Caesarea in honour of Rome's first emperor, Augustus (27 BC–AD 14), who had raised Juba in Rome and arranged his marriage to Cleopatra Selene. Twin daughter of Cleopatra VII of Egypt and her Roman lover Mark Antony, Cleopatra Selene was the only known child of Cleopatra to have survived the civil war that destroyed her mother and her Roman lover.[15] Juba enjoyed the status of "client king" of Rome, that is, a ruler with a measure of local autonomy acting independently of Roman administrators within the empire. (Another, coeval client king was the biblical Herod the Great.) Juba furnished his maritime capital city as a miniature Alexandria, Cleopatra VII's former capital and still a leading focus of culture and learning. Juba was himself a passionate intellectual and bon vivant. Cherchel was given a new theatre and a circus, and it is likely that the much later depiction of the circus at Volubilis, made by mosaicists who had probably never seen a building of this kind, was modelled on the circus at Cherchel, even at roughly 900 kilometres distant the nearest example of the genre. In fourth-century Cherchel itself, wealthy householders looked back to the kingdom of Juba as a golden age. As noted, three marble portraits of the ruler have been discovered in private houses of the period.

Objects of Value

The marble portraits in Cherchel and the bronze bust of Juba from the House of Venus in Volubilis appear to have been made during the king's reign (25 BC–AD 25), long before the houses in question were built. The portraits were thus curated through the period of rule by Juba's son Ptolemy (AD 25–43) and the subsequent absorption of the Mauretanian kingdom within the Roman Empire, to reappear as ornaments in private houses nearly three hundred years later. Their significance, then, was never forgotten, and they were valued enough to survive the lime kiln, the destiny of many marble images that had lost their context, and the foundry where so many discarded bronzes were simply melted down for repurposing.

Mosaic pavements did not suffer such a fate, as their tesserae had already been recycled from building material, glass, and ceramics. Unlike marble, which in any case hardly reached a city as far inland as Volubilis, mosaics were not dependent on the viability of long-distance trade networks developed in the early Roman Empire. Making successful pavements of course depended on the skill sets of craftsmen, and we see in the House of Venus some distinction between mosaicists specialising in pictorial scenes and those with greater skill in geometrical patterning. We also see the difficulty of making a successful image of an unfamiliar building such as the circus. Other mosaics in peripheral areas of the Roman Empire show similar challenges in representing known individuals whose lives were distant in time or place, as well as exotic animals.

The Long History of the House of Venus

The House of Venus was excavated in the last years and aftermath of World War II. The date of its initial construction has been much disputed: a likely opportunity for the development of the northeast quarter of Volubilis, where the house lies, is the extension in the AD 160s of the city walls to form a salient to the northeast. The house plans look as though they came from a template similar to that used to design the new city of Italica in southern Spain earlier in the second century. More recent finds of pottery below the outer wall of the House of Venus suggest that the construction could go as far back as the late first century AD. But however early the first construction of the house is placed, the date cannot be pushed back to the time its bronzes were commissioned. The portrait of Juba goes back to his reign in 25 BC–AD 25, and that of Cato is a posthumous work most likely commissioned in the middle decades of the first century AD. The fisherman and the lion reflect the eclectic tastes of Juba's day, respectively for Hellenistic Greek genre figures and lions imitating a style popular in fifth-century BC Etruria, and the surviving bronze couch ends from the dining room also appear to be of Juba's era. The bronzes, then, must have been brought to the house after they were discarded elsewhere in Volubilis; their original site remains unidentified. We may judge that the fourth-century owner was seeking a deliberate re-creation of the ambiance of a house of Juba's day, not only in the bronzes but also in the choices of the subjects of the mosaic pavements.

It has been claimed that the mosaics date to the late second century AD, that is, they were installed at the time the house was built (if we follow the most likely occasion described above). Nonetheless the closest comparisons for them and their choice of subjects are seen in pavements installed in the fourth century. Moreover, it is clear that the outer west wall of the House of Venus, which divided the house from the trapezoidal open space linking it with the House of the Bronze Bust, had to be demolished to accommodate the mosaics and the installation of the pedestals. It may be the case that the demolition was actually occasioned by the even larger project of installing the adjacent bath suite. In the rear rooms the sequence of work saw first the installation of the pictorial mosaic panels of Diana and Hylas, then the rebuilding of the outer west wall, then the positioning of the pedestals against the new wall, carefully relating the bronzes to the principal figures in the mosaics. Finally the unsatisfactory geometric surrounds to the floor panels were laid. Sadly the interior wall decoration and any lighting arrangements have not survived. The Venus panel of the dining room that gave the house its modern name was transferred to the Kasbah Museum in Tangier in 1960, and the other pavements were carefully restored and left on site at the time.[16]

The Owner(s)

Unfortunately no written documents survive from fourth-century Volubilis to give us the name of the owner of the House of Venus at the time of its major re-formation. He or she was clearly a person of culture and no little wit, with ample financial resources and the local power to commandeer fine bronzes of a much earlier age to decorate the guest rooms and to commission ambitious figural mosaics, some of the finest in the city. The owner was steeped in the pre-Roman history of the kingdom of Mauretania and appreciated decorative art of the time of its most distinguished ruler, Juba II.

We may distinguish several phases of redecoration of the house, a subsequent owner adding in later decades of the fourth century the circus mosaic and the carpet mosaics around it linking the principal court with the bath suite. A small panel of the cat and rat may be later still, a reflection of the ever-popular world of the amphitheatre. This survived until at least the 1950s, but its present location is unknown.

Despite the amusing jokes, an air of self-mocking desperation pervades the house, strongly reminiscent of the climate before the fall in 30 BC of Antony and Cleopatra's Alexandria to Octavian, later the first Roman emperor Augustus, a mood captured at the time by Antony's and Cleopatra's ironic reference to themselves as the society of inimitable livers,[17] and more recently by the Alexandrian Greek poet Constantine Cavafy's "Waiting for the Barbarians."

What are we waiting for, assembled in the forum?
> The barbarians are due here today. . . .
Why have our two consuls and praetors come out today
wearing their embroidered, their scarlet togas?
Why have they put on bracelets with so many amethysts,
rings sparkling with magnificent emeralds?
Why are they carrying elegant canes
beautifully worked in silver and gold?
> Because the barbarians are coming today
> and things like that dazzle the barbarians. . . .[18]

The End of the House of Venus

At some time, probably in the early fifth century, the house was abandoned. Someone, perhaps a raiding tribesman with little time to spare and no local knowledge, collected most of the bronzes together in the southwest corner of the principal courtyard, no doubt with a view to melting them down for recycling. But the melting and repurposing didn't happen, nor was this person or persons able to access the rooms with the busts of Juba and Cato. The hero of Utica was still swaying precariously on his pedestal when Thouvenot uncovered the house in the middle years of the twentieth century. Another fate, then, may be entertained for the House of Venus and the surrounding city: recent excavation on the slopes of the wadi to the west suggests that an earthquake happened in the early to mid-fifth century AD. Such an event, and a further earthquake in the eighteenth century, might explain the unusually high rate of survival of ancient bronzes at Volubilis and the lack of medieval occupation of the ancient city.[19] The later inhabitants of the wadi slope seem to have been content to leave the ancient city alone, the ghost of a sophisticated pagan past, where wildflowers grew over the ruined houses and families of storks still nest on the tops of teetering columns.

3

A House of Air

HERMIONE LEE

Penelope Fitzgerald, English novelist and biographer, published her first book when she was nearly sixty, in 1975, a life of the painter Edward Burne-Jones. In her biography, and in a talk she gave many years after publishing it, she vividly evokes the life of The Grange, the big eighteenth-century house in North Fulham where the Burne-Jones family lived from 1867 until he died there in 1898. At that time North Fulham was in the country, and she describes the market gardens, horse dealers, walnut orchard, and briar roses that surrounded the house, the lovely garden full of "white lilies, stock, lavender, acacias and a great mulberry tree," the shadowy deep-green painted rooms where, as one visitor said, "the house seemed to be holding its breath," the little Giorgione shining on the wall, the smells of paint and turpentine, and the turbulent life of the household. Before she describes it, she tells us that the site "is now part of a council estate, one block of which is named Burne-Jones House." The Grange, she says, has become "a house of air." It is all the more vivid to her mind's eye because it is not there anymore. Kipling, who had paid happy visits there as a child, asked if he could have the bellpull for the entrance to his house, Bateman's. "It is all that is left," says Fitzgerald, "but it means that anyone who goes to Batemans can feel they have at least been in touch with The Grange."[1]

Fitzgerald's evocation of "a house of air" is done in as much loving detail as possible, to make you feel you have "at least been in touch with" the place where her subject lived longest. The sadness of its disappearance is mixed up with the pleasure of re-creating it. So it is with most imaginative returns to a lost home: the excitement and interest of dreaming one's way back into the past life of the house also involve emotions of longing and missing. Fitzgerald's account of the painter's vanished house reminds me of an anecdote Virginia Woolf tells about her mother, Julia Stephen, which has the same atmosphere of poignant joy. This is also a story about a house where Burne-Jones spent some time, Little Holland House, in Melbury Road in Kensington. Like The Grange, this was a house of artists, where the Prinseps (aunt and uncle of Julia Stephen) gave the painter G. F. Watts house and studio room, and created what Fitzgerald calls "a centre of eccentric yet stately hospitality," frequented in the 1860s and 1870s by Holman Hunt, Tennyson, Julia Margaret Cameron, and the Pre-Raphaelites. For the young Julia Jackson it was a romantic second home. Virginia Woolf remembered her mother taking them as children to Melbury Road. Little Holland House was long gone. "When we came to the street that had been built on the old garden she gave a little spring forward, clapped her hands, and cried 'That was where it was!' as if a fairyland had disappeared." Woolf—writing in 1939, at the outbreak of World War II—re-creates the long-lost Victorian house as a "summer-afternoon world," full of crinolines, and gentlemen in peg-top trousers and whiskers, and great bowls of strawberries and cream, with the distant sound of Joachim playing the violin and poetry being recited. Her mother is "a vision" in the centre of it all. "I dream: I make up pictures of a summer's afternoon." The trigger for her dreaming re-creation of that "house of air" was her mother's "little spring forward," which, fifty years later, is the moment of memory that frees Woolf to spring backwards into a lost past.[2]

Those are Victorian scenes, re-created by twentieth-century writers trying to reimagine their way into the tone and feeling of the past. Nineteenth-century poetry often spoke of lost homes and long-gone childhoods. The sentiment might be for a happier lost time, as in Thomas Hood's much-loved tearjerker:

I remember, I remember,
The house where I was born,

The little window where the sun
Came peeping in at morn . . .

Or, more complicatedly, the loss of the childhood family home and garden is bound up with a feeling of alienation, a loss of self, as the remembered place now belongs to someone else, and is going in time to
be the site of *their* nostalgic memory, *their* sense of loss. No one conveys
that sense of strangeness better than Tennyson, as when he writes in *In
Memoriam* about the abandoned garden of childhood as an image for separation and mortality:

Unwatched, the garden bough shall sway,
The tender blossom flutter down,
Unloved, that beech will gather brown,
This maple burn itself away;

. . . .

Till from the garden and the wild
A fresh association blow,
And year by year the landscape grow
Familiar to the stranger's child

. . . .

And year by year our memory fades
From all the circle of the hills.[3]

Alan Hollinghurst takes the phrase as his title for his novel about biography's fallible attempts to re-create the vanished life of a writer and
his era. *The Stranger's Child* ends with a return to a much-changed house,
where a bonfire is consuming the secrets of the past.

Emotions about our lost houses and gardens have to do with growing old and acquiring guilt: we are always leaving our first home and
lamentingly looking back to it. The whole point of the Garden of Eden
is that we are going to leave it, and then spend the rest of our time wish-
ing we could return to it. There is a salutary dry warning by the great
Anglo-Irish novelist Elizabeth Bowen against thinking that you ever can
go back. In an essay of 1946 called "Out of a Book," she sounds the alarm

against trying to crawl back inside the books, gardens, and houses we loved as children. She says: "It is not only our fate but our business to lose innocence, and once we have lost that, it is futile to attempt a picnic in Eden."[4]

All the same, the impulse to return is a very strong one. Revisiting one's own lost home, in the imagination or the mind's eye, or in reality, is an intensely private and emotional experience, in which the past rushes up to meet the present self. Virginia Woolf lost her childhood summer home in Cornwall, Talland House, at thirteen, when her mother died in 1895. She revisits it, physically, at various moments in her life, and she invokes it over and over again, in fiction and autobiography, always with intense memories of childhood happiness.

> If life has a base that it stands upon, if it is a bowl that one fills and fills and fills—then my bowl without a doubt stands upon this memory. It is of lying half asleep, half awake, in bed in the nursery at St Ives. It is of hearing the waves breaking, one, two, one, two, and sending a splash of water over the beach; and then breaking, one, two, one, two, behind a yellow blind. It is of hearing the blind draw its little acorn across the floor as the wind blew the blind out. It is of lying and hearing this splash and seeing this light, and feeling, it is impossible that I should be here; of feeling the purest ecstasy I can conceive.[5]

Making a pilgrimage to a writer's house is an attempt by the visitor, whether devotee or descendant, friend or biographer, to enter into that kind of emotion, to understand the life of the other person, to find out more about them—and to pay tribute. These motives may be mixed, or obscure. Why do millions of people visit Shakespeare's "birthplace"? To see if something will rub off on them? To try to get the key to the vanished genius? It is a strong but muddled impulse, a mixture of awe, longing, desire for inwardness, and intrusive curiosity.

Expectations are always high for such pilgrimages, and disappointment can be correspondingly sharp. The famous writer's house you long to see may have vanished, but the urge to go to the site still remains.

Chaucer's rooms above Aldgate in the City of London, where he lived in the late fourteenth century, were long gone, until vividly conjured out of thin air by his twenty-first-century biographer Paul Strohm. Nothing is left of Pyrford Place in Surrey where Donne wrote his poetry at the start of the 1600s, except for a little summerhouse. Only the famous grotto at Twickenham remains of the Palladian villa and garden where Alexander Pope lived and wrote from 1719—though there is, of course, an Alexander Pope Hotel.

Even when famous, legendary houses remain, the experience they provide can sometimes be bitterly unsatisfactory. Such disappointing encounters with sacred sites make interesting reading. Keats looked forward intensely, on his Scottish journey in the summer of 1818, to visiting Robert Burns's birthplace—he hoped it would be as rewarding as his visit to Shakespeare's birthplace in Stratford. "One of the pleasantest means of annulling self," he wrote to his friend Reynolds, "is approaching such a shrine." But at the cottage there was a boring old drunk telling repetitive, miserable anecdotes about Burns, and it all seemed flat: "O the flummery of a birth place! Cant! Cant! Cant!" Keats wrote what he called a bad sonnet about being in the very place where Burns lived, stamping his foot on his floor and looking out of the window at his view but finding himself unable to "see." He invokes the legendary dead poet with disappointed irony: "O smile among the shades, for this is fame!"[6]

However disappointing it may be, the attempt to imagine back into the life of a past house is something almost all biographers feel the need to do. Life-writing usually involves thinking about houses: places of growing up, domestic life, leaving (and sometimes returning), deathbeds, afterlives. The "Romantic Biographer" of Shelley and Coleridge, Richard Holmes, famously turned the quest for the writer's places into an essential part of life-writing. But, in his book about questing, *Footsteps*, he also touchingly lamented the fact that the quest always has a kind of built-in futility or disappointment. We cannot reenter the past, just as he cannot cross the broken bridge at Avignon:

You could not cross such bridges any more, just as one could not cross literally into the past. . . . For me, [biography] was to become a kind of pursuit, a tracking of the physical trail of someone's path through the past, a following of footsteps. You would never catch them; no, you would never quite catch them. But maybe, if you were lucky, you might write about the pursuit of that fleeting figure in such a way as to bring it alive in the present.[7]

My biographical quests have been in search of writers who lived between the late nineteenth century and the twentieth century, so many of their houses still stand, giving off the illusory sense that one could almost step back into the lives lived there. Still, my pilgrimages for writers' homes in America, France, Ireland, and England have been mixed experiences.

In the late 1980s, I pursued Willa Cather's trail in Nebraska, Arizona, New Mexico, and New York. In Red Cloud, Nebraska, the small country town near the Kansas border where she lived as a child in the 1880s after the family moved in from the countryside, Willa Cather has been reverentially memorialised. The image of the plough against the sunset, which in *Ántonia* invokes the heroic labour and endurance of the pioneers who carved their homes out of the land, is everywhere. There are signs directing pilgrims to the "Willa Cather Memorial Prairie," the "Willa Cather Pioneer Memorial Museum," and the "Cather Childhood Home." In this neat little house, a kindly local lady played a worn-out tape that told a reverential story of Cather as a Nebraskan heroine.

Cather's marvellous fiction beautifully invokes the life and spirit of the pioneers and the landscape of the Nebraskan prairie. But as an awkward, clever, ambitious young woman she rages, in letters and stories, against the provincial, constricting life of her small midwestern town. She leads her early life in revolt against all the conventions of Red Cloud, longs to get out, and is terrified when she goes back that she will never be able to leave. As with Joyce, Lawrence, or Mansfield, the childhood home, which she couldn't wait to put behind her, would then become one of her deepest inspirations. But it seemed ironic that the little house where she spent so many restless, angry hours, dreaming of another life, is now a shrine to her memory.

Edith Wharton, whose childhood homes could not have been more different from Cather's, is a writer deeply interested in and involved with the lives of houses. She designed at least five homes in her lifetime (1862–1937), in America and France, including her famous New England house, The Mount. She wrote books on "the decoration of houses" and on Italian villa styles. She places her characters, in novels like *The House of Mirth* and *The Custom of the Country* and *The Age of Innocence*, in thickly described, minutely detailed architectural settings. Her novels slice down through the surface of domestic decoration and house styles to the ways of life and behaviour they reflect. A writer of secrets, loneliness, and thwarted love, she once compared a woman's nature to "a great house full of rooms," where most people only get as far as the reception rooms but "in the innermost room, the soul sits alone and waits for a footstep that never comes."[8]

Her own houses have had mixed afterlives. Because of the perpetual tearing down and building up of late nineteenth-century New York, which so amazed her generation, who had grown up in the demure brownstone houses clustered around Washington Square, most of her New York sites have been demolished or very much altered. For instance, the first house she "did up" as a young married lady in the 1890s, a newly built Queen Anne style house at 884 Park Avenue, not only has disappeared, but the very house number no longer exists. The row of small houses from 882 to 888 Park Avenue gave way to bigger buildings in the 1920s, and a cross street now cuts through what would have been number 884. Her houses outside New York in Newport, Rhode Island, where she spent unhappy married years, still stand but are privately owned and show no trace that one of America's leading novelists once lived there. The Mount is another matter. After many changes of fortune, it is now a magnificently preserved and active centre of the Wharton industry in America. When you are there, it feels as if this was Wharton's most important home. Yet, because of her move to France and the breakdown of her marriage, after pouring her money and energy into its making in the early 1900s, she lived there, intermittently, only until 1911.

In France, the grand apartment she lived in on the Rue de Varenne, in the elite left-bank Faubourg district, has a respectful French plaque memorialising the *Romancière Américaine* who became a heroine in France because of her dedication to the French cause during the Great War. The two houses still remain that she acquired and redesigned after the war, one an elegant eighteenth-century "Pavillon" in St.-Brice, on the outskirts of Paris, and the other a Provençal house high up over the Mediterranean, built just below a ruined castle, in old Hyères. The Pavillon Colombe and "St.-Claire-le-Château" are still recognisably her houses, though one is now privately owned and the other is the office of the Parc National. The beautiful gardens she created for both of them have not disappeared, though in the eighty years or so since her death there have of course been changes. When I went to visit the Pavillon Colombe in 2002, I was ushered in by the butler, in full uniform, complete with gloves, and made welcome by its owner, the Princess of Liechtenstein, who enjoyed visits from Wharton scholars. The Princess told me that the house had been much redesigned by the Duchesse de Talleyrand, and then by herself. She did not think much of Wharton's taste in furniture. But the garden was being lovingly kept up, and from the bedroom where Wharton died, I looked out at the pond where she used to feed the fish, with the scents and sounds of the garden coming up through the windows. Some things had had to go: the Princess told me that, unlike Wharton, she disliked white dahlias but, in tribute to her predecessor, had obtained satisfactory replacements. Sure enough, out on the terrace, there were two rather shamefaced-looking white peacocks, pretending to be dahlias.[9]

The Pavillon Colombe is not an inviting-looking house. It presents itself to the street as a blank north wall with a massive carriage door. Only once inside the interior cobbled courtyard do you get a sense of the elegance and charm of the house, with its classically elegant, formal, wood-carved suite of rooms and its high French windows at the back, looking on to an orderly, extensive garden. To my Wharton-saturated imagination, it spoke of a life of privacy, reserve, impeccable high taste, and loneliness. It is a big house for a long-divorced woman living on her own, though she was visited often by dear friends and

FIGURE 3.1. Pavillon Colombe. (Credit: Beinecke Rare Book and Manuscript Library)

well known in the outside world. It feels like a shelter or a retreat, a house where perhaps no one ever penetrated to the secret innermost room of its remarkable owner.

In my quests for women writers' homes on this side of the Atlantic, the houses that most haunt me are the ones that have vanished. Virginia Woolf's places, in London, Cornwall, and Sussex, are mostly still there, and when I was researching her life in the early 1990s, fifty years after her death, she still felt within touching distance. Monk's House in Sussex is carefully maintained by the National Trust. There are blue plaques on her childhood Kensington home, 22 Hyde Park Gate (though in the 1990s the plaque only celebrated her father, Leslie Stephen), and on her Bloomsbury home in Fitzroy Square. The flat she and Leonard lived in for many years in Tavistock Square was bombed in the war and replaced, after the war, by an ugly hotel, but a bust of Virginia Woolf now stands in Tavistock Square gardens. Hogarth House in Richmond, where she and Leonard lived from 1915 to 1924 on an annual rent of £150, and founded the Hogarth Press, has a blue plaque to them both. When I was questing after Woolf it was an architect's office, but, renamed Leonard House and knocked together with the house next door, it recently went on the market as a much-refurbished four-bedroom Georgian town house, for well over £3 million.

Talland House in St. Ives still stands but has not always had owners who recognised its significance. Legend has it that one of its inhabitants put up a sign reading: "Home of Virginia Woolf, wife of the famous novelist." When I went on my pilgrimage there twenty-five years ago, the exasperated owner shooed me away. He said that when he had bought the house he had "never heard of the bloody woman," but he soon realised his mistake: "Every time you turn round, there's Americans in the living room! Australians in the bathroom!" Later owners became more welcoming to Woolf pilgrims.

But the house of Virginia Woolf's that haunts me most is the elegant little Sussex house called Asheham, the first country home she lived in with Leonard. Built in 1820 under the shadow of the Downs, it was a remote, damp, rather mysterious house, supposed to be haunted. Leonard Woolf described it as "romantic, gentle, melancholy, lovely." They lived there, on and off, from 1911 to 1919, years of war and illness, and, though these were difficult times, she became very fond of it. They left it for Monk's House, but Asheham survived, hidden inside a spindly wood and up a muddy track, for many years afterwards. It was bought up by a cement works in the 1930s and became the property of the Blue Circle Cement Works and Waste Management. In 1993, I made my way into the closed-off and boarded-up house, past the "No Trespassing" signs, and snuffed up the atmosphere of silence, decay, and forlorn beauty. The following year it was demolished. In a tiny story published in 1921, "A Haunted House," Woolf imagines a ghostly couple returning to a house like Asheham, looking for something, revisiting their past lives, sensed by the couple who are living there: "not that one could ever see them." "Wandering through the house, opening the windows, whispering not to wake us, the ghostly couple seek their joy."[10]

Penelope Fitzgerald, my most recent biographical subject, had mixed feelings about Virginia Woolf and Bloomsbury, partly because of their privileged social status. Fitzgerald, like Woolf, came from a professional,

FIGURE 3.2. Asheham House. (Credit: MS Thr 557 [191], Houghton Library, Harvard University)

literary, upper-middle-class family. She grew up in a nice house in Hampstead. But because of the war and her husband's drastic ill fortunes, she fell through the bottom of her social class into poverty and, for a time, homelessness and brought her children up under great difficulties. It is a painful and surprising story. In later life, when she had become an admired novelist and a public literary figure, she never acquired a house of her own. She lived in a rented flat, or in rooms or annexes attached to her married daughters' homes. She regretted this and wished she had more to offer her children and grandchildren. She wrote sadly to her older daughter: "I have failed to produce the fur coat, the crocodile bag, the little freehold property in good condition, all the things I dreamed of. Instead of that, you know I'll help if I can."[11]

In her extraordinary novels, she wrote more about the unhoused, the struggling, the transient, and the poor, those who are "clinging on for dear life," than she did about the settled, the comfortable, or the privi-

FIGURE 3.3. Signpost to Bowen's Court. (Credit: Jane Fallon)

leged. One of her novels, *Offshore*, which won the Booker Prize in 1979, was closely based on her experiences of living, from 1961 to 1963, on an old leaky barge called *Grace*, moored at Chelsea Reach. The life she and her family led there was bleak, poor, hand-to-mouth, and even dangerous. In the end, the barge sank, with most of their possessions, leaving them homeless. Yet she was fond of *Grace*, and the novel she sets amongst the boat owners on the Thames in the early 1960s is full of affection and nostalgia for that ramshackle, misfit community living between land and water, for the endurance of their "crazy old vessels," the sounds and moods of the river, and "the sodden, melancholy and yet enduring spirit of the Reach."[12] Now, Chelsea Reach is a place of expensive, well-maintained, fashionable houseboats. It is utterly changed from the time of Fitzgerald's sunken barge, poor *Grace*, a house of water.

Of all the vanished houses I have visited, the most powerfully present is Elizabeth Bowen's Irish home, Bowen's Court. Bowen writes, many times, and with strong and mixed feelings, about the eighteenth-century Anglo-Irish "Big Houses." These houses, she says, built by incoming settlers and founded on a social ideal of European culture and civilization, were planned for "spacious living" and hospitality. But the Big Houses were separate and withdrawn from the surrounding countryside, haunted by the ghosts of the past and viewed with resentment and hostility by the "native" Irish. Many of them went into decline through debt, historical struggles, and isolation. Some of them were burned down, some fell into ruin. Yet, as long as their houses stood, their owners went on trying to keep up a good face to the world, even "with grass almost up to their doors and hardly a sixpence to turn over."

Her own "high bare Italianate house," built in the northeastern corner of County Cork in the 1770s, and the family who lived in it are typical of a class that came to full flower in the late eighteenth century, went into decline thereafter, and was, by the 1920s, an isolated minority cut off from the country it had once dominated. In *Bowen's Court*, with energetic physical detail and dramatic characterisation, Bowen told the often violent, fanatical, and feuding story of her family's history in the house from the 1770s to the 1950s (and by inference the whole story of the Anglo-Irish). The story ends, touchingly, with the lives and deaths of her parents and her inheriting of the house.

Elizabeth Bowen always felt like a semi-stranger, caught between two countries. (In that respect, she resembles Edith Wharton.) When she was a child, because her father was ill, she and her mother spent several years away from Bowen's Court, in Kent. Her mother died in 1912, when she was thirteen. After that she went back and forth between England and Ireland. When her father died in 1930, she inherited the house, but her marriage and the war kept her in England. She began to write *Bowen's Court* in 1939 and published it in 1942. Ten years later, she and her husband decided to live there permanently. But he died very soon after that. From 1952 to 1959 she tried to keep up the house alone but could not manage it. In 1959 the house was sold and then demolished. Her book was reissued in 1964 with an afterword in which she explains why she had not changed the description of the house from the present tense of the first edition:

> When I think of Bowen's Court, there it is. . . . Knowing, as you now do, that the house is no longer there, you may wonder why I have left my opening chapter, the room-to-room description of Bowen's Court, in the present tense. I can only say that I saw no reason to transpose it into the past. There is a sort of perpetuity about livingness, and it is part of the character of Bowen's Court to be, in sometimes its silent way, very much alive.[13]

FIGURE 3.4. Bowen's Court. (Copyright © the British Library Board 10390.i.2)

Forty years after Bowen's Court was demolished, in 1999, I was invited to give a talk in memory of Elizabeth Bowen at her local church in the tiny village of Farahy, where she is buried, and I went, as other Bowen pilgrims have done, the short distance from Farahy Church to the site of Bowen's Court. What I saw was an empty field in North Cork, surrounded by trees, with a heap of stones in one corner, in which there were a few last fragments of the building. What does it mean to visit a field full of stones, because a much-written-about house once stood there? I had been affected by Bowen's own passionate investment in things and places and in the lives of houses, and by the discomforting mixture of reality and strangeness, ghosts and presences, that there is in all her work. Bowen's Court is long gone. But "there it is," still, in Bowen's memory and her mind's eye, in her writing, and in the imagination of those who write about her life and work: her house of air.

Family Houses

4
My Mother's House

MARGARET MACMILLAN

It was my father's, too, of course because they had been a partnership from the moment he knocked her down outside the University of Toronto Medical School, but it was, always, her domain. Like all the fathers in the Toronto of the 1940s and 1950s he went out to work every day and she, like almost all the mothers, ran the household. Sometimes the mothers had help, young women emigrating from the British Isles—who soon found they could get better jobs in the shops and offices and factories of a booming postwar economy—or what we called in those days DPs. Only later did we understand that stood for Displaced Persons who might have survived in an occupied Holland or who had memories of fleeing the Russian troops in the centre of Europe.

We were privileged although it took us some time to realize it. Our father had come home from the war, and Canada seemed far away from the trouble and war-torn parts of the world. And we were middle class, perhaps even upper-middle class, although Canadian society did not like to reflect on such gradations. The house was not like some of the grander ones in Toronto which aspired to be southern mansions or Tudor manor houses. Yet it was big enough with five bedrooms and what was in those days an exceptional three bathrooms. We had a separate dining room and what my mother always called the drawing room, although in Canada it was a living room or a parlour or the front room.

My mother had not expected to find herself in Toronto, which in those days was a dull, provincial, and smug town where everything closed on Sundays and we all tended to judge each other, usually unfavourably.

(People from Montreal, which had a zip and a style, always made fun of us.) She had grown up in London in a warm, funny, complicated, and worldly family, but the war, as it did to so many millions, swept her up and deposited her many miles from home. She came to Canada on a school girls' trip in 1939, a present from her parents before she went to university and then, at the end of August, found she could not get home. She was so young and very beautiful. She could have married (and perhaps nearly did) a rich, stuffy, Toronto young man, but by luck and because she was an acute judge of people she married my father, who for the next half century thought almost everything she did was perfect and admirable.

So she took our boring 1920s house and turned it into something quite unlike anything else in our sedate neighbourhood. You could see that when you first drove or walked down our quiet street. All the other front gardens had immaculate lawns trimmed like so much felt. Occasionally a wild burst of creativity had left a few impatiens in a disciplined row and from time to time a hydrangea bush, trimmed and shaped into regular shapes never seen in nature. Our garden was exuberant and colourful and spilled over onto the sidewalk. Iris, tulips, peonies, larkspurs, roses, candytuft, poppies, and chrysanthemums came and went while at the other houses the impatiens and the grass remained stuck in their deadly order. Our front door was bright red; others on the street were olive or dark brown or black. And only our house had splashes of white paint where my youngest brother and a friend had tried to paint the stone door frame.

Inside the house she defied all local rules of what was proper and expected, to make it as colourful and as friendly as her garden. Our dining room, like so many in the Toronto of those days, was panelled with dark wood. She simply painted it, pale violet at first but always light colours. Along one wall she put a Welsh oak tridarn, quite unlike any of the sideboards in the other houses. And no one else had a collection of pewter and Staffordshire jugs. We had special meals there for birthdays, for example, but the table was often covered with homework or school projects. My father loved tinkering and kits would arrive from the United States with thousands of tiny parts that he would slowly build with the help of a soldering iron into radios and hi-fis.

Over time our kitchen became where we took most of our meals because, long before anyone else was doing it, she had the back of the house built out and a big table—made as I remember from a large door—brought in. Almost every night we five children and often a friend or two ate dinner there with our parents. In the winters (was there always snow and ice in those days?) we came into the kitchen in skates, just off the rink that our neighbour across the back fence made every year. She never minded. We argued, talked about the day, and watched for the warning signs that my two youngest brothers were about to fight as each slipped lower in his chair better to be able to kick the other. My, your children make a lot of noise, another neighbour told her.

When we went to other houses we were always struck by the living rooms which had no signs of life at all. The carpets were invariably broadloom—wall to wall was the proud boast. And the rooms were im-maculate and ordered with their coffee tables covered with what were in those days the inevitable cigarette boxes and ashtrays; sometimes a curio cabinet that held various treasures, seashells, mementoes collected on travels, or a few ornaments, Royal Doulton figures of, say, an old balloon seller or a bunch of flowers; and perhaps a painting or two. A sofa and chairs were set out carefully around the room in such a way that no one could ever comfortably have a conversation. And in any case the furniture was often covered with sheets or, in one house where I babysat, plastic.

Our living room was where we lived much of the time. My mother had bookcases put in all along one wall. Our coffee table was covered with magazines—and not the *Reader's Digest* or *Lady's Home Journal* fa-voured in other homes we knew but the *New Statesman* or the *New Yorker*. She left the floor bare and put down carpets, some that her father had bought years ago in Mesopotamia. We too had a couch but it was well worn and, because we all loved to jump on it, often propped up by a log of wood where we had managed to break off a leg or two. She found comfortable armchairs at an auction and covered them with bright chintz. Every Saturday my mother would put on the Metropolitan Opera broadcast and the music would fill the downstairs.

When we were young we often turned the chairs over and covered them with sheets to make forts. Or we moved everything around to stage plays. When my father came home from work the boys would rush at him and ask for a play fight. Often their friends would ask if they could join in too; their fathers never did such things. He would roll around covered with boys. My mother never minded any of it.

In the winters we sat by the fire in the evenings with our books. My mother would not have a television in the house until we could all read and my youngest brother refused to read anything until he was ten years old. So we all became readers, even eventually the recalcitrant one. Sometimes we took turns reading to each other. We chatted a lot too and laughed.

She let us do what we wanted with our bedrooms. My youngest brother lived in a cave of black and orange. When I was fifteen she let me choose my own wallpaper and for years after I had to live with knots of pussy willows and violets tied with bows. Were there kittens on my walls too? I think there may have been. I cannot remember what my sister who shared the top floor of the house had but I do remember the two of us as teenagers leaning out our bathroom window to smoke stale cigarettes we had stolen from the box even our house had in the living room.

In her house my mother celebrated birthdays—we could each choose our favourite meals—and all the annual festivals that Protestant Toronto had. (Not as many as the Catholics, who went to separate schools and had an enviable number of religious holidays.) So we had pumpkins at Halloween and turkeys at Thanksgiving. We dyed hardboiled eggs for Easter and had chocolate bunnies when we woke up on the day. But the best of all was Christmas.

Years later she told us how much she hated it because it made her think back to when she was young and carefree and someone else had to worry about making everyone happy. Perhaps she was more ambivalent than that because she threw herself into getting the house ready. She made Christmas cakes months before. In December she brought in pine and spruce boughs and decorated every picture and surface she could find. On the dining room table she added candles, a small Santa Claus and reindeer, and a white wooden church which played a tinny "Silent Night" over and over. She brought out—this once a year only—the pair of silk Persian carpets her father had given her. She made cookies shaped like holly, bells, and angels which we all decorated. We sat around the kitchen table and made marzipan fruits and vegetables and groaned when my father produced strange shapes in lurid colours which he said were diseased appendixes or rare snakes. And of course we had a tree, propped unsteadily in one corner of the living room with bits of string tied by my father to the window latches. (On one memorable year it fell over, leaving shattered balls all over the floor.) The other trees on our street never dreamed of doing such a thing and their decorations, all matched in colour and size, stayed firmly in place. Our tree had battered paper chains and plasticine figures we had made at school and a wonderfully eclectic range of decorations from huge painted balls to small spikes and strings of lights that blinked in no particular order. It had lots of tinsel everywhere and on the top a peroxide blonde angel who rested at a dangerous angle like a tipsy Marilyn Monroe.

We all grew up and moved away, but we came back to the house often but particularly at Christmas. We expected, I think, that my parents would always be there and our bedrooms, still filled with our old books and odds and ends, would never change. One day my mother said they were moving to the country, to a farm that had belonged to our grandparents, and gave us a deadline for collecting all our stuff before she threw it out. We were shocked and perhaps dismayed. No house, we thought, could ever mean the same to us.

This usurper, this second house, was built sometime in the 1840s, old by Ontario standards, and in style Georgian not Victorian or Edwardian. It was, we had to admit, much lovelier than the city one. Her Welsh furniture, the armchairs, the pictures all looked much nicer than they had in the city. She now had the space to garden on the scale she had always longed for. Year by year she put in more flower beds, more trees, more hedges, a pool with water lilies. And we still came back and still had evenings reading and gossiping and celebrations such as Christmas and, increasingly, weddings of the new generation that was coming along. Like us they sometimes made the mistake of thinking it was the house that drew them when really it was our mother.

5
At Orchard House

MAURA DOOLEY

—if you are a skilful gleaner, you may get many a pocket-full
even of grafted fruit, long after apples are supposed
to be gone out-of-doors.

—Henry Thoreau, *Wild Apples*

FIGURE 5.1. Orchard House.

Visiting Orchard House, Concord, Massachusetts

A mother, a fever,
a tattoo of feet on stairs
then round the banisters
down to a fire in the parlour
or out to the apple orchard
a plait of voices, laughter,
anger, always forgiveness in
a mother's voice, reading

reading of one whose shoes
you stood in to be bold
or sensible or dreamy but not
the one who had you sob at night,
or was that the blazing star, soft muzzle
of Blackie or Jack or Beauty,
another time, another story,
or both times, now, entering here

just as you'd imagined,
buttoned boots in a sisterly row,
Marmee's spice chest out on the table,
Baldwin trees bright with blossom
the trill and tang of remembered voices
each a braid in your own mother's voice,
every room a new chapter
or, not at all as you'd imagined

desk, hearth, shelf of books,
planting of seeds, swell of ideas,
winter evenings of notions and plans,
but through an open door
how well you seem to know it
all that was sharp, then rosy, then ready

for the taking was there all the time
in your mother's voice reading,

reading through fever and fear
and here now where a father lit
winter evenings with notions, plans
but no regard for the doctor's bill
as the orchard turned from green to gold
it's Louisa who gathered the fruit carefully—
so easy to harvest all that surrounds you,
harder to send it ripe and delicious down the years.

6

Romantic Home

FELICITY JAMES

Sometimes I give in to temptation and I type the postcode into Google. I take the turning off the A50, passing all the old remembered, altered places, the farms that have been turned into footballers' mansions, the ponds and hollows and haulage depots all mixed together in the long unlovely Manchester hinterland. I turn into the dead end that once led home.

Look: it's still here.

I remember how amazed, and affronted, my mother was when I showed her on Street View that the house had been immortalised: with the washing on the line, too. April 2009, says the time stamp. The incurious, all-seeing camera holds the whole scene. There's her dark green Rover on the drive. There's my father's work van, the last of the work vans, with its back door open and his toolbox visible inside. Four years before she died; when we were still able to explain away Dad's forgetfulness. When they were still living inside the stories of home they'd made for themselves, back when Dad had built the house in the pure plate-glass optimism of the 1960s. When he was making good money wiring shopping centres and high street stores and neon-lit car showrooms, and building a little kingdom out here in the fields, where he could ensure his children were set on a trajectory well away from the building site into piano playing and poetry reading, university and culture and a good profession.

Greedily, guiltily, I look all round at lost home. The overgrown flower beds. The traces of the swallows' nests, up under the eaves. The flowering cherry trees. And all the daffodils they planted, hundreds of them, lapping the edges of the lawn, beneath the trees, in the bit of field my father marked out as his orchard, grandly planting rows of apples like a patriarch, so that my mother spent all her autumns in a frenzy of jelly and juice and pudding making. The freezer, when we sent it to the tip, was still filled with decades of labelled, hoary bags of past seasons' produce; the cupboard under the sink stacked with jam no one could bring themselves to eat. There's no one who will pick the apples; no one who will admire the unfashionable ranks of daffodils. And yet they will be getting ready to flower again now, suspended in the dark Cheshire earth, ready to burst out in a riot of heartless yellow frill.

All that poetry reading my parents encouraged me into couldn't help with the boiler maintenance or the rotting windows or the leaking bath as the sad familiar story of decline unfolded. But it has helped me understand something of the nature of that nostalgia for home. Something, too, of what my parents were trying to create for themselves. Old-fashioned even for their time, they were participating in a larger myth of going home to the country. Their carefully constructed rural idyll was deeply informed by my mother's *Palgrave's Golden Treasury*, and by the poems she had learned by heart at school in the 1930s—by Thomas Hood's memories of the house where he was born, its roses, red and white, by A. E. Housman's cherry trees, and, especially, by the Romantic poets' faith in the nourishing power of nature. The house in the country wasn't simply an aspirational emblem, a compensation for grief and loss and wartime penury, but a step to a better moral life, particularly for the next generation. My mother took quite literally the insistence of "Frost at Midnight" that Coleridge's baby Hartley will be tutored by nature:

> For I was rear'd
> In the great city, pent mid cloisters dim,
> And saw nought lovely but the sky and stars.
> But *thou*, my babe! Shalt wander, like a breeze,

By lakes and sandy shores, beneath the crags
Of ancient mountain, and beneath the clouds,
Which image in their bulk both lakes and shores
And mountain crags . . .[1]

It's this Romantic vision of being at home in nature that I want to explore in this chapter. "Frost at Midnight," one of a group of blank verse "conversation" poems by Coleridge, comes out of that year of intense collaboration and idealism in 1797 and 1798, when Wordsworth and Coleridge were living within easy walk of each other in the Somerset-shire countryside. This was a period of great productivity, in the face of Revolutionary disappointment and wartime uncertainty: alongside, and intertwined with, the *Lyrical Ballads*, and the start of the larger writing project of *The Recluse*, come a series of homecoming poems written by Wordsworth and Coleridge. From "The Eolian Harp" through "Frost at Midnight," "Tintern Abbey," and "Home at Grasmere," it is possible to trace the image of Romantic home evolving through the later 1790s, passing from Coleridge to Wordsworth, from Wordsworth to Coleridge, and then back again. What Coleridge and Wordsworth create, I think, is a powerful myth of Romantic home—one that also, however, has its darker aspects, its pressures and hidden griefs, fears that are there from the start.

These poems of homecoming start with Coleridge's works of 1795 and 1796, as he struggled with his vocation after leaving Cambridge: American settler? Political journalist? Newspaper editor? Unitarian preacher? Alongside the political and philosophical writings of, for instance, *The Watchman*, he was also feeling his way into his poetic identity—and searching for a home. One great early expression of this is "The Eolian Harp," which he began writing in November 1795 just as he contemplated moving to a cottage in Clevedon, in the country-side outside Bristol, with the woman he was about to marry, Sara Fricker:

My pensive SARA! thy soft cheek reclin'd
Thus on mine arm, most soothing sweet it is
To sit beside our cot, our cot o'er grown

With white-flower'd Jasmin, and the broad-leav'd Myrtle,
(Meet emblems they of Innocence and Love!)[2]

The marriage to Sara and the retreat to the country were the last remnants of the Pantisocratic scheme of utopian community Coleridge, Robert Southey, and other friends had imagined, "trying the experiment of human Perfectibility on the banks of the Susquehanna."[3] The move to the cottage in Clevedon was a symbolic one, indicating his ongoing sympathy with those ideals. He was trying to form a new sort of society based in rural domesticity: a break with his urban, radical identity as a Bristol writer, journalist, and preacher.

It was also about making a home for himself in the traditions of English poetry. The "cot" almost smothered in greenery is a version of Adam and Eve's "blissful Bower" in Book IV of *Paradise Lost*, thickly woven with myrtles and Gessamin. It's redolent, too, of eighteenth-century refuges of sensibility: Werther's doomed search for domestic happiness in nature; the celebration of rural haunts in the sonnets of William Lisle Bowles and Charlotte Smith; or Cowper's "loop-holes of retreat" that allow the poet to train a creative vision on the world in a place free from distraction.[4] In Cowper's Olney sanctuary, the poet creates a writing bower "where only my Myrtles presume to peep in at the window," in which he can dream up new relations between poetry and the world, the internal and external.[5] Similarly, as the poet of "The Eolian Harp" looks at the landscape around the cottage, those slightly stagey inherited "emblems" of nature become something more organic and deeply felt, as he imagines new ways in which man, like the harp set in the window of the cottage, might respond to nature. The image of the connection between nature and the divine would be one Coleridge returned to again and again, revising "The Eolian Harp" right up to the end of his life: so too, in less obvious ways, would the image of the home in nature as the starting point for such insight. The house becomes a symbol of poetic vocation, not a retreat but a position from which to write outwards, and influence the world.

Coleridge's doubts about this continued, however. They're visible in the slightly later poem, "Reflections on Having Left a Place of Retirement," which was, tellingly, first published as "Reflections on Entering into Active Life." The drama of hesitation between the home in retirement and a more active life is acted out in the poem itself, which begins, of course, with an image of the Clevedon house:

> Low was our pretty Cot: our tallest Rose
> Peep'd at the chamber-window. We could hear
> At silent noon, and eve, and early morn,
> The Sea's faint murmur. In the open air
> Our Myrtles blossom'd; and across the porch
> Thick Jasmins twin'd.[6]

The myrtles and jasmines have lost their emblematic quality and are beginning to blossom into something more natural: the rhythms of the later conversation poems. Nevertheless, they are still descendants of the thickly twining shrubs of Adam and Eve's connubial bower in *Paradise Lost*, with its high roses that shower themselves upon the happy couple. There is also a hint of something more threatening in this paradise—the murmur of the sea "at silent noon, and eve, and early morn," which inescapably carries an echo of Milton's falling angel, "from Morn, / to Noon he fell, from Noon to dewy Eve" (Book I, 742–43). The suspicion of temptation grows throughout the poem, as Coleridge fears he is enjoying "the Valley of Seclusion" too much, until by the end he resolves to quit his "dear Cot." Inveighing against what he describes as the "rose-leaf Beds" of "slothful loves and dainty Sympathies!" the poet turns away towards active life, albeit with a few backward glances towards the "sweet Abode," "Thy Jasmin and thy window-peeping Rose."

But the following year, Coleridge determined to attempt, again, the ideal of a rural idyll, this time enabled by his friend Thomas Poole, who found him a cottage near to his own in Nether Stowey, Somerset. Here Coleridge the poet-farmer set out to eschew "poetic Vanity" and "political Furore," professing instead his ambition to be rather "an expert, self-maintaining Gardener than a Milton, if I could not unite both."[7] His repeated invocation of hard manual labour in the garden bears witness to a longer classical tradition—Virgil's *Georgics*, and their redefinition in Cowper's *The Task*—but it was also his way of calming his own anxieties, refuting his fears of slothfulness and indulgence. This new life would be one of "honourable toil," intimately involved with poetic composition and child-rearing, as he tells Thelwall, "You would smile to see my eye rolling up to the ceiling in a Lyric fury, and on my knee a *Diaper* pinned, to warm."[8]

Although the early letters of the residence are full of references to his gardening ambitions—potatoes, vegetables, corn, an orchard, two pigs—a callus on his hand seems to have been the only tangible agricultural product of the period. He was soon channelling his powers of cultivation into a new project: persuading William Wordsworth and his sister Dorothy to join him in Somerset. This succeeded in summer 1797, when he wrote triumphantly to Southey and Thelwall that he had persuaded them to settle nearby. "Frost at Midnight" was written that winter and bears witness to the power of his conversations with the Wordsworths. The silent evening, as the poet sits at the cottage fireside, baby Hartley sleeping "cradled by my side," opens out into the past and the future, momentarily crystallised, like the icicles outside the door, in a single creative vision of his child, at home in nature. Yet at the point he wrote it he hadn't even visited the mountain country he evokes: those crags and lakes and clouds are a reflection of Wordsworth's yearning for the Lakes, a beautiful articulation of another's dream of home.

"Frost at Midnight" found an answer in Wordsworth's poem of summer 1798, "Tintern Abbey," which begins with the poet looking back across five years of Revolutionary disappointment and loss but ends by finding consolation in family love, in the figure of his "dear, dear Sister." She will become his reminder of a perfect relationship with nature, both now when she is free to enjoy solitary moonlit walks and "misty mountain-winds" and in later years

> when thy mind
> Shall be a mansion for all lovely forms,
> Thy memory be as a dwelling-place
> For all sweet sounds and harmonies.[9]

Those words, "mansion" and "dwelling-place," with their biblical resonance, show how strongly his sister was associated with homecoming.
This was literally realised in December 1799, as William and Dorothy
returned to settle in the Lakes, and set up house together, "a home within
a home."

The journey is mythologised in "Home at Grasmere," a long poetic
fragment which reminds us that, like Coleridge's home-making in
Clevedon and Nether Stowey, this house-move came freighted with
poetic intent. This would not be a retreat or retirement but a conscious
choice of vocation, continuing the quest begun in Coleridge's poetry of
the 1790s. Coleridge himself had begun to turn away from that poet-
gardener ideal, but his belief in the vision of retreat became still more
intense as it was projected onto Wordsworth, who would now be the
one to justify poetic retirement and "ameliorate mankind" in the shape
of *The Recluse*.[10] We know, from the manuscript copies, that "Home at
Grasmere" was intended as a part of this blank verse epic, and this ideal
helps us understand the movement of the poem, as the Lakes landscape
enfolds the poet, nourishing him spiritually and creatively, in a sort of
liberating enclosure: "Embrace me then, ye Hills, and close me in." It
is one of Wordsworth's great poems of vocation, as he turns away from
the world and pledges himself both to his art and to the landscape of his
childhood, the two thoughts inextricable from one another as he decides
that "here / Should be my home, this Valley be my World."[11]

This is evident from the very start of the poem: a stop. A running
schoolboy, cresting the brow of a hill and brought up, short, by the view
laid out below:

And, with a sudden influx overcome
At sight of this seclusion, I forgot
My haste, for hasty had my footsteps been,
As boyish my pursuits; and sighing said,
"What happy fortune were it here to live!" (174)

Thus, the homecoming is presented as a return in some ways to the pure
"boyish" happiness of childhood: it would, indeed, be a chance for the
Wordsworths to recapture a sense of security and closeness lost in

childhood. Brother and sister had been separated early and traumatically, losing first their mother, then their father, William sent away to school, Dorothy to live with relatives. "You know the pleasure I have always attached to the idea of home, a blessing which I so early lost," Dorothy wrote to a friend in 1795 when she first went to live with her brother, rejoicing at the prospect of "a comfortable home, in a house of my own."[12] Since that time, brother and sister had searched for a permanent place to settle. They found it in Grasmere, in the shape of a little white cottage, a former inn called the Dove and Olive Bough. William and Dorothy lived there from December 1799 to May 1808, joined by Mary Hutchinson, whom William married in 1802. As the increasing number of children meant space became tight, they moved on from the house, which was immediately occupied by Thomas De Quincey, for whom the rooms were "hallowed" by their association. Later in the nineteenth century, a public appeal established the house as a museum, to "preserve [Wordsworth's] humble home for England."[13]

Wordsworth describes the difficult journey towards the cottage almost as a test of strength and fortitude, as the pair win their way towards it through the winter storms.

> Bleak season was it, turbulent and bleak,
> When hitherward we journeyed, and on foot,
> Through bursts of sunshine and through flying snows. (179)

He describes the "frosty wind" driving them onwards, even the icy trees and naked brooks questioning their determination and intent, "Whence come ye? To what end?" When they finally reached the cottage, the weather briefly cleared:

> bright and solemn was the sky
> That faced us with a passionate welcoming,
> And led us to our threshold, to a home
> Within a home, what was to be, and soon,
> Our love within a love. (180)

The language of passion, of threshold and love, presents this as a wedding journey, an epithalamium with the house as an abashed bride, "disturbed, uneasy in itself" and its new inhabitants. In the letters of the period, particularly a long joyous celebration of their arrival to Coleridge written on Christmas Eve 1799, Wordsworth describes a process almost akin to wooing the house: "am I fanciful when I extend the obligation of gratitude to insensate things? May not a man have a salutary pleasure in doing something gratuitously for the sake of his house, as for an individual to which he owes so much?"[14] This isn't simply taking possession: this is a coaxing into relationship that shows the deep feeling the pair had for this house. As "Home at Grasmere" goes on to relate, brother and sister would be put to the test through a long Lakes winter, "two months unwearied of severest storm," but they were, in a significant choice of words, "found faithful" both to the house and to the poetic vocation it embodied, as the cottage hears:

The Poet mutter his prelusive songs
With chearful heart . . . (180)

In "Home at Grasmere," then, Wordsworth suggests that the homecoming has been a triumph: that dedication to country life has enabled true poetic vision.

The story was borne out by subsequent pilgrims, such as Thomas De Quincey, who would go on to take over the tenancy of the cottage, literally inhabiting the Wordsworthian ideal of home. His *Recollections of the Lakes and the Lake Poets* vividly re-enacts the journey undertaken in "Home at Grasmere" as he recalls the "almost theatrical surprise" of the Vale of Grasmere laid before him with the "little white cottage" at its centre. Inside:

One window there was—a perfect and unpretending cottage window, with little diamond panes, embowered at almost every season of the year with roses; and, in the summer and autumn, with a profusion of jasmine and other fragrant shrubs.[15]

This is not simply a visit to Wordsworth *en famille*: it is a re-creation of the paradisal, Miltonic vision first encountered in "The Eolian Harp," with the embowered poet at the centre. And when in the 1890s Queen Victoria's chaplain Stopford Brooke began the campaign to save the

FIGURE 6.1. Dove Cottage, Grasmere, Wordsworth's home from 1799 to 1808, as pictured in Stopford A. Brooke's 1895 pamphlet raising funds for its preservation. (Copyright © the British Library Board 10362.gg.1)

house for the nation, he too returned to the image of the embowering flowers, quoting De Quincey alongside "Home at Grasmere." Urging readers to save this "hallowed ground" blooming with "memories like flowers," Brooke sees the house as testament to plain living, high thinking, poetic vocation, and family love:

> In poverty, in simplicity of life, in quiet duty done in obedience day by day, in love, is the strength of life. There is no greater object-lesson of this truth than Dove Cottage and Wordsworth's life in it.[16]

Visiting the Dove Cottage website now, the image of the roses at the window is prominent; the cottage is introduced through a quotation from "Home at Grasmere," and visitors are urged, just as in Stopford Brooke's pamphlet, to enter into the cottage and muse on the "many years of 'plain living and high thinking'" spent by William and Dorothy.[17]

But for all the quiet domestic content celebrated at the cottage, it had its own stories of loss, disappointment, grief, and hard labour. There were absences in this home: their brother John, who had intended to settle with them but who was lost at sea in 1805; more covertly, William's first child, Caroline, his illegitimate daughter by Annette Vallon, with whose family he had stayed in Orleans in 1791. An instruction to Dorothy in late 1800 reads, "When you are writing to France say all that is affectionate to A. and all that is fatherly to C."[18] This home-making, then, was carried out while also acknowledging the ideals and the relationships that had been left behind across the Channel. As William's instruction also suggests, the home at Grasmere was primarily sustained by female duty and hard work. Dorothy's diary entries reveal all the occluded labour behind the poetic vision: the washing, scouring, sewing, weeding, child-rearing, copying, and correspondence. They also show the bodily toll of this rural life, the cold, the physical hardships, the toothaches and headaches and gloom and sickness. Dorothy's life from 1829 was increasingly curtailed by illness, probably pre-senile dementia, leading to complete invalidism in her later years.

It is worth remembering the potential for loss and disappointment and failure of expectation that is ever present in the Romantic home. What, for instance, of Hartley Coleridge, the child who is so beautifully imagined in "Frost at Midnight" wandering "like a breeze," perfectly at home in the landscape of the Lakes? He seems to have lived out the injunction literally, never managing to escape the promise of his childhood, despite considerable accomplishment as a scholar and poet in his own right. He spent his later life lodging around Grasmere, often sleeping in barns and ditches, and in his poems he compulsively returns to the imagery of his father's work, so that it is unclear whether the wandering image acts as a prophecy or a curse.

A lonely wanderer upon earth am I,
The waif of nature—like uprooted weed

Borne by the stream, or like a shaken reed,
A frail dependent of the fickle sky.[19]

So powerful had the myth of being at home in nature become that it seems to have stopped him finding a home anywhere else.

Perhaps we shouldn't be surprised at the ways in which Romantic home might prove a difficult ideal. Coleridge's Clevedon poems of rural bliss were, after all, shaped by the language of paradise lost: even as the rural bower, with all its roses and myrtles and jasmine, is celebrated, the fate of its first Edenic incarnation is uneasily remembered. The Wordsworths' passionate attachment to place notwithstanding, the Romantic home may always have been most powerful simply as an imaginative ideal: already nostalgic from the start. *The Recluse* was never completed, despite all Coleridge's cajoling and admonition; "Home at Grasmere" was not published in its own right until later in the nineteenth century. It was in the frustrated idolatry of De Quincey, and the devotion of Victorian pilgrims, readers, and editors—Stopford Brooke, Matthew Arnold, William Knight—that the sanctification of the Dove Cottage home really took shape.[20] When we go back to the poetry, whether that is the Miltonic bowers of Coleridge's 1790s poetry or the unfinished nature of "Home at Grasmere," what emerges is something more tentative, more alert to its own storytelling and the ways we create our narratives of home.

I still have Google Street View open on the browser. I take a last look: the rose bushes; the apple trees just knobbling into bud; all those flowers. I banish the thought of the skip on the drive and the estate agent's sign at the gate, and instead I take down the *Golden Treasury* from my shelf. Book IV, where Wordsworth and Shelley and Keats and Thomas Campbell all jumble together in a parade of cottages, nooks, cuckoos, beech trees, daisies, daffodils:

For oft, when on my couch I lie
In vacant or in pensive mood,
They flash upon that inward eye
Which is the bliss of solitude

And then my heart with pleasure fills,
And dances with the daffodils.[21]

Like Wordsworth lying in the little room at home in Grasmere, hearing Dorothy read over the journals of the past, reliving walks they'd taken years before, those daffodils can only really be enjoyed in retrospect. Nostalgia is the true condition of Romantic home.

Dream Houses

7
At Home with Tennyson

ROBERT DOUGLAS-FAIRHURST

Between 2006 and 2009 the *Guardian* ran a series of articles titled "Writers' Rooms." Each week there was a fresh invitation to look around a room where a particular writer worked, and by implication to poke around inside their heads. Together they revealed a whole world of interiors. Simon Callow chose his dressing room in the Haymarket Theatre, where he was busy typing out the latest sections of his Orson Welles biography in between scenes playing Pozzo in *Waiting for Godot*: one strolling player trying to pin down another; one seemingly endless task intercut with another. Alexander Masters explained that "there's no pattern to the way I write" and offered as evidence the barely controlled chaos of his bedroom, where the star attraction was a crocodile skin nailed to a wall. It was the same specimen he had earlier put on the cover of his first book, *Stuart: A Life Backwards*, and in the published photograph it still looked as if it was on a blank page waiting to be surrounded by words. Miranda Seymour devoted most of her account to things that couldn't be seen in the newspaper, such as a window from where she watched "birds scooting about on the surface of the lake," or the picture above her desk of "an Italian landscape on the morning of the last eclipse," both of which playfully drew attention to what all writing does: making present what is absent; making a world of paper and ink seem as real as a desk or a chair. But despite many differences between these rooms in terms of architectural style and personal taste, all of them touched on a common set of questions. When someone is writing, where *do* they live: in the real world or in a self-created elsewhere? And are stories or poems shaped by the pressures of external reality, or do they discover that shape by pressing back against the world in which they find themselves?

Such questions were central to Victorian discussions over the "place" of literature, an idea that included the physical environment in which it was produced as well as the cultural position it attempted to uphold. This took on various forms. For example, *The Empty Chair* (1870), Sir Samuel Luke Fildes's watercolour of Dickens's study at Gad's Hill Place, depicts the novelist's chair pushed back from his desk, as if he has just left the room and will return at any moment. R. W. Buss's *Dickens's Dream* (1875) is similarly open-ended: here the novelist is pictured fully, but the characters swarming out of his head are incomplete, like a set of ghosts from the stories he didn't have time to write. Tennyson's study was an even more popular subject for Victorian artists and journalists, not to mention the dozens of friends whose accounts of his prickly hospitality gradually turned it from an ordinary room into a place as legendary as Fingal's Cave. To take just one example, in 1884 *The Graphic* pictured Tennyson in his study at Aldworth, the French-style Gothic house he had built in 1869 as a writing retreat, as part of a series titled "Celebrities of the Day." "The accessories of this charming room were such as one naturally expects to find in a poet's study," noted the journalist F. G. Kitton: "Books and magazines, covering shelves and tables, were abundant, and, besides antique chairs and tables, there was a pair of large globes (terrestrial and celestial), mounted on stands."[1] Clearly in Kitton's eyes Tennyson's study wasn't a neutral space; it was steeped in history, geographically far-reaching, and thick with words: just like the poetry produced there. Kitton's conclusion was that "surely nothing could be more conducive to poetic thoughts and inspirations than such a delightful environment as that enjoyed by the Laureate in his Surrey home," and the newspaper's illustration reinforced this idea that readers had stumbled into a place that was set at an angle to the real world, where poets gazed off into the distance in search of somewhere that existed far, far away, or perhaps could only exist in the space between their ears.

Figure 7.1. "Celebrities of the Day—Lord Tennyson, Poet Laureate," from *The Graphic*, 22 March 1884. (Copyright © the British Library Board MFM.MLD46)

Tennyson's early descriptions of where poetry was made had been far more vague: in a "lonely place," according to "The Poet's Song," or "Not wholly in the busy world, nor quite / Beyond it" in "The Gardener's Daughter," which was hardly a helpful set of directions.[2] But as his career developed, readers were increasingly keen to pin him down to somewhere more specific—not only Aldworth but also Farringford, his home on the Isle of Wight and the subject of an article written by Grant Allen in 1892,[3] where Tennyson wasn't pictured but the desk chair was again positioned at an inviting angle, and everything else could be treated as an enduring emblem of the poems assembled there: order, comfort, learning, a clear view. It was another attempt to offer some insight into the mysterious process of composition, and another example of a developing trend in which Victorian journalists sought to give their readers a simulacrum of intimacy with famous writers. Tennyson had invited them into his home, and they could now reciprocate by cutting out this picture and sticking it onto their walls. It was both a window into his life and a virtual extension of their own homes.

Tennyson wasn't the only writer who was subject to this sort of intrusion. Charlotte Boyce has pointed out that "houses associated with writers such as Wordsworth and Byron became popular stopping-off points on Britain's tourist trail,"[4] and later in the century Haworth Parsonage became the site of dedicated literary pilgrimages, including sentimental books like *Charlotte Brontë at Home* (1899). There was a similar appetite for poking around living writers' houses through publications such as William Howitt's *Homes and Haunts of the Most Eminent British Poets* (1847), as well as series such as the *Idler*'s "Lions in Their Dens," the *Strand Magazine*'s "Illustrated Interviews," and the *World*'s "Celebrities at Home."[5] Nor was Tennyson immune to this fashion for literary tourism. According to his son, he was filled with "awe and sadness" when he visited the "low dark room" that had been Goethe's "sacred study," and on a visit to Lyme Regis he insisted on being shown "the steps from which Louisa Musgrove fell" in Jane Austen's *Persuasion*.[6]

But although Tennyson occasionally—grudgingly, grumblingly—allowed journalists into his home, he was far less hospitable to the crowds of ordinary readers who tried to hunt him down. The periodical press and contemporary memoirs include many stories in which souvenir hunters are caught stripping branches from the tree planted at Farringford by Garibaldi, or are seen spying on Tennyson as he eats his breakfast, or so terrify him that he flees from what he thinks is a crowd of them advancing on him but turns out to be a flock of sheep. In this atmosphere of literary stalking and door-stepping, even polite brush-offs could be burnished into anecdotes. A visiting American bishop named Gilbert Haren reported knocking on the poet's door to ask "if Mr. Tennyson is at home" and was told that he was; he waited excitedly as his card was taken into the house and was then told that in fact Mr. Tennyson was *not at home*—a slight change of emphasis from geographical location to social acceptance that he seems not really to have understood.[7]

Other writers stuck to virtual tourism. John Walters's illustrated book *In Tennyson Land* (1890) was only one of several attempts to trace the poems to specific locations, which in this case meant arguing that all the houses Tennyson describes were "echoes" of "the home of his youth"—that is, Lincolnshire, which Walters dutifully trudged through with a camera to capture the supposed originals of places like Locksley Hall and Audley Court. For him Tennyson's poems were photographic memories that had been filtered through a lyrical lens. For those who knew Tennyson, on the other hand, his homes were not only places that had inspired poems. They *were* poems: buildings imbued with a literary atmosphere that was as powerful and intangible as old pipe smoke. Perhaps that is why some visitors' memories naturally slipped into a kind of prose poetry, as if trying to make their writing style fit in with their host's lifestyle. After a visit to Farringford, H. D. Rawnsley pointed out that "when one came upon the lawn it seemed more velvet and mossy silent than woodland lawns are wont to be": a description that drifts in and out of dreamy blank verse and with "mossy silent" makes Tennyson's garden sound like the sort of place where you might bump into a figure like his Mariana, whose "flower-plots" are crusted with "blackest moss." Lady Ritchie went even further, describing Farringford as "a charmed place" with "green walls without, and speaking walls within," as if she was half expecting to find a fairy-tale princess living there rather than an old man downing port and peering at her through plainly inadequate spectacles.[8]

Of course it isn't just the Victorians who suffered from this sort of confusion. The popular association of houses and writers is something that continues to exert its influence, through not only tourist attractions like Anne Hathaway's Cottage but also contemporary building projects like Laureate Gardens in Henley-on-Thames: a new development of thirty-four homes grouped together in architectural clusters with names like Tennyson House and Wordsworth Court. But if Victorian readers were especially prone to associating Tennyson and the home, that's probably because he too kept returning to the subject in his writing, like a creative itch he could never scratch away.

He enjoyed settling the word "home" in different places, using compounds that included "home-bred," "home-circle," "home-return," and "home-voyage." Nor was he above exercising a kind of literary hospitality: "The moanings of the homeless sea" is a line from *In Memoriam* that borrows "the homeless sea" from Shelley, so that even as Tennyson is describing the endlessly shifting surfaces of the sea he is finding them a new home on the page. He was equally good at evoking home when it existed only as an idea, as in "The Lotos-Eaters," where so much of what the speaker broods over—"roam," "foam," "honeycomb"—has the word "home" flickering through it like a nagging but elusive memory. "How they got home you must read in Homer," one reviewer wittily pointed out,[9] but that journey is not part of Tennyson's story, because in this poem home is less a place than a state of mind. Then there's the fact that Tennyson was clearly interested in what one might call—reversing the title of one of Ruskin's early essays—the architecture of poetry. So, at a crude level, joining words together could be compared to joining bricks together, and the relationship between ordinary and more unusual words could be compared to the relationship between solid everyday building materials like wood or stone and more fanciful decorative details. There's an example in Tennyson's early poem "The 'How' and the 'Why'":

> Why a church is with a steeple built;
> And a house with a chimneypot?

This is the first recorded use of "chimneypot" in the *OED*, and although it's unlikely Tennyson invented such a homely compound, it does show his awareness of post-Romantic debates over the kind of materials a poet should be using, whether new or reclaimed or a mixture of both.

Other early poems, like "The Deserted House," are even more self-conscious about their status as literary constructions:

> Close the door, the shutters close,
>> Or through the windows we shall see
>> The nakedness and vacancy
> Of the dark deserted house.

FIGURE 7.2. *Home Sweet Home*, painted by W. Dendy Sadler; etched by W. H. Boucher. (Courtesy of the Library of Congress)

Here the house represents the body deserted by the spirit at death, but the door and shutters could just as easily refer to the mouth and eyelids, traditionally closed at death, or to a real door and real shutters, sealed as a sign of mourning. Again the ambiguity makes Tennyson's house into both a place and an idea. But the fact that "close" and "house" fail to match up properly, like the patterns on badly laid wallpaper, also seems significant, and it reveals a surprising pattern that reaches across his career.

Like his hero in "The Wanderer," in poem after poem Tennyson "wanders on from home to home," but very rarely do these poems comfortably settle into or settle for the period's typical domestic ideals. Usually they strain and chafe against them. And one symptom of this is that when Tennyson tries to engage with the idea of home, often his verse slips out of its usual groove, producing the impression of a voice that is not at home even in its own form. Some examples should make this a bit clearer. To begin with, there's Tennyson's interest in homelessness: the "homeless ocean" of "The Voyage" and "homeless plant" of "Despair," as well as the "homeless sea" of *In Memoriam*, not to mention all those voyagers and explorers for whom home lies over the horizon and beyond the final lines of their poems. Then there's the lingering association in Tennyson's mind of home with death or decay: Simeon Stylites complaining about "the home of sin, my flesh" that is gradually rotting away; Rizpah stealing her son's body and boasting, "I have taken them home, I have numbered the bones"; "Crossing the Bar" and the ship that "turns again home"; "Home they brought the warrior"—for a celebratory knees-up? Waving palm leaves and ostrich plumes? No: "Home they brought the warrior dead." There are also the odd little rhymes he invented, such as this couplet:

> Home is home, though never so homely,
> And a harlot a harlot, though never so comely.

Tennyson came up with this in response to a planned home for fallen women, and the gap between ideals and actuality that dominates so many discussions of such issues in the period can be heard in that slightly skewed rhyme of "homely" with "comely." There are also whole poems, like his early lyric "Home," which reaches its conclusion with a triumphant exclamation mark, like a little firework being let off on the page, but only after asking a far less convincing set of questions:

> What shall sever me
> From the love of home?
> Shall the weary sea,
> Leagues of sounding foam?
> Shall extreme distress,
> Shall unknown disgrace,
> Make my love the less
> For my sweet birth-place?

It goes on like this for several more lines, but what prevents it from turning into a sentimental squib are the number of jerky rhythms and wonky rhymes it contains. The result is a poem that sounds like a half-hearted impression of something more convincing, literary karaoke, as Tennyson mouths a set of platitudes that in effect have an invisible set of quotation marks around them.

In Memoriam is equally unwilling to settle on home as an idea or even as a word. On five of the seven occasions "home" appears in this poem, it is the last word in a line, but four out of these five examples follow it with something other than a full stop, and in each case the reader, like the speaker, is forced to carry on. Elsewhere, even when Tennyson narrows his architectural range to a single room the results have a similarly Beckett-like ambivalence, producing a voice that is keen to create a nest of words for itself but also appears to be nervously eyeing up the lines of each stanza like a little set of prison bars:

> O darling room, my heart's delight,
> Dear room, the apple of my sight,
> With thy two couches soft and white,
> There is no room so exquisite,
> No little room so warm and bright,
> Wherein to read, wherein to write.

The critic Herbert Tucker has described "O Darling Room" as "teasingly camp,"[10] which nicely captures its combination of the overemphatic and the uncommitted. At a simple level it is a celebration of writing and the power of poetry to create a world of its own. The final word, "write," is also the seed from which everything else springs: a whole stanza (the Italian word literally means "a room") in which words create everything from the couches to the temperature. You can even shuffle the lines around like pieces of furniture without any great loss of sense. But again we notice that one word is clearly out of place. John Wilson Croker certainly spotted it when he first reviewed the poem in 1833—"*this little room so exquisite*," he trilled meanly.[11] In context the word looks like an angular modern chair in a shabby sitting room: it is not quite at home. And when we read the poem neither are we.

Why this sort of awkwardness when Tennyson writes about home? Partly, I think, it is because what the home typically represents in the Victorian imagination—stability, security, and so on—is perfect for

FIGURE 7.3. *Enoch Arden: The Hour of Trial.* (Courtesy of the Library of Congress)

generating moods but not for generating stories. One might even say that home is a good environment for lyric but no place for narrative. And for Tennyson that meant it usually had to be deferred or denied if the writing was to retain any narrative interest. One of the traditional nursery rhymes he collected was this:

> Come home, father, come home
> Come home, father, come home
> Bring baby a spice cake
> And pussy a boulderstone

If this is a prayer or magical incantation it is clearly one that fails: four times the father is asked to come home, and each time all that returns is the phrase "Come home." (The fact that these words are so close in appearance but will never produce a proper rhyme makes such a failure sound even sadder.) This keeps a mild sort of narrative interest going, as also happens when Tennyson makes Mariana repeat "He cometh not . . . he cometh not" in her poem, because here too a refrain is the only kind of return that she can control. But what both poems might remind us, through their lyrical patterns, is that although it's easy to make home the setting for a story, it is far harder to make it the subject of a story.

Put simply, a poem is where words dwell: it is where they live but also where they stay on, not only through the sheer persistence of print but also through rhyme and refrain and all the other ways in which poetry encourages words to extend themselves beyond their usual limits. That can make a poem a good place to celebrate the home as restful, harmonious, and so on, but it's far harder to use it in the way Tennyson's critics repeatedly urged him to—that is, to find a compromise in his poetry between reflection and action, or still life and process. His solution, it seems, was to take the idea of home and twist it to be far more unsettled and unsettling. Like the hero of Tennyson's *Enoch Arden*, who towards the end of the poem finds himself peering in through his living room window and realizing he's been displaced from his own household, it was to write poems that stop us feeling too much at home.

8

Chartwell

Winston Churchill's Dream House

DAVID CANNADINE

"If only," Clementine Churchill wrote longingly to her husband, Winston, in September 1922, "we could get a little country house within our means and live there within our means it would add great happiness and peace to our lives."[1] At that time, Winston and Clementine needed some significant injection of happiness and peace into their existence. In the previous year, Churchill's mother, Jennie, had died at sixty-seven; Winston and Clementine's fourth child, Marigold Frances, had succumbed to septicemia of the throat, aged only two years and nine months; and Clementine's thirty-four-year-old brother, Bill Hozier, had committed suicide in a Paris hotel room. These private family sorrows were accompanied by serious setbacks in her husband's public career. In the autumn of 1922, the Lloyd George Coalition fell, Churchill relinquished his position as colonial secretary, and a general election ensued. Soon after, he was operated on for appendicitis, he was voted out by the electors in his Dundee constituency, and he began his "re-rat" from the Liberals back to the Conservatives, which would take him two years to complete. "In the twinkling of an eye," as he later recalled, "I found myself without an office, without a seat, without a party and without an appendix."[2] He might have added that he was without a country house, too.

During Churchill's bachelor years as a soldier, journalist, young MP, and ambitious politician, he had never enjoyed a permanent home, fixed address, or settled abode, and this peripatetic existence had continued after he married Clementine in 1908. Here, indeed, was a deeper explanation for his wife's heartfelt wish to settle down fourteen years later. There was always Blenheim Palace in Oxfordshire, the grand, Olympian ancestral pile of the Dukes of Marlborough, where Churchill had been born and had proposed to Clementine, and which they would frequently visit for lengthy stays. But when it came to their own domestic arrangements, Winston and Clementine, and their growing family, were often on the move during their early married years. In London they had set up home in Eccleston Square but later relocated to Admiralty House in Whitehall, then to Arlington Street, to the Cromwell Road, and finally to Sussex Square; while in the country they had rented places in Norfolk and Surrey, and late in 1916 they had acquired a dilapidated medieval farmhouse at Lullenden, which had turned out to be a very costly white elephant, and which they sold with relief and at an unexpected profit three years later.[3]

One reason for this constant movement was that, as Clementine soon learned, her husband's finances were far from robust, and maintaining a town house and a country house, both appropriately staffed with servants, was a serious burden, given the limited and unreliable nature of their resources. Churchill earned money from his books and journalism, he was paid as an MP, and he also received a ministerial salary while in government. But his authorial income fluctuated unpredictably, he had ceased to draw any official stipend in 1922, and, to Clementine's lifelong dismay, he liked to gamble in the casinos on the French Riviera (and later would speculate unwisely on the New York Stock Exchange). There was also the residual estate of his father, Lord Randolph Churchill, who had died in 1895, which was worth £42,000 by the time Winston married (approximately £5 million in current values) and was held in trust for him and his younger brother, Jack. Churchill could apply to the trustees for loans towards house purchases, but they would have to be repaid. More promising was an unexpected legacy from an unmarried distant kinsman, Lord Harry Vane-Tempest, who had been killed

in a railway accident early in 1921, and who had left Churchill his
Garron Towers estates in County Antrim, which brought in an income
of £4,000 a year (well over £150,000 in today's money).[4]

The result, as Clementine noted with relief, was that "haunting care"
had "vanished forever from our lives," as this surprise windfall might
make possible the longed-for settled existence, "within our means," that
she craved.[5] Yet such hopes would prove vain, for the country house
the Churchills eventually acquired meant that for most of the next quarter of a century, they would not be living within their means but considerably beyond them. Enriched by the Vane-Tempest legacy, Winston
and Clementine looked at several properties, but it was Chartwell Manor
by which Churchill was completely smitten. It was a Tudor house, with
subsequent enlargements and additions, set in eighty acres of grounds,
and although only twenty-four miles from London it commanded magnificent views over the Weald of Kent. Just a few days after Clementine
had sensibly urged the need to get only "a little country house within
our means," Churchill bought Chartwell for £5,000 (approximately
£250,000 in today's values), *and he did so without telling her*. It was the
only occasion during their marriage when he was not straightforward
with her, and Clementine was appalled by his behaviour and extrava-
gance. In the words of Stefan Buczacki, "the purchase of Chartwell revealed Churchill at his most implacable, his most egotistic, his most
deaf and blinkered to outside reason and influence."[6]

As Clementine had feared, Chartwell proved to be a money pit, with
expenditures soon spiralling out of control. The renovations and exten-
sions overseen by the architect Philip Tilden eventually cost in the region
of £25,000 (or substantially more than £1 million at current prices), and
at further expense, the grounds were adorned with ornamental lakes
and a swimming pool, and the estate was stocked with a variety of fish,
animals, and birds. The running costs were also prohibitive, since the
house required a full-time staff of eight indoor servants, three gardeners,
two secretaries, and a chauffeur.[7] And as befitted someone who once
remarked "my tastes are simple: I am easily pleased with the best,"
Churchill liked to live well. He expected the food to be delicious, the
wine and spirits to be excellent, and the supply of cigars to be abundant.

FIGURE 8.1. Churchill bricklaying, Chartwell, 1930. (Courtesy of the Churchill Archives Centre, The Broadwater Collection, BRDW 1/2/141)

As a result, Chartwell became the centre of Churchill's life: his private sanctuary, the place to which he returned in days of triumph and failure, of joy and sorrow, of health and sickness. "Every day away from Chartwell," he once observed, with some exaggeration (what about twenty-four hours in 10 Downing Street?), "is a day wasted." But Clementine, who was responsible for running the house, saw things very differently: instead of bringing her the peace and happiness her husband undoubtedly found there, Chartwell was a constant source of worry and strain.[8]

In order to pay for the money pit, Chartwell became what was known as Churchill's "word factory," where he poured out books, articles, and speeches. He completed *The World Crisis* in five volumes (1923–31), produced *Marlborough: His Life and Times* in four volumes (1933–38), and worked on a first draft of his *History of the English-Speaking Peoples*

(1937–40). He also published *My Early Life* (1930), *Thoughts and Adventures* (1932), *Great Contemporaries* (1937), *Arms and the Covenant* (1938), and *Step by Step* (1939). In addition, there were articles for a wide range of newspapers on a wide range of subjects, often ghostwritten by his former private secretary Eddie Marsh. There were many reasons why Churchill produced so much: he was genuinely creative and loved putting words together in arresting patterns and phrases, he sought to celebrate his family and justify his own political conduct, *and he needed to make money.* Yet although he was very well paid for his books and articles, the cost of keeping Chartwell meant Churchill's finances became increasingly chaotic, and they were made worse by his losses on the American stock exchange in 1929 and 1938. As his debts mounted, he mothballed Chartwell in 1929–30 and was driven to put it on the market in 1937, when only the timely intervention of Sir Henry Strakosch, an Austrian-born financier who took responsibility for his liabilities, saved Chartwell (and also Churchill's career).[9]

Of all the books that Churchill produced at Chartwell during the 1920s and 1930s, the most revealing, in terms of what it did and did not say, was *My Early Life.* It was written in a beguilingly self-deprecating tone and was a nostalgic evocation of youthful adventure in the late nineteenth century on the frontiers of empire—a world that had been largely eclipsed by World War I and by the financial downturn and economic collapse that began in 1929. In dealing with his schooldays, Churchill exaggerated his scholarly shortcomings, and he also gave a very selective account of his relationship with his parents. In the case of his mother, who invariably put her crowded and demanding social life ahead of her maternal duties and obligations, Churchill was correct in observing: "She shone for me like the evening star. I loved her dearly—but at a distance." However, he did not mention the many sad and pathetic letters he wrote her when he was away at school, begging and craving for the replies, the attention and the affection that she rarely provided.[10] Such attention and affection as young Winston did receive came from his nanny, Mrs. Everest: he remained devoted to her for as long as she lived, paid for the upkeep of her grave, wrote a moving tribute to her in *My Early Life*, and kept a photograph of her on his bedside table ever after.[11]

Winston's relations with his father had been even more distant, for Lord Randolph was not only an absentee parent but also, when he chose to focus on his elder son at all, extremely critical and negative. When he finally scraped into Sandhurst, at the third attempt in 1893, Lord Randolph wrote him a cruel, scathing, and heartless letter, denouncing his "slovenly, happy-go-lucky, harum-scarum style of work," deploring the "idle, useless, unprofitable life you have had during your school-days," and predicting that he would become "a mere social wastrel," degenerating into "a shabby, unhappy and futile existence," for which he would "have to bear all the blame for such misfortunes himself."[12] Small wonder that Churchill would later write, in the first volume of *Marlborough*: "It is said that famous men are usually the product of un-happy childhood" and that "the twinges of adversity, the slights and taunts in earlier years are needed to evoke the ruthless fixity of pur-pose and tenacious mother-wit without which great actions are seldom accomplished."[13] Much of the energy, ambition, drive, and resolve that Churchill would display in later life came from a determination to prove that Lord Randolph had been wrong and to win from him a sort of posthumous approval that he had never gained while his father had been alive.

Yet Churchill also idolized Lord Randolph, even as he knew he was such a disappointment to him: according to Violet Bonham Carter, "he worshipped at the altar of his unknown father."[14] When Lord Randolph died in 1895, still only in his mid-forties, from a degenerative disease of the brain that may have been brought on by syphilis, Winston was desolate. "All my dreams," he later wrote, "of comradeship with him, of entering parliament at his side and in his support, were ended. There remained for me only to pursue his aims and vindicate his memory."[15] In preparation for the parliamentary career on which he had set his heart, he memorized many of Lord Randolph's speeches, dressed up in similar clothes, used many of the same gestures, and espoused his cause of Tory democracy. And he ended his maiden speech in the House of Commons early in 1901 by thanking MPs for "the kindness and patience" with which he had been heard, "not on my own account, but because of a certain splendid memory which many honourable members still preserve." (In fact, many politicians who remembered Lord Randolph did not recall "a certain splendid memory" but someone of overweening ambition, unstable temperament, and wayward judgement, and they soon began to say the same thing about Winston.)[16]

Throughout the 1900s, Churchill remained in thrall to Lord Randolph's example. "I took my politics almost unquestioningly from him," he would later write, and when his first child was born in 1911, he would name him Randolph, in further homage to his father. By then, he had written a two-volume life of Lord Randolph, which was published in 1906.[17] From one perspective, it was a deeply sanitized and highly selective work of filial piety, ignoring his father's many defects of character, omitting episodes from which he had not emerged with credit, failing to understand why so many people had disliked and distrusted him, and implausibly depicting him as a self-made man, valiantly but vainly battling against the entrenched but outmoded Conservative "old gang" led by Lord Salisbury and his network of aristocratic relatives. As Churchill's cousin Ivor Guest perceptively remarked, "Few fathers have done less for their sons. Few sons have done more for their fathers."[18] But at the same time, Churchill also used this biography as a way of justifying his own decision to leave the Conservatives and join the Liberals, on the (implausible) grounds that he, too, was being held back by the still outdated party leadership and that the best way to promote Tory democracy in the 1900s was to cross the floor and join the Liberals.

Thereafter, Churchill continued to hero-worship his father, even as he never quite got over the scornful treatment he had received at his hands as a boy. Having returned to the Conservative Party and to Parliament in 1924, the prime minister, Stanley Baldwin, invited him to be Chancellor of the Exchequer, the very post Lord Randolph had (briefly) held and from which he had resigned in 1886. "This fulfills my ambition," Churchill responded. "I still have my father's robes as Chancellor." His mother had carefully preserved them in case her son might need them, and he would later wear them on ceremonial occasions as

Chancellor of Bristol University, to which he was appointed in 1929.[19] Yet the scars from the paternal scoldings he had suffered in his childhood remained unhealed. "We have," Winston told his own son Randolph, after dinner à deux in the late 1930s, "this evening had a longer period of continuous conversation together than the total which I ever had with my father in the whole course of his life."[20] But even amidst the stresses of the final stages of World War II, he still remembered that 24 January 1945 was the fiftieth anniversary of Lord Randolph's death; and on VE Day, the one figure he would most have wished to have been present to witness his moment of supreme triumph was his father.

~

World War II transformed Churchill's fortunes not only metaphorically but also literally. He became the heroic figure that he had always wanted to be and that he had imaginatively anticipated in his only novel, *Savrola* (1900). From 1945 until his death twenty years later, Churchill was the most admired, honoured, and famous man in the Western world, one indication of which was that he was awarded the Nobel Prize for Literature in 1953 "for his mastery of historical and biographical description as well as for his brilliant oratory in defending exalted human values." The many hours he had spent dictating in his study at Chartwell during the 1920s and 1930s had certainly paid handsome dividends, while his long column inches of sometimes ghosted journalism were conveniently forgotten. By the end of the war, Churchill's finances were also transformed, thanks to the sale of the film rights on his earlier books, which meant his accumulated debts were paid off and his bank balance was well in credit for the first time in a long time. And the deals that were subsequently made for the worldwide publication of his war memoirs (6 vols., 1948–54), and remade for the *History of the English-Speaking Peoples* (4 vols., 1956–58), meant that in later life, Churchill did become a wealthy man for the first time.[21]

This transformation in Churchill's circumstances was also accompanied by a transformation in his relation to Chartwell. In the short run, things had not looked all that good for him in the aftermath of VE Day. He was defeated in the general election held soon after, and it would be another year before the lucrative deals for his war memoirs were finally completed. In the meantime, Churchill once again decided that Chartwell would have to be put up for sale. But the press baron Lord Camrose, proprietor of the *Daily Telegraph*, thought it deplorable that the man who had led Britain through its darkest days to final victory, only to be dismissed by the electorate, should also have to sell his home to make ends meet. With the help of fifteen friends from business, industry, and finance he raised £85,000 (more than £3 million in today's values), of which £35,000 was paid to Churchill for Chartwell and £50,000 was given to the National Trust as an endowment for its upkeep. Churchill even offered to "throw in the corpse as well," and be buried there, and for the rest of his life, he would continue to live at Chartwell as a tenant of the Trust. The details were only made public many years after his death, and a circular slate plaque was eventually mounted on the east wall at Chartwell, recording the names of those who had given.[22]

This arrangement did much—but never enough—to allay the anxieties by which Clementine had constantly been beset before 1939, trying to balance the household accounts, deal with the servants, and keep the place functioning, when it was often unclear where the money would come from. And while, during the 1930s, Chartwell had been the expensive place of retreat for an ageing politician widely regarded as having a brilliant future apparently behind him, it was increasingly seen after 1945 as a secular shrine to "the greatest Englishman of his time" and "the saviour of his country"—a status that was guaranteed by the deal reached with the National Trust.[23] (Chartwell was also the place where he would spend much of the summer of 1953, recovering in seclusion from the stroke about which very few people were told at the time.) As his finances prospered, Churchill extended the Chartwell estate, buying up neighbouring farms and entrusting their management to his son-in-law Christopher Soames. He took up racing, some of his horses were stabled near Chartwell, and during his peacetime premiership, he would attend race meetings with the queen, their horses competing against each other. By then, Churchill not only could afford his country house but possessed sufficient resources to take up country pursuits as well.[24]

It was, appropriately, at Chartwell, late in 1947, that Churchill made a final attempt to come to terms with Lord Randolph. When asked by his daughter Sarah whom he would most wish to meet at dinner, he replied, "Oh, my father of course," and he went on to explain that he had recently dreamed that the ghost of Lord Randolph had visited him, while he had been painting in his studio. Churchill subsequently wrote an imaginary account of their conversation, which was never published in his lifetime.[25] Much of their talk was concerned with what had happened since Lord Randolph's death: the strengthening of the monarchy, votes for women, two world wars, the holocaust, the end of British rule in India, the decline of British global power, the advent of a bipolar world dominated by the United States and Communist Russia, and the election in Britain of "a Socialist government with a very large majority." But the central conceit of the story is that Lord Randolph never guesses, and at no point during these exchanges does Churchill let on, that he had far surpassed his father in his achievements. "I really wonder," Lord Randolph concludes, "why you didn't go into politics. . . . You might even have made a name for yourself." At which point his apparition vanishes, leaving Winston bereft once more.

The story makes plain that, despite the global acclaim and celebrity he was now enjoying, Churchill still yearned, over half a century since his death, for the posthumous approval from his father that he had never won or received while he had been alive. "I was," he makes Lord Randolph recall, "not going to talk politics with a boy like you ever. Bottom of the school! Never passed any examinations, except into the Cavalry! Wrote me stilted letters. I could not see how you could make your living." But although Lord Randolph never realises how much his son has achieved, he does offer an apology and attempt a reconciliation: "Of course you were very young, and I loved you dearly. Old people are always impatient with young ones. . . . I never expected that you would develop so far and so fully." When asked by friends whether what became known as "The Dream" was fictional, Churchill would smile and say, "Not entirely." But one final act of homage and reconciliation remained, for Churchill to make in fact, unlike his father in fiction. On 24 January 1953, he told his Joint Principal Private Secretary, Jock

Colville, "It's the day my father died. It's the day I shall die, too."[26] Soon after, he decided against being buried at Chartwell and settled on Bladon churchyard instead, in sight of Blenheim Palace, next to the graves of his mother and father.

Early in 1965, Churchill suffered a massive stroke, but he held on long enough to die, as he had predicted, on 24 January, the seventieth anniversary of Lord Randolph's death. After a magnificent state funeral, he was buried, as he had wished, next to his parents—closer to them in death than he had ever been in life. A year later, "The Dream," which had been discovered by Randolph Churchill in a locked box, was published for the first time. Clementine did not spend another night at Chartwell after her husband's death, and having been restored to its 1930s heyday, the house was opened to the public in the middle of 1966. It attracted 150,000 visitors during its first five months, and half a century on, it continues to draw more than 200,000 visitors each year.[27] It is not grand or splendid like many National Trust properties (or, indeed, like Blenheim Palace), but it is so much Churchill's domain that it remains suffused by his presence. There is no such monument to any other British prime minister of modern times, and along with Franklin D. Roosevelt's home at Hyde Park on the Hudson River, Chartwell is the most renowned house in the Western world for its historic twentieth-century associations. But if Churchill had not been a writer as well as a statesman, and if Clementine had not been so forgiving and so loyally long-suffering, this might never have happened. For Chartwell was both her nightmare and his dream.

Creative Houses

9

The Quangle Wangle's Hat

Edward Lear in the Villa Emily, San Remo

JENNY UGLOW

On the top of the Crumpetty Tree
    The Quangle Wangle sat,
But his face you could not see,
    On account of his Beaver Hat.
For his Hat was a hundred and two feet wide,
With ribbons and bibbons on every side
And bells, and buttons, and loops, and lace,
So that nobody ever could see the face
    Of the Quangle Wangle Quee.

"What do you think as I have been & gone & done?" Edward Lear asked
a friend on May Day 1870. "I grow so tired of noisy lodgings, & yet am
so more & more unable to think of ever wintering in England—& so
unable to bear the expense of two houses & two journies annually, that
I have bought a bit of ground at San Remo and am actually building a
house there." He drew a nonsense picture of his plans, with the house
like a large square head, with doorbells swinging from its ears, and joked
about living on figs in summer and worms in the winter, planting twenty-
eight olive trees and an onion bed, and having "a stone terrace with a gray
Parrot & 2 hedgehogs to walk up & down on it by day & by night."[1]

In his late sixties, Lear had bought his first house. Having made his
name as a natural history artist, at the age of twenty-five he had headed
for Italy to become a landscape painter and from then on he stayed mostly

abroad. He lived in Rome until the revolutions of 1848–49; he travelled in Greece, Albania, Egypt, Palestine, and Lebanon; from the mid-1850s he was based in Corfu, until the Ionian Islands were handed back to Greece in 1864. Since then he had drifted between various places on the Riviera. His restless, voluntary exile was partly for his painting and partly for his health, but in dodging the British fogs he was also escaping the strictness of English society, so intolerant of eccentrics. He was adept at hiding his face, presenting a series of different selves: the artist, the traveller, the joker. Beneath these façades teemed anxieties stemming back to his childhood, to his father's financial ruin and his mother's rejection of him—he was brought up by his eldest sister, Ann—and to the curse of epilepsy, a burden that he kept secret all his life.

Lear had many friends but no partner, male or female. The man he loved most, Franklin Lushington, was now married with young children, and Lear had retreated in agonised uncertainty from proposing to Augusta Bethel, "Gussie," who would certainly have accepted him. His conclusion, as he told his friend Chichester Fortescue, was that "if you are absolutely alone in the world, & likely to be so, then move about continually & never stand still. I therefore think I shall be compulsed & more especially by things on the horizon."[2]

Travel had given him freedom but now he was tired of chasing the horizon. He thought of buying a place in England, or in the south of France, Corfu, or Corsica. Then at the end of February 1870, in San Remo, just across the Italian border with France, he met an English resident, Walter Congreve, who showed him land overlooking the sea. A month later, over a weekend in late March, he took the plunge and decided to buy. His plot was on a narrow lane to the west of the old town, winding down from the Corso degli Inglesi where rich English families built villas surrounded by gardens, with turrets and balconies gazing down at the bay. Below his own garden was a patch of land dotted with olives, and beyond it, across the road and the railway, lay the beach. "There is great charm in the quiet olive branches," he wrote, "& seen through their network, the quiet sea."[3]

His house would be called the Villa Emily—named, he said, for a New Zealand great-niece but, as everyone who knew him worked out, really for his great friend Emily Tennyson, who was, he wrote in his diary, "singularly good & kind—that woman is 10,000 angels boiled down— an essence of goodness."[4] The land cost £400, and the house would be £1,200, leaving him money to spare from his savings. First he was exhilarated. Then he panicked. Then he called in the builders. He designed the house himself: "worked hard at copying my two plans," he wrote in late April, and he employed a local architect to supervise the work.[5] While he waited he spent the summer in the cool of the mountains, in an exuberant burst of creativity, putting together a new book of nonsense, including the songs of the wanderers that he had written over the previous few years: "The Owl and the Pussy-Cat," "The Jumblies," and "The Duck and the Kangaroo" who hop the whole world round.

He sent these to his publisher Robert Bush, along with nonsense botany and recipes and alphabets, and a hundred new limericks, which Bush persuaded him to hold back for a separate book. But while *Nonsense Songs, Stories, Botany and Alphabets* was published for Christmas 1870, the Villa Emily was not quite ready, and, he groaned, "My only remaining fig tree was accidentally smashed by a lad with a ladder, so that figuratively speaking I now cut a figless figure."[6] Though he joked, he did feel exposed, and worried. But by now his furniture, prints, and books had been shipped out from London duty free, thanks to Frank, who was now a London police magistrate and got Lear a certificate of London residence. Another load arrived from Cannes by train, and Lear and his servant of many years, the volatile Giorgio Kokali, were "working like slaves," unpacking cases and putting thousands of drawings into cabinets and crates.[7]

On 26 March 1871 Lear finally moved in: "so, exactly a year from the day I decided on buying the ground, I am living in the house built on it!"[8] It was a new beginning. A few days later, he brooded in his diary, "Rose at 6.30. One does not know how to begin life daily in the new house."[9]

For Lear the Villa Emily would be a house of art, of solitude, of visits, of friendship, of nonsense. It was not precisely a hundred and two feet wide, like the Quangle Wangle's Hat, but it was long and low, gleaming white with a long balcony and a shady verandah. It had good rooms for friends to stay and, best of all, at last he had the perfect studio:

> I never before had such a painting room—32 feet by 20—with a light I can work by at all hours, and a clear view south over the sea. Below it is a room of the same size, which I now use as a gallery, and am "at home" in once a week—Wednesday: though as Enoch Arden said in the troppicle Zone "Still no sail, no sail," and only one £12 drawing has been bought.[10]

Since sales proved so slow, he sent pictures back to his dealer in London and sought commissions from friends and patrons. At the same time, he returned to an idea that he had outlined to Emily almost twenty years earlier, of illustrating Tennyson's poems—a task that would occupy him in various forms for the rest of his life.

Lear loved his Riviera garden, putting in shrubs and flowers and planting seeds that friends sent from England and his sister Sarah from New Zealand. He found that San Remo suited him, "for we are all humdrum middle class coves and covesses, and no swells."[11] He was constantly paying calls on local families, having guests for lunch and going out to dinner, and he became increasingly close to Walter Congreve and his two small sons, Hubert and Arny, who lived just up the hill. At lunchtime, Hubert remembered, Lear often dropped in for a glass of Marsala, talking about travels, birds, botany, and music, and making terrible puns, and in the evenings he strolled over and stayed late, singing his settings of Tennyson poems, and comic songs, including their favourite, "The Cork Leg." Back in the Villa Emily, he loved the quiet: only birdsong broke the silence.

Life settled into a routine. Lear worked on his paintings, pottered in the garden, wrote letters, read quantities of books, and became busily caught up in local gossip. Over time, he also acquired a cat—or three. The first wandered off; the second, Potiphar, "Potta," disappeared when Giorgio took him to Corfu for the summer; and as a replacement, the Congreves' governess brought over his twin brother, with his cut-off tail. They called him Foss, short for "Adelphos," Greek for "brother."

~

The Quangle Wangle said
   To himself on the Crumpetty Tree,—
"Jam; and jelly; and bread;
   Are the best of food for me!
But the longer I live on this Crumpetty Tree
The plainer than ever it seems to me
That very few people come this way
And that life on the whole is far from gay!"
     Said the Quangle Wangle Quee.

When Giorgio was in Corfu with his family, Lear either returned to England to sell his paintings and see friends or went up to the mountains. But although he was busy, melancholy was part of his nature. Friends came to stay, including Frank Lushington, Chichester Fortescue, and, in later years, Gussie. When they left, weariness poured into his diary, as he confessed in his "How Pleasant to Know Mr Lear":

He weeps by the side of the ocean,
   He weeps on the top of the hill;
He purchases pancakes and lotion,
   And chocolate shrimps from the mill.

One spring day soon after he moved in, when his gardener Bernardino was clipping the olive trees, he noted, "Many little birds sing in the trees, & in one is a nest."[12] The image slid into nonsense. "Going up & down stairs worries me," he confessed to Chichester Fortescue, conscious of creeping age, "& I think of marrying some domestic henbird & then of building a nest in one of my many olive trees, whence I should only descend at remote intervals during the rest of my life."[13]

But there came to the Crumpetty Tree,
   Mr. and Mrs. Canary;
And they said,—"Did ever you See
   Any spot so charmingly airy?

May we build a nest on your lovely Hat?
Mr. Quangle Wangle, grant us that!
O please let us come and build a nest
Of whatever material suits you best,
    Mr. Quangle Wangle Quee!"

When the visitors left and the cold winds came, Lear took solace in nonsense—the characters arrived without a summons, nesting in his imagination. The hybrid beings, vociferously alive, became internal markers. When he liked the look of a visitor, Miss Poynter, he sighed, "Too late—oh far too late, Mr Yonghy-Bonghy-Bò"; when he thought a spell in the Tasmanian bush might suit Hubert, he added, "but his aunt (Jobiska) thinks not"; when he worried about new furniture and curtains he groaned,

When all these people come to be paid
    What a horrible bore t'will be—
      Said the Quangle Wangle Quee.[14]

The poems he wrote in the Villa Emily are autobiographical, but they are sunset poems, full of understanding of those who hanker for a home and long to look like other people, as well as for those who abandon ideas of settling and succumb to the urge to travel. Full of sympathy, too, for the people who hide their face, who create behind a mask.

    Can contentment be bounded by a nest? "Mr and Mrs Spikky Sparrow" salve their anxieties by dashing to Moses' wholesale shop, to buy hat and bonnet "and a gown with spots upon it."

Then when so completely drest,
Back they flew, and reached their nest.
Their children cried, "O Ma and Pa!
How truly beautiful you are!"
Said they, "We trust that cold or pain
We shall never feel again!
While, perched on tree, or house, or steeple,

We now shall look like other people,
    Witchy witchy witchy wee,
    Twikky mikky bikky bee,
      Zikky sikky tee!"

Their witchy song belies their attempt to fit in. It is scratchy rather than melodious, an alarm call rather than a joyful tune. Maybe their perch, their "sikky tee," is really a sickly tree?

In the winter of 1871–72 Lear wrote another poem about a dreamed-of home. On Christmas Eve he made a fair copy of "Mr and Mrs Discobbolos."[15] For these people-creatures, married life is precarious. They aim high, like the Discobolos, the lost Greek bronze of the javelin thrower. They climb up, like so many of Lear's limerick people, like Lear himself in his olive-tree dream.

Mr and Mrs Discobbolos
    Climbed to the top of a wall,
  And they sate to watch the sunset sky
  And to hear the Nupiter Piffkin cry
    And the Biscuit Buffalo call.
They took up a roll and some Camomile tea
And both were as happy as happy could be—
    Till Mrs Discobbolos said—
    "Oh! W! X! Y! Z!
  It has just come into my head—
Suppose we should happen to fall!!!!!
    Darling Mr Discobbolos!"

It is never safe, with Lear, to say "happy as happy could be." The family can stay up there safely, above the worry of life and household cares—from on high they see no trouble ahead, no "Sorrow or any such thing." But always there is the threat of falling, of breaking into pieces like those final, separate letters of the alphabet, with their spearing exclamation marks.

In the Villa Emily, where Lear was busily sorting out curtains and chairs and cutlery, he wrote two other poems that undercut the bliss of the settled state, "The Broom, the Shovel, the Poker and the Tongs" and "The Table and the Chair." In the latter, the furniture with "legs" long to walk:

Said the Chair unto the Table,
"Now you know we are not able!
How foolishly you talk,
When you know we cannot walk!"

Said the Table with a sigh,
"It can do no harm to try,
I've as many legs as you,
Why can't we walk on two?"

Movement—flight—is the great escape. In "The Courtship of the Yonghy-Bonghy-Bò," Mr. Bò, in his home on the Coast of Coromandel, is also defined by his furniture, "Two old chairs, and half a candle / One old jug without a handle / These were all his worldly goods." When his proposal to Lady Jingly Jones is rejected, he leaves all these goods behind, fleeing on a "large and lively turtle," abandoning Lady Jones to weep on the shingly shore.

Through the silent-roaring ocean
    Did the Turtle swiftly go;
        Holding fast upon his shell
    Rode the Yonghy-Bonghy-Bò.
        With a sad primaeval motion
Towards the sunset isles of Boshen
        Still the Turtle bore him well.
        Holding fast upon his shell
        "Lady Jingly Jones, farewell!"

Said the Yonghy-Bonghy-Bò,
Said the Yonghy-Bonghy-Bò.

The distant isles become the refuge of "Bosh," nonsense. And perhaps, in those sunset isles, one can find peace and make sense of past life, like the heroine of one late limerick, writing as the sun sinks into the sea.

There was a Young Person whose history
Was always considered a mystery;
She sate in a ditch, although no one knew which,
And composed a small treatise on history.

In the Villa Emily, Lear was considering his own history, painting watercolours based on a lifetime of sketches that made him revisit past times. He remembered all the places, and the charm of travel, but also his suffering at rejection, his abandoned hope of love. His poems touch on this, and of the danger of adventure, like the tale of emasculation and rescue in the two versions of "The Pobble Who Has No Toes."

The Pobble who has no toes
    Was placed in a friendly Bark,
And they rowed him back, and carried him up,
    To his Aunt Jobiska's Park.
And she made him a feast at his earnest wish
Of eggs and buttercups fried with fish;—
And she said,—"It's a fact the whole world knows,
That Pobbles are happier without their toes."

The urge, for most readers, is to reject Aunt Jobiska's brisk and blithe consolation. But if the Villa Emily was a park, a nest, a place for Lear to hide his loneliness and heal his fragmented self, it was also a place to show off, to display to his friends and neighbours. He was proud of his library, his dining room with its steps onto the terrace, making fun of its grandeur, its "parble massage with glass daws."[16] Yet this too was a device of concealment. As he knew from long experience one can hide beneath display, as the Quangle Wangle ducks beneath his hat with its bells and loops and lace. In his first winter at the villa, he wrote his mysterious poem "The Scroobious Pip," showing the Pip surrounded by beasts and birds, fish and insects, all crying out in frustration:

> Tell us all about yourself we pray!——
> For to know from yourself is our only wish——
> Are you Beast or Insect, Bird or Fish?
>
> The Scroobious Pip looked softly round
> And sang these words with a liquid sound——
> "Plifatty flip——Pliffitty flip——
> My only name is the Scroobious Pip."

We must accept the name, and hear the liquid song——but not enquire too far into the nature of his being.

There was one great break in Lear's years in the Villa Emily: in 1873–74 he and Giorgio travelled round India for fourteen months, courtesy of his old friend Thomas Baring, Lord Northcote, then viceroy of India. And there was one last heartache: in 1877 his neighbour's son, young Hubert Congreve, decided to study in London, depriving Lear of a surrogate son and a beautiful young man who had become part of his life. Distraught, he wept bitterly.

But Hubert remained close, and the people Lear loved turned up in San Remo—Frank Lushington and his daughter Gertrude, Chichester Fortescue, Northcote, and Gussie. When they left he felt alone again. The beings who never left him belonged to his nonsense. In "The Quangle Wangle Quee," the denizens of both the natural and nonsense world make their way to his wildly bedecked hat:[17]

And besides, to the Crumpetty Tree
   Came the Stork, the Duck, and the Owl;
The Snail, and the Bumble-Bee,
   The Frog, and the Fimble Fowl;
(The Fimble Fowl, with a corkscrew leg;)
And all of them said,—"We humbly beg,
We may build our homes on your lovely Hat,—
Mr. Quangle Wangle, grant us that!
     Mr. Quangle Wangle Quee!"

And the Golden Grouse came there,
   And the Pobble who has no toes,—
And the small Olympian bear,—
   And the Dong with a luminous nose,
And the Blue Baboon, who played the flute,—
And the Orient Calf from the Land of Tute,
And the Attery Squash, and the Bisky Bat,—
All came and built on the lovely Hat
   Of the Quangle Wangle Quee.

In 1876, seeing his recent poems mounting up, Lear began planning a new book, and for it he wrote his greatest ballad. On 24 August he worked on drawings of Hyderabad, from his Indian trip, "After which I quite concluded 'The Dong with the Luminous Nose'—& so also ends the new Christmas book."[18] He walked on his terrace in the evening cool:

> Wrote to F. Lushington enclosing the Dong, for Gertrude, also to R. J. Bush, with the Dong, his portrait, the music for Lady J Jones, & the Pelicans. . . . After wh—lunch on bread & cheese with Foss, & am now mostly mooning about & hoping for the Post. . . . Later a walk on the Terrace, moonlight.[19]

The Dong was not a new character: he had been among the throng dancing on the Quangle Wangle's hat five years before. But now he had a poem of his own. He shares a Learical geography with the other nonsense beings—stretching from the Coromandel coast to the Great Gromboolian Plain and the Jelly Bo Lee—and falls in love with the

Jumbly Girl with her sky-blue hands and sea-green hair. But the Jumblies sail on:

> And the Dong was left on the cruel shore
> Gazing,—gazing for evermore,
> Ever keeping his weary eyes on
> That pea-green sail on the far horizon.

The rhyme is absurd, but so is the Dong, searching for a love that he knows has gone: "What little sense I once possessed / Has quite gone out of my head." Yet that non-sense drives his quest and spurs the creation of his luminous nose, his guiding light in the darkness, his visionary self:

> And all who watch at that midnight hour
> From Hall or Terrace, or lofty Tower,
> Cry, as they trace the Meteor bright,
> Moving along through the dreary night,—
>> This is the hour when forth he goes,
>> "The Dong with a luminous Nose!
>> Yonder—over the plain he goes;
>>> He goes!
>>> He goes;
>> The Dong with a luminous Nose!"

The Dong's weird personal oddity becomes a heroic attribute. And in "How Pleasant to Know Mr. Lear," Lear came to terms, wryly, with his own oddities—or almost. His house soothed him. In October 1878, marvelling at his garden, Lear wrote, "altogether I should be rather surprised if I am happier in Paradise than I am now."[20]

Paradise was threatened. A huge hotel was to be built just below his garden, blocking his view of the sea. This disaster felt like treachery, as Lear had been promised that nothing would be built there apart from low-roofed villas. Carts arrived, rocks were blasted, trees were felled. Scaffolding and gaping windows faced him, and whitewashed walls glared into his rooms.

In his misery, he took up a suggestion from Wilkie Collins that he should finish the story of Mr. and Mrs. Discobbolos. In the poem's second part, which he copied out in mid-October 1879 for Collins and for his American publisher James Field, the couple have lived on their wall for twenty years, and more, "Till their hair had grown all pearly grey / And their teeth began to fall." Then, in a fury, spurred by his wife's assertion that their children have no chance of a normal life—"Surely they should not pass their lives / Without any chance of husbands or wives!"—Mr. Discobbolos acts. Drastically.

Suddenly Mr Discobbolos
    Slid from the top of the wall;
  And beneath it he dug a dreadful trench,
  And filled it with Dynamite gunpowder gench,—
    And aloud began to call,—
"Let the wild bee sing and the blue bird hum!
For the end of our lives has certainly come!"
    And Mrs Discobbolos said,
    "O! W! X! Y! Z!
  We shall presently all be dead
On this ancient runcible wall—
    Terrible Mr Discobbolos!"

Pensively, Mr Discobbolos
    Sate with his back to the wall;—
  He lighted a match, and fired the train,—
  And the mortified mountains echoed again
    To the sounds of an awful fall!
And all the Discobbolos family flew
In thousands of bits to the sky so blue,
    And no one was left to have said
    "O! W! X! Y! Z!
  Has it come into anyone's head
That the end has happened to all
    Of the whole of the Clan Discobbolos?"

In imagination at least, he had dynamited the monster hotel, but the violent end of the runcible wall echoed all the crashes and falls that had seared his spirit from childhood on.

Seeing his despair, friends and patrons clubbed together, commissioning pictures and organising loans so that he could build a new house. He chose a plot a little nearer the town, lower down the slope so that his view of the sea was safe, "unless the Fishes begin to build, or Noah's Ark comes to an Anchor below the site."[21] The plans copied the Villa Emily, to make it easier, Lear said, for Foss to find his way around, but the rooms were in reverse order, to fit the ground. In late February 1880 he wrote, "*the walls of the Villa Oduardo was really begun yesterday*: certainly I am making a leap in a kind of darkness."[22] Soon he settled on a name, not his own "Oduardo" but the partner of the Villa Emily—the Villa Tennyson. Slowly he moved his books and possessions and drawings. On 31 May 1881 he wrote, "Dined for the last time at the Villa Emily." He would live in the Villa Tennyson until his death in February 1888.

In his distress Lear had blasted and shattered his imaginary world and all its beings: "Has it come into anyone's head," went his verse, "That the end has happened to all / Of the whole of the Clan Discobbolos?" After he left the house, although he fiddled with rhymes and limericks, and wrote his last great autobiographical poem, "Some Incidents in the Life of My Uncle Arly," he wrote no more songs. He left them behind, to live on in the empty Villa Emily, and in his books:

And the Quangle Wangle said
    To himself on the Crumpetty Tree,—
"When all these creatures move
    What a wonderful noise there'll be!"
And at night by the light of the Mulberry moon
They danced to the Flute of the Blue Baboon,
On the broad green leaves of the Crumpetty Tree,
And all were as happy as happy could be,
    With the Quangle Wangle Quee.

10
Benjamin Britten in Aldeburgh

LUCY WALKER

Britten's Houses

21 Kirkley Cliff Road, Lowestoft (1913–30/on and off until 1935)

Various, London plus Peasenhall Hall, Suffolk from 1937 (1930–38)

First Purchase: The Old Mill, Snape (1938–39/1942–47; rented out from 1939 to 1942)

Various, United States (1939–42)

Crag House, Crabbe Street, Aldeburgh (1947–57)

The Red House, Golf Lane, Aldeburgh (1957–76) (plus Chapel House, Horham, for composition, 1969–76)

"If I may say so, what a nice town it is!"[1]

In Britten's remarks on his hometown, his various houses, and his role as an artist in the world, the word "roots" or "rootedness" appears with remarkable frequency. It is particularly noticeable in his speech on accepting the Aspen Award in 1964, at the end of a thoroughgoing description of what he believed his duty was as a composer ("I want my music to be of use to people, to please them, to 'enhance their lives'"). As an exemplar of the utility of music (and the arts generally) in society, Britten spoke not only for his times. His words also have great resonance today. A recent book, *Beyond Britten: The Composer and the Community*, followed on from and expanded the ideals laid out in the Aspen

Award speech, ideals anyone can aspire to.[2] But for Britten "the community," which he refers to in that speech, was not merely an abstract concept but a real, physical, and specific place: Aldeburgh and its near environs. The town in which he lived for the last thirty years of his life was at the root, as it were, of his "rootedness" in home and utterly central to all aspects of his life. Each physical location he planted himself in reflected, or actively shaped, his musical and cultural output, as well as confirmed his attitude to "home," what it represented to him, and how important the domestic spaces were to his equilibrium. The painful absence of such security often found its way, menacingly dramatized, into his stage works.

The first home he purchased in Snape was a welcome respite from the busyness and emotional complications of London life. His coastal homes (in Lowestoft and Crag House in Aldeburgh) met a powerful need to have regular contact with the sea. Even during his brief non-Suffolk residency in the United States (1939–42) he hopped from one coast, with its proximity to the Atlantic Ocean, to the other, spending the summer of 1941 in California. Otherwise, though, the American years are an anomaly: three remarkable years in which he composed some of his most enduringly popular works (such as the violin concerto, *Sinfonia da Requiem*, and *Seven Sonnets of Michelangelo*), far away from home while war raged across Europe. His letters to family and friends back in the UK are shot through with longing (to his sister Beth, "I feel *terribly* homesick, my dear. Yearning for things to get all right & so that we could meet again, & go on living as before"), plans to ship his sister over to create a home-from-home in the United States ("I think we'll *have* to arrange this, Beth, you come over & keep house for Peter & me!"), and to his friend Enid Slater a heartfelt desire to see Suffolk again ("It pleases me to hear you talk about Snape & Suffolk . . . I've been horribly homesick for it recently!").[3] A brief stay in a bohemian household in Brooklyn further helped Britten realise what he did *not* want from a domestic space.[4]

During the Californian summer—as a result of both a chance purchase in a Los Angeles bookshop and an article by E. M. Forster in *The Listener*—Britten reencountered the works of the eighteenth-century

FIGURE 10.1. The Red House as it is today. (Photograph: Britten-Pears Foundation)

Suffolk poet George Crabbe. Crabbe's lengthy poem *The Borough* contained the seeds of Britten's first "Suffolk" opera, *Peter Grimes*. Reading Crabbe, Britten felt even more homesick. He began to plan his return home with more earnestness, eventually journeying back across the Atlantic as part of a vulnerable naval convoy in April 1942. Shortly after his return he reclaimed his home in Snape, more or less opposite what is now Snape Maltings Concert Hall. His next home, Crag House ("bang on the sea in Aldeburgh"),[5] from 1947 to 1957, was a permanent base in Aldeburgh, allowing him to more or less abandon London except when he needed to be there. As even this home became too public he retreated further inland to The Red House, alongside the golf course and down a quiet residential lane. There he found tranquillity and dark and silent nights, inspiring a group of haunting, nocturnal works.

"I've always felt I wanted to live by the sea. I've tried living away from the sea but something has gone slightly wrong."
—"People Today: Benjamin Britten" in Kildea, *Britten on Music*

It has become something of a cliché to link Benjamin Britten with the sea—to "hear" it in his music and to enjoin others to do the same. Joseph Cooper, interviewing Britten in 1957, asked, self-deprecatingly, "Would you say that the salt tang has got into your composition, or would you say that was a silly remark?" Britten somewhat endorsed the comment, "silly" or not, by immediately playing "Dawn," one of the *Sea Interludes* from his "salty" opera *Peter Grimes*.[6] As a literal presence in his music, it certainly features strongly in three operas—*Grimes*, *Billy Budd*, and *Noye's Fludde* (a planned *Sea Symphony* much later in his life did not get further than an initial selection of poetry). But it is more palpable in his words: in letters, speeches, interviews, and other public declarations.

He was born opposite the North Sea on 22 November 1913. The family home, 21 Kirkley Cliff Road in Lowestoft, directly faced the sea, and Britten's childhood bedroom looked out over it, captured in an early artistic effort (see figure 10.2). Almost forty years later he was made "Freeman of Lowestoft" and waxed long and lyrical about the county of his birth:

> Suffolk, the birthplace and inspiration of Constable and Gainsborough, the loveliest of English painters; the home of Crabbe, that most English of poets; Suffolk, with its rolling, intimate countryside; its heavenly Gothic churches, big and small; its marshes, with those wild sea-birds; its grand ports and its little fishing villages. I am firmly rooted in this glorious county. And I proved this to myself when I once tried to live somewhere else. Even when I visit countries as glorious as Italy, as friendly as Denmark or Holland—I am always homesick, and glad to get back to Suffolk.
>
> . . . I treasure these roots, my Suffolk roots; roots are especially valuable nowadays, when so much we love is disappearing or being threatened, when there is so little to cling to.[7]

Other than the three-year interlude in the States, he lived in Suffolk for most of his life, although not always directly on the coastline. *Peter Grimes* emerged while he was living in Snape, though it is more romantic to imagine he composed it within sight of the North Sea, its pages literally imbued with a "salt tang." He fashioned a sinister community in The Borough (Aldeburgh by another name), and only a rough shack for his

THE BRITISH FLEET SIGHTED

FIGURE 10.2. "The British Fleet Sighted," painted when Britten was around eight or nine while living at 21 Kirkley Cliff Road, Lowestoft. (Credit: Britten-Pears Foundation)

troubled hero. Grimes disappears into the sea at the end, unable to live with the community that needs him so badly to be their scapegoat. For tenor Stuart Skelton, a regular inhabitant of the role, Grimes returns to the elements that forged him: rock, saltwater, and brine; merely dispensing with the "character" of Grimes and melding back to his primal state.[8] Britten responded to the particular properties of *this* sea—not a gentle lapping at a sandy beach but as full of rage as Grimes himself:

[Grimes's apprentice] strove with terror and awhile prevail'd;
But new to danger on the angry sea,
He clung affrighten'd to his master's knee:
The boat grew leaky and the wind was strong,
Rough was the passage and the time was long . . .[9]

Crag House (4 Crabbe Street), Aldeburgh: "The walls will be white with an offness of pink."

—Benjamin Britten to Peter Pears, 4–12 September 1947, reproduced in *My Beloved Man: The Letters of Benjamin Britten and Peter Pears* (Suffolk: Boydell, 2016), 102

The Old Mill had been purchased in 1937 after the death of Britten's mother. Searching for a larger home ten years later he found (for a time) utter perfection in Aldeburgh. From there he wrote reams of letters, puppyish in his enthusiasm for his new home. He wrote to Peter Pears about the development of new works, as well as critical appraisals (to put it politely) of other performers, mixed with instructions for curtain measurements. He wrote to his publisher, Ralph Hawkes, thanking him for forwarding a large sum in anticipation of future royalties: "I shall gradually shift my focus from London to here, incidentally good for composition too! Thank you, Ralph, more than I can say for making it possible for me to come here."[10] He wrote vividly to his friend Elizabeth Mayer (see also figure 10.3):

> The new house (with its lovely 4 Crabbe Street address!) is turning out a great success. I had in a way outgrown the Mill. I still have it—friends from Switzerland have rented it—but I wanted something simpler, bigger & above all in front of the sea as before! It is next door to the Grimes "Moot Hall" too, like this.
>
> Aldeburgh is a sweet little town, & the beach & sea full of fishing-business—not at all "quaint" though.[11]

Several months later he explained to her that for him a sea view is as natural a part of life as "eating & sleeping":

> Peter will have told you all about this house—it is a real pleasure to us, & every day becomes more appreciated. The view as I sit at my desk writing is beyond description—a deep blue-green sea, flat as a pond, with big ships out at sea, & small fishing boats being launched from the beach & fishing right along-shore, with all the seagulls hovering around them. *Not a striking breathtaking view which distracts, but a part of one's life, like eating & sleeping!* Morgan Forster has got to love it too—he comes in a day or so again. You must get to love it too![12]

E. M. Forster was at the time working with Britten and co-librettist Eric Crozier on *Billy Budd*, another seafaring opera. Photographs of the

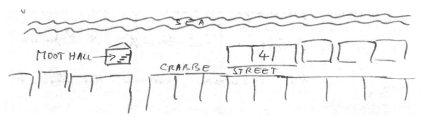

FIGURE 10.3. Britten's drawing of the location of his new home in Crabbe Street.
(Credit: Britten-Pears Foundation)

three men at work (or staged to look like it) appeared in a 1950 edition of *Picture Post* in one of the upstairs rooms at Crag House, striped beach huts standing decoratively in the background.

A double-paged spread in the *Woman's Journal* in 1952 titled "Benjamin Britten at Home" shows photographs of the rooms and is very complimentary about their décor and comfort. Jeremy Cullum, Britten's secretary in the 1940s and 1950s, remembered the striking view from the front rooms "which was fatal actually because we used to get in the middle of a letter and something would be happening at sea and everything would stop for a quarter of an hour while we watched it."[13] The house was for work as well as for retreat, its three storeys providing space for Britten to compose as well as for Pears to rehearse without disturbing him. The daily routines of the household were infused with music of all kinds; the Aldeburgh Music Club meetings were held there, and, as Arthur Oldham described, there was much music-making: "Each day, after lunch, Ben would play a Mozart piano concerto with Peter at the other piano."[14] The casual mention of the "other piano" tells us that by this stage Britten could not only afford a three-storey house on Aldeburgh's seafront but furnish it with more than one piano. He could also afford staff: Nellie Hudson (always and only known as "Miss Hudson") arrived in 1948, as she recalled some years later: "Somebody said to me, 'Are you looking for a job? . . . Well, there's two gentlemen on the front, you know, these artists, musicians and that.'"[15] Miss Hudson remained with the "two gentlemen" until her retirement in 1973.

FIGURE 10.4. Britten and Pears playing recorders at a meeting of the Aldeburgh Music Club at Crag House in 1954. (Photograph: Roland Haupt, courtesy of the Britten-Pears Foundation)

"Red House, Aldeburgh," for Next Letter Please!

In the great floods of January 1953, the sea broke into the house at Crabbe Street. The downstairs rooms were flooded. The composer and conductor Imogen Holst, who worked for Britten throughout the 1950s, wrote in her diary on 4 February 1953:

> Everything still in a state, and Miss Hudson looking weary. Ben had spent most of Tuesday trying to clean out the cellar. He said that after dark (the electricity was off) he went up to the Potters [at The Red House] and Mary gave him an extra stiff drink and he managed to write Concord's song [from the opera *Gloriana*].[16]

This large house, uphill and at less risk from the floods, was to become his own home four years later. Britten wrote to Elizabeth Mayer,

[Peter] has been enjoying planning the great move . . . we go up the hill to the Potters' house, Red House, next week!! Mary & we swap houses. It should be lovely, but of course it will take time to get straight & comfortable. The move is endlessly complicated, & there'll be lots to do when we get in. I, for instance, am having a studio built, & we are knocking walls down, redecorating; etc., etc.: but, it is such a sweet place, such a lovely garden, and so quiet after this house, which has become more & more public these last years.[17]

He had been on the lookout for a different house as early as May 1956, commissioning his friend George Behrend to find somewhere for him. He rejected Theberton Hall at Eastbridge as being too dilapidated, and also too far inland; in the end, he did move away from the sea but only a mile or so and within easy walking distance. His friend Mary Potter, recently separated from her husband, Stephen, had lived in The Red House from 1951 and wanted to find somewhere smaller; Britten, meanwhile, was looking for somewhere larger and away from town—thus a swap was effected. (Mary Potter later moved back to the Red House grounds, into a studio Britten and Pears had built for her.) While Pears was choosing curtains and carpets in his favourite reds and greens (some of which remain in the house today), Britten set about constructing an idyllic composer's residence in this former farmhouse. A studio away from the main house, designed by H. C. "Jim" Cadbury-Brown, was built over the garage (where he housed his Rolls-Royce); a former cow shed was converted into a gracious library; and in the absence of the North Sea, a bracing open-air swimming pool was dug out between the house and the outer buildings.

The first piece completed there was *Noye's Fludde*, a distillation of two of Britten's preoccupations: the sea and usefulness to the community. Recent memories of the 1953 flood no doubt inspired the turbulent evocations of rising waters (more apocalyptic here); and the opera was designed as a "community project," including children, audience participation, and DIY instruments. It was also a specifically *Suffolk* enterprise at its first performance: "the handbells from Leiston Modern

School, which heralded the appearance of the rainbow; the percussion group from Woolverstone Hall, with its set of slung mugs for the raindrops which start and end the storm; the recorders from Framlingham College which vie with the wind; the bugles from the Royal Hospital School, Holbrook."[18]

But most of the pieces composed at The Red House were more inward-looking. Paul Kildea, in *Britten on Music*, remarks that "the many 'night pieces' for different instruments in [the Red House years] were an extension of Britten's fascination with hidden worlds, far from public gaze; this same feeling, after all, had led to his move in 1957 from Crag Path to the privacy of the Red House at the edge of Aldeburgh."[19]

A consequence of his growing fame and his international reach was that his attachment to this particular corner of Suffolk became more entrenched. It was for the people in this specific community that he composed. From *Noye's Fludde* onwards, nearly all of his dramatic works were premiered in this area (in Aldeburgh itself, in Orford Church, only a few miles away, and later on at Snape Maltings). Introducing one of the "nocturnal" works, *A Midsummer Night's Dream* (1960), Britten wrote, "We are taking the 'Midsummer Night's Dream' to Holland immediately after the Aldeburgh Festival. . . . But the new opera was really written as part of the Aldeburgh Festival, for the reopening of the Jubilee Hall." He ends, perhaps surprisingly, "Ultimately, it is to me the local things that matter most."[20]

A few years later, towards the end of his Aspen speech, he declared: "I do not write for posterity—in any case, the outlook for that is somewhat uncertain. I write music, now, in Aldeburgh, for people living there, and further afield, indeed for anyone who cares to play it or listen to it. But my music now has its roots, in where I live and work." Where he lived and worked became the only place he wanted to be, and he organised it precisely to his liking. His housekeeping staff moved with him—Miss Hudson, cooking her "safe," nursery food; and Heather Grant (née Bryson), who arrived in 1961 at age fifteen and stayed at The Red House long after Britten died. Britten, as Pears cheerfully admitted, could barely boil an egg and managed to keep about him a group of devoted staff, nearly all women, who looked after the domestic side of his life. After Miss Hudson's retirement Britten and Pears built a home for her in the grounds of The Red House, which she christened Cosy Nook. With Mary Potter installed in Red Studio on the other side of the grounds, and later on with the constant presence of his nurse Rita Thomson at The Red House when his health failed, Britten was comfortably surrounded by nurturing, congenial women. As W. H. Auden perceptively, if brutally, wrote to him towards the end of their friendship: "you are and probably always will be surrounded by people who adore you, nurse you and praise everything you do . . . you are always tempted to make things too easy for yourself in this way, ie to build yourself a warm nest of love."[21]

⁓

"We're now on the telephone Aldeburgh *323*"
—Britten to Pears, 28 October 1948, reproduced in *My Beloved Man*, 120

The most central relationship of his home life, and a major component of the "warm nest," was Peter Pears. They had begun their relationship in the United States in 1939 and remained together until Britten's death in 1976—a significant and enduring gay partnership in the context, for many years, of illegality. Their correspondence was published in 2016 and provides an insight into their affection for each other over the years. They referred to themselves as "married" as far back as 1943. They loved using pet names and endearments for each other, right to the end: "My darlingest P.," "Darling Honey Bun," "My own honey bee." There is nothing clearly discernible in the letters regarding their necessary discretion, although Pears at one point declares, "Why shouldn't I recognise that you are such a large part of my life that without you my life is dry and stupid and dull."[22] And when a telephone was installed at Crag House in 1948, Britten tellingly wrote to Pears that he would rather exchange letters, as "I prefer them to a hectic 3 minutes with fading, & not daring to say what I really feel,"[23] as if concerned about being overheard.

Their life together was not exactly secret. In 1956 the *Woman's Journal* noted that they shared the home together. In the Britten-Pears Archive, which holds a startlingly large collection of household receipts,

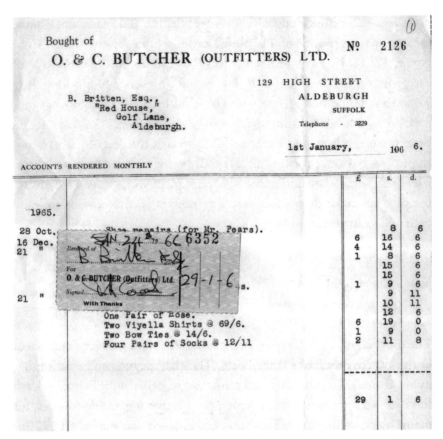

FIGURE 10.5. An invoice from O&C Butcher, held in the Britten-Pears Archive.

one invoice sent to Britten at The Red House notes "Shoe repairs (for Mr Pears)" at the top of an itemised bill for Britten's bow ties and dress shirts.

Yet for the purposes of outward appearances and, for instance, room inventories for house insurance, there was a bedroom for Mr. Britten and another for Mr. Pears. Britten was apparently interviewed by Scotland Yard in 1953 during a period of high-profile arrests of homosexual men including Alan Turing and John Gielgud, and homosexuality was only partially decriminalised in 1967. So for most of Britten and Pears's thirty-seven-year relationship they lived under the threat of exposure and prosecution. Yet at the same time, their home life conformed to the most conventional routines and most middle-class of structures. In his music, as well as in his life, Britten fluctuated between being progressive and entrenched. He also moved between an absolute rootedness in East Anglia and a wanderlust that took him to the Far East, Russia, South America, and Australia, amongst many other parts of the world. He required stability and security in order for adventure and risk.

It may also be that, despite the threat to his and Pears's privacy, his stability at home allowed him to explore the absolute opposite of domestic safety in his work. Assaults of a psychological as well as physical nature abound, as well as more systemic violence and cruelty, against a backdrop of highly privileged if unconventional familial setups. The rapist Prince Tarquinius intrudes into the all-female household of *The Rape of Lucretia*, while the men are away at war. An elaborate and overpolite "good-night" takes place before the drama builds up to its central episode, the prince being made comfortable in this home before violently abusing the hospitality of its chatelaine in her own bedroom. The house at the centre of *The Turn of the Screw*—the first of two haunted operas—is inhabited by two orphaned children, their housekeeper and governess, and the ghosts of two previous employees. As the residents gradually depart, Miles, the young boy, is menaced to death by either one of the ghosts or his obsessive governess. In *Owen Wingrave*, the other haunted opera, the titular character is attacked from all quarters, including ultimately by the house itself: at its dark centre is a locked room from which nobody can emerge alive. In *Peter Grimes* the town turns on the protagonist, forcing him from his dwelling into a final resting place at sea. In *Billy Budd* suppressed longing, displaced rage, and mob mentality boil over in the floating "home" of the *HMS Indomitable*.

⁓

> "I find as I get older that working becomes more and more difficult away from . . . home."
> —"On Receiving the Aspen Award," in Kildea, *Britten on Music*, 262

These scenarios are the furthest possible distance from Britten's safe, cosy retreats, set up exactly as he wanted, shared (albeit discreetly) with

Figure 10.6. Aldeburgh. (Illustration by R. K. R. Thornton)

a loving partner and cared for by a variety of comforting women, wrapped up in a "warm nest of love." Yet it was precisely this that enabled him to venture into such troubling territory. Today, The Red House is open to visitors, who are often struck by its "lived-in" quality as well as by the juxtaposition of fine art (the collection amassed largely by Pears includes works by John Piper, John Craxton, William Blake, and Gwen John) with homely lamps, kitsch ornaments, and classic 1970s upholstery. The rest of the site, comprising his workplaces—studio and library—and the comprehensive archive he left behind, relates the story of Britten the composer (and performer, recording artist, and administrator) and his remarkable international reach, both when he was alive and today. But for Britten, accepting the Freedom of Aldeburgh in 1962, it was the "Aldeburgh-ness" of his life and increasingly of his work that mattered the most:

As I understand it, this honour is not given because of a *reputation*, because of a chance acquaintance, it is—dare I say it?—because you really *do* know me, and accept me as one of yourselves, *as a useful part of the Borough*—and this is, I think, the highest possible compliment for an artist.[24]

11
77 St. Mark's Place

SEAMUS PERRY

W. H. Auden had rented variously inadequate apartments since arriving back in New York at the end of the summer of 1945, and had most recently been living with Chester Kallman in a warehouse building on Seventh Avenue, an especially unsatisfactory place that lacked both hot water and a functional front door.[1] So when he and Chester moved to 77 St. Mark's Place on the Lower East Side, in February 1954, it promised to be a significant improvement; and he was certainly very pleased with the place from the start—"my N.Y. nest," he called it.[2] He would stay there until his ill-fated departure for Oxford in 1972, making it his longest single habitation. From 1949 he summered in Europe—in Ischia until 1957, when he bought a small farmhouse in Kirchstetten in Austria, which delighted him: he devoted a sequence, "Thanksgiving for a Habitat," in his collection *About the House* (1965), to a celebration of his domestic existence there. It was in these summer houses that he tended to write poems: New York was largely for his distinct life as a "man of letters," a label he applied to himself.[3] "It is a sad fact about our culture," he once wrote, "that a poet can earn much more money writing or talking about his art than he can by practicing it";[4] but at the same time he prided himself on his professionalism as a reviewer, essayist, anthologist, and commentator, work which in turn often suggested subjects for poems; and that work principally happened in St. Mark's.

Freshly installed, he excitedly invited round his young friend Charles Miller ("Come! I'll take you on a tour"):

FIGURE 11.1. Auden and the mailman John. (Photo credit: Karl Bissinger Papers, University of Delaware Library, Newark)

The large first (entry) room with high ceiling had a green marbled fireplace flanked by built-in bookshelves, which also incorporated Wystan's battered turntable with speaker equipment and his much-used collection of records and albums. A big shabby sofa and a swamped antique coffee table centered the cluttered room. I followed Wystan through an arch into a similar room at the front with another green marbled fireplace. This room was hardly furnished, except for built-in bookcases and Wystan's small work table just touched by sunlight from the generous nineteenth-century windows. To the right of this room, as we faced Saint Mark's Place, was a small room with its door to the stair hall nailed shut; the room had only a cot bed, on which Wystan slept, he said.[5]

Just touched by sunlight, one imagines: as an undergraduate at Oxford, Auden had preferred to keep his curtains drawn at all times, and he seems to have adopted the same policy in America. When Stephen Spender had visited him in the 1940s he unwisely attempted to open the curtains and brought them crashing to the ground: "You idiot!" Auden scolded him, "Why did you draw them? No one ever draws them. In any case there's no daylight in New York."[6] Wystan's succession of rooms gave his friend Margaret Gardiner "the sensation of brownish caverns, a brown that seemed to pervade everything, even the air itself."[7]

Auden's territory was the front of the apartment; Chester's the kitchen and the music room at the back of the flat, where there were also separate bedrooms for Kallman and for a tenant. Auden was especially pleased with the fireplaces, and he liked the porcelain tiles in the kitchen. The area had lots of Italian, Polish, and Ukrainian stores selling good food. And the building even had a history: Trotsky had once published works from its basement, a fact that seemed to please Auden; and, some more recent colour, an illegal abortionist had been its previous inhabitant. (The flat was buzzed from time to time by would-be clients.)[8] Auden placed his father's barometer on the mantelpiece, and hung over it a watercolour by Blake, *The Act of Creation*, a present from his rich patron Caroline Newton.[9] But his evident pride in the place did not translate into any instincts to be house-proud, as Charles Miller's retrospective account, despite its touches of fine writing, communicates well enough:

> The coffee table bore its household harvest of books, periodicals, half-emptied coffee cups scummed over with cream, a dash of cigarette ashes for good measure, and a heel of French bread (too tough for Wystan's new dentures?). An oval platter served as ashtray, heaped with a homey Vesuvius of cigarette butts, ashes, bits of cellophane from discarded packs, a few martini-soaked olive pits, and a final cigarette stub issuing a frail plume of smoke from

FIGURE 11.2. Auden in his apartment. (Photo credit: Donal F. Holway/*New York Times*/ Redux/eyevine)

the top of the heap, signature of a dying volcano. This Auden-scape reeked of stale coffee grounds, tarry nicotine, and toe jam mixed with metro pollution and catshit, Wystanified tenement tang.[10]

And this was his *new* flat. "The speed with which he could wreck a room was barely credible, certainly dangerous," observed his friend James Stern. He spoke from experience. On one occasion he had left Auden in his flat for the day, dropping back shortly afterwards to pick something up: "if it hadn't been for the pictures on the walls I wouldn't have known where I was," Stern remembered: "Frustrated burglars could not have created greater chaos . . . God, Wystan, was a mess! 'My dear, I do love this apartment, but I can't understand why it doesn't have more *ash*trays!'"[11] The St. Mark's apartment rapidly came to resemble what Robert Craft, Stravinsky's right-hand man, had witnessed with some incredulity in Auden's previous place, a litter of "empty bottles, used martini glasses, books, papers, phonograph records." Dinner with them would be boozy and delicious (Kallman was an excellent cook); but the cutlery would be greasy and the plates often only imperfectly washed. "He is the dirtiest man I have ever liked," said Stravinsky of Auden, a touching if qualified mark of regard.[12]

Auden and Kallman had not been lovers for some time; but they lived in a cranky kind of marital household, to which Chester would often introduce the latest conquest. At the housewarming, according to a neighbour, he brought along a handsome sailor of his acquaintance: after three of the lethal cocktails on offer (a mixture of English tea, white wine, and vodka) the young man slipped into stockings and, making inventive use of a kosher salami, gave a hearty rendition of "Anchors Aweigh!" Auden, apparently mostly cross about the misuse of the salami, which had been a gift, instructed Kallman to "get that hidee-ola out immediately."[13] (In "Music Is International," Auden had given as an example of being moral "looking pleased when caught / By a bore or a hideola"; but perhaps the salami was a step too far.)[14] The story is probably too good to be true; but it does at any rate show the kinds of stories that were told. There were large birthday parties every year, mixing up Auden's eclectic circle of friends and acquaintances, flush with Californian champagne; and they often involved incident. At one, the émigré Russian writer Yanovsky remembered, a woman inadvertently opened the door to Auden's cell-like bedroom: "He screamed in anger and outrage . . . Chester very expertly calmed him down."[15]

The anecdote is a slight one, but it does suggest something about the strength of Auden's, admittedly eccentric, sense of propriety and rule, something about which the household revolved. Louis Kronenberger, his collaborator on the *Faber Book of Aphorisms*, observed of him: "He showed almost no interest in possessions, or in living at all splashily, or even in what might be called upper-Bohemian comfort. . . . he was himself no real Bohemian: if rumpled-looking in appearance, he lived no gypsy life within; it was orderly, not to say regulated."[16] Auden had lived in seriously Bohemian circumstances at one point in his earlier life: shortly after leaving England he had joined a famously colourful household at 7 Middagh Street in Brooklyn Heights, a place he shared with, amongst others, Benjamin Britten and Peter Pears, Carson Mc-

Cullers, Golo Mann, the strip-tease artiste Gypsy Rose Lee, and for a time a trained chimpanzee. The more punctilious Britten and Pears had soon had enough of the mayhem and left; but Auden positively took to it—less as a simple participant, however, than in a newfound role as domestic goddess-cum-headmaster. He organised the meals, ensuring they were punctual; he barked instructions to the unruly company from the head of the table; he calculated and then collected payments from the inmates; and generally he kept things as shipshape as the comically disreputable circumstances would allow.[17] As he once said, "Sorry, my dear, one mustn't be bohemian!"[18]

He thus established what would become his lasting mode within doors, one that translated to the St. Mark's apartment. Amidst the proliferating chaos that surrounded him, the day ran to a strict timetable. He could work for eight or ten hours with half an hour for lunch;[19] and callers were emphatically not welcome. There was an open-house hour at 4:00, which students and admirers might attend, a session referred to with Edwardian formality as "teatime" though other things might be offered; and then "always a cocktail hour at five o'clock and dinner had to be served exactly at six."[20] He never worked in the evening: "Only the Hitlers of this world work at night; no honest artist does," he told his friend Orlan Fox, who had dinner with him every Friday.[21] Dinner was always at a set time: he could not bear meals to be late any more than visitors; and when bedtime (which grew earlier and earlier, from eleven to ten to nine-thirty to nine) came round, he went off to bed regardless of the company. On one occasion, when a party of Chester's friends showed no sign of leaving the dinner table despite the hour, Auden went off to his bath, making a spectacular appearance shortly afterwards covered only in bubbles: he strode purposefully across the apartment casting a disapproving look at the nightbirds and disappeared into his bedroom; the effect was hilarity, but the guests soon headed off. (Bubble bath, which Orlan Fox bought him at Christmas from the children's section of Woolworth's, was one indulgence.)[22] Timeliness and routine became something of an obsession: he claimed even to feel hungry according "to the schedule" and said that losing his watch would render him helpless. "He disliked surprises, change, deviations, anything that could throw him off balance," said his friend Yanovsky.[23] Once, when Stravinsky enquired upon meeting, "How are you?" Auden replied, "Well, I'm on time anyway."[24]

"The most dishevelled child of all disciplinarians," Kallman called him, in a sweet-tempered poem written to mark his sixty-fifth birthday.[25] Kallman evidently grew used to the semi-serious domestic tyranny of the regime: "Mother wouldn't like it" became a favourite moral standard to be evoked as necessary.[26] The household turned upon an elaborate and almost sustaining game about bourgeois respectability, a kind of parody of domesticity, in which the matriarchal instructions were both passionately meant and wholly ludicrous: "Miss Master" was Chester's nickname for him when he adopted his disapproving note.[27] In fact, as Robert Craft discerned, any order that the flat retained was largely down to Kallman, who was hardly much of a stickler for tidiness himself;[28] and once Kallman had decided not to winter in New York anymore, from 1963, Auden presided over the household without any mitigating interventions, apart from an agency maid who came in to make little difference once a week.[29] "The kitchen became a complete mess and so did the bathroom," remembered Yanovsky: "'You pee in the toilet?' he asked with dignified surprise, after having heard me flush (the door did not close anymore). 'Yes, how else?' 'Everybody I know does it in the sink. It's a male's privilege,' was his answer, soft and not intended to belittle me."[30] Without Chester the flat slid into ever greater chaos. As the district grew poorer and more run-down, so that apartment grew "darker and dustier than ever," as Margaret Gardiner was sad to see: "there was something very desolate about him then."[31]

"Time and again," wrote Hannah Arendt, one of his shrewdest New York friends,

> when to all appearances he could not cope any more, when his slum apartment was so cold that the water no longer functioned and he had to use the toilet in the liquor store at the corner, when his suit—no one could convince him that a man needed at least two suits so that one could go to the cleaner or two pairs of shoes so that one pair could be repaired, a subject of an endlessly ongoing

debate between us throughout the years—was covered with spots
or worn so thin that his trousers would suddenly split from top to
bottom, in brief, whenever disaster hit before your very eyes, he
would begin to kind of intone an utterly idiosyncratic, absurdly
eccentric version of "count your blessings."[32]

"Life remains a blessing / Although you cannot bless," he had written
many years before.[33] Arendt remained bewildered that he should have
not merely endured but in some way actively created "the absurd circumstances that made everyday life so unbearable for him"; but, after
his death, she made a shrewd connection between the shambles of his
domestic circumstances with what she memorably identified as his ex-
pertise "in the infinite varieties of unrequited love."[34] Had he been regarding someone else, Auden himself would have been the first to speculate sympathetically about the psychopathology at work in such odd
self-punishment; but other observers were less forgiving about the phe-
nomenon of someone setting out to make such a mess of things. Edmund Wilson impatiently thought Auden "deliberately goes in for uncomfortable, sordid, and grotesque lodgings" and that he had "condemned
himself to this, so far as I can see, for all the rest of his life": "in a puri-
tanical way, [he] seems to feel he is acquiring merit by living—with a
touch of fantasy—in the most unattractive way possible."[35]

But the state of the apartment was not only symptomatic of some self-
punishing neurosis: the profuse detritus of his life was also the venue
for an amazing literary intelligence in a way which may not have been
the mere emotional contingency that Wilson took it to be. It would be
a bit too neat to quote Swift's "Such order from confusion sprung," although it is indeed striking that so many of Auden's statements about
poetics—many no doubt typed up on that desk overlooking St. Mark's
Place—repeatedly emphasise the importance of form and order. A poem,
says Auden in many places during this period, transforms your experience of the fallen world, in all its "unfreedom and disorder," into something momentarily redeemed and, within the special precincts of art, a
vision of the good.[36] But then the greatest poets, like Swift and Auden
himself, are conscious of themselves as moral agents as well as poetic

fabricators, and must not let themselves forget the disarray that was the occasion of their poems in the first place: for "nothing is lovely, / Not even in poetry, which is not the case."[37] It is difficult not to believe that in some way the great Auden writings of the 1950s and 1960s, so often preoccupied by the aesthetic end of order and the human reality of its absence, drew in some intuitive way upon the fertile disarray over which he presided in his apartment. Auden himself suggested as much, anyway: he responded to Wilson's obvious disgust at his living conditions, "I hate living in squalor—I detest it!—but I can't do the work I want to do and live any other way."[38]

12
Samuel Johnson's Houses

REBECCA BULLARD

In 1911, the newspaper magnate and newly appointed MP for Luton, Cecil Harmsworth, bought 17 Gough Square, a large and very dilapidated red-brown brick house just off Fleet Street, which had recently been in use as a printer's office. The reason for the purchase and subsequent restoration of this building was that this house had once belonged to Samuel Johnson and was the place where, in the garret, Johnson and a team of literary labourers had compiled the monumental *Dictionary of the English Language* during the late 1740s and early 1750s. In a cartoon drawn in 1915 to mark the opening of the house as a museum the caricaturist Max Beerbohm imagines two possible Johnsonian responses to Harmsworth's purchase. One version of Johnson declares, with evident delight, that "nothing has pleased me half so well since the *Rambler* was translated into the Russian language and read on the banks of the Wolga"—an exclamation based on an anecdote in James Boswell's *Life of Johnson*.[1] On the other hand, Beerbohm also imagines a curmudgeonly Johnson ("puffing, and rolling himself from side to side"), who pronounces that "if a house be not fit for tenancy by Tom or Dick, let it be demolished or handed over without more ado to the rats, which, by frequenting, will have acquired a prescriptive right there." When a diminutive cartoon Boswell protests that "the house of the great Samuel Johnson" ought to be preserved for the nation, Johnson cuts him short with a cod-Johnsonism: "The house is nought. Let us not *sublimify* lath and plaster."

FIGURE 12.1. Dr. Johnson's House. (Courtesy of Dr. Johnson's House Trust Ltd.)

The debate about whether or not we should "*sublimify* lath and plaster" reflects not only on Harmsworth's recent purchase of 17 Gough Square but also on a fashion for "rescuing" the homes of literary luminaries that had taken hold of Britain in the mid-nineteenth century and showed no signs of abating at the beginning of the twentieth. The house in Stratford-upon-Avon in which William Shakespeare had been born was purchased by an organisation that became the Shakespeare Birthplace Trust in 1847 (as was Anne Hathaway's Cottage in 1892); John Milton's cottage in Chalfont St. Giles was bought by public subscription and opened as a museum in 1887; and the Wordsworth Trust bought Dove Cottage, where William and Dorothy Wordsworth spent eight years at the beginning of the nineteenth century, in 1890 and opened a museum there the following year. Johnson's birthplace in Lichfield was

FIGURE 12.2. "In the Shades" by Max Beerbohm, 1915. (Courtesy of Dr. Johnson's House Trust Ltd.)

given to the city in 1901. From 1867 the Society of Arts (later the Royal Society of Arts) erected plaques to mark the places where writers and other notable figures lived, worked, and died—forerunners of the blue plaques that adorn many houses in London, and beyond, today. Johnson's house at 17 Gough Square still bears an early example of this practice. By the second decade of the twentieth century, Milton's belief that books "do preserve as in a vial the purest efficacy and extraction of

FIGURE 12.3. Dr. Johnson's House, plaque. (Courtesy of Dr. Johnson's House Trust Ltd.)

that living intellect that bred them" seems to have been more routinely applied to bricks and mortar than paper and board.[2]

Johnson's own view of the relationship between lives and houses seems at odds with the "blue plaque" impulse of Harmsworth's Britain. In his *Life of Milton* he observes, somewhat archly, "I cannot but remark a kind of respect, perhaps unconsciously, paid to this great man by his biographers: every house in which he resided is historically mentioned, as if it were an injury to neglect naming any place that he honoured by his presence."[3] The fascination of Milton's biographers with his places of residence denotes a misplaced interest on outward conditions of existence and worldly praise rather than on their subject's "moral and prudential character."[4]

In an essay in *The Rambler*, Johnson offers a corrective to this kind of superficial biography. "The business of the biographer," he asserts, is "to lead the thoughts into domestick privacies, and display the minute details of daily life, where exterior appendages are cast aside, and men excel each other only by prudence and by virtue."[5] Homes reveal the most authentic version of a biography's subject, free from mannered or even hypocritical public behaviour. As Johnson himself puts it, "more knowledge may be gained of a man's real character, by a short conversation with one of his servants, than from a formal and studied narrative, begun with his pedigree, and ended with his funeral."[6] Even more importantly, the domestic sphere offers a point of connection between the reader and the subject of a biography. Few readers will have held high office, written literary masterpieces, or acted on stage; almost all will have experienced domestic life in one form or another. If biographers want to tell true and useful stories about their subjects, as Johnson insists they should, it is to the home that they must turn.

If Cecil Harmsworth had wanted to justify his decision to memorialise Johnson in and through his home, he might have turned to Johnson's own writings on biography. Equally, though, he could have represented himself as an heir not so much to Johnson himself as to some of his most significant biographers. Johnson's domestic habits are important to both Hester Lynch Piozzi's *Anecdotes of the Late Samuel Johnson, LL.D.* (1786) and James Boswell's *Life of Samuel Johnson, LL.D.* (1791).

I want to explore the ways in which both of these writers engage with, and to some degree react against, Johnson's own ideas about "domestick privacies" as he expresses them in his biographical writings. I also want to show how Piozzi and Boswell use Johnson's domestic habits to attack one another. In lives of Johnson, the home is a contested space that often generates and barely contains conflict, whether between domestic cohabitants or the biographers who write about them.

Hester Piozzi's *Anecdotes*

Hester Piozzi's *Anecdotes* is a biography born of extended domestic acquaintance. Johnson was a regular visitor to the homes that she shared with her first husband, Henry Thrale, and their children at Southwark and Streatham. He travelled with the Thrales to Wales, France, and Brighton and lived part-time with them at Streatham. Following Henry's death, however, Johnson's fury at Hester's marriage to Gabriel Piozzi, an Italian singing teacher, resulted in their estrangement five months before Johnson's death in December 1784. That death precipitated Hester Piozzi into print for the first time: *Anecdotes* was published in March 1786.

Anecdotes gives a brief account of Johnson's childhood, student days, and professional career, but its peculiar attraction to readers was the glimpse that it offered of Johnson in private circumstances. This view of the biography is one that Piozzi herself encourages; she begins her account by reflecting that "the Preface before a book, like the portico before a house, should be contrived, so as to catch, but not detain the attention of those who desire admission to the family within."[7] Here, Piozzi metaphorically elides home and book, so that the reader is welcomed as a guest. And in this biography we do indeed see Johnson at home—drinking tea, conversing with children, and threatening to burn not only his wig but also the whole house down due to his insistence on trying to read in bed by candlelight.

Piozzi portrays her home as Johnson's sanctuary. She reports that after he had suffered a particularly acute period of mental illness in the late 1770s, she persuaded him "to quit his close habitation in the court, and come with us to Streatham, where I undertook the care of his health, and had the honour and happiness of contributing to his restoration."[8] "The court" here refers to Bolt Court, an enclosed yard off Fleet Street, just around the corner from Gough Square, where Johnson lived from 1776 with a strikingly eclectic group of domestic servants and needy guests. These included Frank Barber, a black servant, who was eventually joined in the household by his wife, Betty; Anna Williams, a poet left blind by an operation for cataracts; Elizabeth Desmoulins, the impoverished daughter of Johnson's godfather; Robert Levet, a surgeon to the poor who moved in with Johnson after his wife was taken up for pickpocketing; and Poll Carmichael, a Scottish woman about whom very little is known. Number 8 Bolt Court housed seven poor and sick people (including Johnson himself), as well as a servant, Mrs. White. In her account of Johnson's household, Piozzi does not give these inmates separate identities, portraying them instead as ungrateful vipers in Johnson's bosom: "he nursed whole nests of people in his house," she reports, "where the lame, the blind, the sick, and the sorrowful found a sure retreat from all the evils whence his little income could secure them."[9] Constant bickering between Johnson's cohabitants "made his life miserable from the impossibility he found of making theirs happy."[10] According to Piozzi, Johnson was trebly trapped in Bolt Court—in the pent-up architecture of London, in an ungrateful, quarrelsome, and oppressive household, and in a mind "oppressed with diseases incident to the most vivid and fervent imaginations." Streatham, where he spent half the week, is portrayed by contrast as a refuge without which "he would scarce have lived . . . and kept his faculties entire, to have written."[11]

Streatham as sanctuary is, however, only half of Piozzi's story; her narrative also reveals that keeping Johnson in good health imprisoned her in her own home. Johnson's horror of being alone, for instance, led him to insist that his friend stay up with him into the small hours, "as I often did in London till four o'clock in the morning. At Streatham indeed I managed better, having always some friend who was kind enough to engage him in talk, and favour my retreat."[12] After Henry Thrale's death she moved to Bath, "where I knew Mr Johnson would not follow me, and where I could for that reason command some little portion of time for my own use; a thing impossible while I remained at Streatham or London."[13] Published in the wake of Johnson's death, Piozzi's biography itself is an assertion of newfound freedom—an act of rebellion against Johnson's disapproval of her second marriage. Her new name, "Hesther Lynch Piozzi," appears prominently on the title page, and she refers explicitly to the fact that she has written *Anecdotes* from Italy, calling it "a piece of motley Mosaic work" that resembles "square pieces of all the curious marbles which are the just glory of this surprising part of the world."[14] *Anecdotes* records Piozzi's former intimacy with Johnson, but it also represents a calculated response to their estrangement.

In *Anecdotes*, Piozzi uses a Johnsonian model of domestic biography to offer her readers both a privileged view of Johnson and an assertion of her independence from him. Her depiction of her oppression at Johnson's hands neatly recalls Johnson's own *Life of Pope*, which he wrote while living with the Thrales at Streatham. Pope, Johnson reports, "was a very troublesome inmate," who insisted on round-the-clock care: "one of his constant demands was of coffee in the night, and to the woman that waited on him in his chamber he was very burthensome."[15] He goes on: "Lord Oxford's domestick related, that, in the dreadful winter of Forty, she was called from her bed by him four times in one night, to supply him with paper, lest he should lose a thought."[16] Both Johnson and Piozzi draw attention to the emotional and practical female labour that underpins masculine literary production, but Piozzi goes a significant step further than Johnson. His female domestic remains nameless, her words (for instance, "the dreadful winter of Forty") rendered in free indirect discourse rather than direct speech. Piozzi's book, on the other hand, allows the author to articulate her own unique role in facilitating Johnson's career. It offers, as the word "anecdotes" suggests, a secret history of Johnson's literary career that gains power through its appropriation of Johnsonian domestic biography.

James Boswell's Life

In a very self-conscious passage of her *Anecdotes*, Hester Piozzi suggests that domestic biography has limitations:

> In giving little memoirs of Mr Johnson's behaviour and conversation, such as I saw and heard it, my book lies under manifest disadvantages, compared with theirs, who having seen him in various situations, and observed his conduct in numberless cases, are able to throw stronger and more brilliant lights upon his character. . . . Mine is a mere *candle-light* picture of his latter days, where every thing falls in dark shadow except the face, the index of the mind.[17]

When she alludes to other writers who "can throw more brilliant lights" upon Johnson, Piozzi gestures towards James Boswell—not to the *Life of Johnson* (which had not been published when she wrote her *Anecdotes*) but rather to his first published account of Johnson in *Journal of a Tour to the Hebrides*, published in October 1785. Here, Boswell depicts a dynamic Johnson who loved riding in carriages at speed, who journeyed hundreds of miles on horseback, scrambled in and out of boats, explored caves, and conversed with people from lairds to crofters, including the Jacobite heroine Flora MacDonald. Taken at face value, Piozzi's account of her own "*candle-light* picture" of Johnson suggests its inferiority to the vigorous *Journal*. And yet, for all her self-deprecation, Piozzi uses domestic biography to assert her own privileged relationship with Johnson to the extent that she gives an "index of the mind" of her subject.

Relations between Boswell and Hester Thrale were strained but polite while Johnson was still alive. After his death and the publication of

Anecdotes, they became increasingly rancorous. Boswell hated Piozzi's *Anecdotes*. He thought it partial, inaccurate, and deeply disrespectful. In his *Life of Johnson* he repeatedly contradicts her versions of events, justifying his decision to do so by referring to the authority conferred on her by domestic acquaintance:

> It is with concern that I find myself obliged to animadvert on the inaccuracies of Mrs. Piozzi's *Anecdotes*. . . . But as from Johnson's long residence under Mr. Thrale's roof, and his intimacy with her, the account which she has given of him may have made an unfavourable and unjust impression, my duty, as a faithful biographer, has obliged me reluctantly to perform this unpleasing task.[18]

In writing his own biography, Boswell navigates a careful course as he depicts Johnson at home, guided on the one hand by his respect for Johnson's interest in domestic intimacy and on the other by his antagonism towards Piozzi's manipulation of her privileged relationship with him. The result is a peculiarly uneasy engagement with the domestic sphere.

Early on in his *Life*, Boswell approaches the topic of Johnson's homes with a degree of circumspection:

> As there is something pleasingly interesting, to many, in tracing so great a man through all his different habitations, I shall, before this work is concluded, present my readers with an exact list of his lodgings and houses in order of time, which, in placid condescension to my respectful curiosity, he one evening dictated to me, but without specifying how long he lived at each. . . . To some, this minute attention may appear trifling; but when we consider the punctilious exactness with which the different houses in which Milton resided have been traced by the writers of his life, a similar enthusiasm may be pardoned in the biographer of Johnson.[19]

Boswell's allusion to Milton here harks back to Johnson's own *Life of Milton*. But while Johnson, as we have already seen, expressed scepticism towards the blue-plaque impulses of Milton's previous biographers, Boswell embraces the kind of antiquarian methods that justify a fascination with any and every scrap of Johnsoniana—including a list of his addresses. It is in keeping with the antiquarian mode that, when Boswell gives this list later in his narrative (noting that he wrote it on Sunday, 10 October 1779), it takes the form of a footnote (1035). As he gives the list he refers once more to Johnson's *Life of Milton*—this time quoting from it directly. Again, though, he uses Johnson's words to justify his own decision to include, rather than pass over, trivial details about Johnson's places of residence. Just as Piozzi uses a Johnsonian model to rework the genre of domestic biography, so Boswell uses the *Life of Milton* in order to question some of Johnson's ideas about biography. But where Piozzi used domestic biography to paint Johnson as an overbearing household guest, Boswell rejects Johnson's ideas about the value of the domestic precisely in order to portray Johnson as a "great man."

When Boswell does treat Johnson's domestic circumstances in the *Life*, he does so in such a way as to distance himself from them. Writing about the year 1778, he observes:

> We surely cannot but admire the benevolent exertions of this great
> and good man, especially when we consider how grievously he was
> afflicted with bad health, and how uncomfortable his home was
> made by the perpetual jarring of those whom he charitably accom-
> modated under his roof. He has sometimes suffered me to talk
> jocularly of his group of females, and call them his *Seraglio*. He thus
> mentions them, together with honest Levett, in one of his letters
> to Mrs. Thrale: "Williams hates every body; Levett hates Desmou-
> lins, and does not love Williams; Desmoulins hates them both;
> Poll loves none of them."[20]

Boswell seems both amused and bemused by Johnson's domestic circumstances. He clearly admires Johnson's benevolence, but even as he looks on in wonder he also emphasises his exclusion from this strange household. Suggesting that the women around Johnson form a seraglio is, as Boswell notes, a joke, but it is one that draws attention to Boswell's status as outsider—a (virile) man shut out from a domain associated, he implies, with women and eunuchs. It is notable that Johnson's epigrammatic catalogue of complaints about his lodgers is rendered in a letter to "Mrs. Thrale." This kind of domestic sphere, he seems to imply, is her domain, not his.

Indeed, even though Boswell was given an apartment in Johnson's lodgings for a time, Johnson's home in Boswell's *Life* comes most clearly into focus when Johnson is not there. On one occasion, for instance, Boswell visits Johnson's library while its usual occupant is away from home:

> Mr. Levet this day shewed me Dr. Johnson's library, which was contained in two garrets over his Chambers. . . . I found a number of good books, but very dusty and in great confusion. The floor was strewed with manuscript leaves, in Johnson's own handwriting, which I beheld with a degree of veneration, supposing they perhaps might contain portions of *The Rambler* or of *Rasselas*. I observed an apparatus for chymical experiments, of which Johnson was all his life very fond. The place seemed to be very favourable for retirement and meditation.[21]

Boswell's incursion into Johnson's library feels something like a sanitised and reverent version of Swift's poem "The Lady's Dressing Room," in which a young man named Strephon explores (with a mixture of fascination and disgust) private apartments that have been vacated by his lover, Chloe. Boswell's preferred way of seeing Johnson in domestic circumstances, it seems, is when the great man is out of them. He distances his account of Johnson both from Johnson's own view of biography and from Piozzi's domestic portrait by dwelling on his own exclusion, and on Johnson's absence, from home.

Back to 17 Gough Square

Samuel Johnson, Hester Piozzi, and James Boswell held very different views of the relationship between life-writing and houses, but they could agree on some things. All of them, for instance, regarded the home somewhat paradoxically as a place both of retreat or refuge and of inconvenience and interruption. In his *Life of Milton* Johnson expresses scepticism towards the accounts of John Milton's "domestick habits, so far as they are known," from earlier biographies because the life of a "severe student" who keeps strictly regular hours was, to Johnson's mind, impossible in a private house:

> This even tenour appears attainable only in Colleges. He that lives
> in the world will sometimes have the succession of his practice broken and confused. Visiters, of whom Milton is represented to have
> had great numbers, will come and stay unseasonably; business, of
> which every man has some, must be done when others will do it.[22]

Johnson's present tense ("He that lives in the world . . .") is Milton's
too, in spite of the century between them: the familiarity of the domestic setting allows Johnson to assert fundamental human connections
across time and space that extend as far as Johnson's own readership.
As Piozzi and Boswell show, however, residents in a house were as likely
to "have the succession of [their] practice broken and confused" by cohabitants as much as by visitors. Living in houses, all three writers suggest, means dealing with other people, being imposed on and imposing
on others, mutual dependence and mutual forbearance. Houses are
important not for their lath and plaster but because of the human relationships that are forged in and through them.

The Dr. Johnson's House Museum captures very beautifully something of all three writers' ideas about the life of houses. These days, it
is dwarfed by the towering plate glass, brick, and cladding of the office
blocks that surround Gough Square. Number 17, by comparison, feels
like a house on a human scale—indeed, as a man of significantly more
than average height, Johnson must have struggled to negotiate the rather
low-ceilinged and narrow staircase that winds up three floors from the
entrance to the garret. Its fabric still reveals some of the ways in which
its former inhabitants handled one another and the world outside. A huge
chain on the front door and iron bars above it hint both at the threat of
unwelcome incursion (from burglars, rather than visitors) and at the idea
of the house as a kind of sanctuary. A set of doors at the top of the first
flight of stairs offers the drawing room an improvised kind of privacy,
as well as rudimentary protection from the east wind blowing through
the front door. In the drawing room itself, ingenious folding doors offer
the possibility of partitioning the available space in a number of differ-

ent ways—opening it up to larger groups or closing off sections for social or thermal reasons. These material features capture something of
the ways in which residents and visitors navigated not just the space of
the house but their relationships with one another. By contrast, the garret where Johnson worked on the *Dictionary* still feels like something of
a retreat. Though it lacks the manuscripts and experimental equipment
that Boswell admired in the garret at 8 Bolt Court, it is not difficult to
imagine Johnson rolling and puffing his way up here. His absent presence feels as humane as his *Life of Pope*, as uncomfortable as Piozzi's
Anecdotes of Johnson, as awkwardly heroic as Boswell's *Life*.

House-Proud

13
The Manor

SIMON ARMITAGE

What a prize prick he's made of himself,
trudging a dozen furlongs across the plain

to the widowed heiress's country estate
just to be turned away at the lodge, to stare

from the wrong side of the locked gates.
The plan—admit it—was to worm his way in:

to start as a lowly gofer and drudge, then rise
from gardener to footman to keeper of hawks—

her hooded merlin steady on his wrist—
to suddenly making his way upstairs after dark,

now soaping her breasts in the roll-top bath
with its clawed gold feet, now laying a trail

of soft fruit from her pillow to his, his tongue
now coaxing the shy nasturtium flower of love.

Here he is in the dream, gilt-framed, a gent
in her late husband's best brown suit,

the loyal schnauzer gazing up at his eyes.
And here's the true him tramping the verge,

frayed collar and cuffs, brambles for hair,
the toes of his boots mouthing like grounded fish.

A pride of lions roams the walled parkland
between this dogsbody life and the next.

14

At Home with
the Disraelis

DAISY HAY

In the spring of 1862 Mary Anne Disraeli decided to organise a surprise for her husband. In an atmosphere of intense secrecy she commissioned an obelisk for the park at Hughenden in Buckinghamshire to commemorate the life of Disraeli's father, Isaac. She enlisted the help of her lawyer, Philip Rose, who later wrote an account of the project. "Her idea was in favour of a tall column or monument on the top of the Hill which would be conspicuous over the neighbouring County," Rose recalled. "I pointed out the difficulties of the secrecy she required, particularly as her husband would wish to go down at Easter. She had thought of this. Nothing Dizzy disliked so much as the smell of paint, and she intended to do some painting inside the house at that time.'" Rose duly found an architect and arranged for the monument to be constructed some way from Hughenden, "with no local man being employed."[1] In August that year the Disraelis travelled together to Hughenden and on their way through the park Mary Anne was able to point out the completed monument to her husband. "I hasten to tell you we are delighted, perfect success," she wrote to Rose. "Mr Disraeli says he sees no fault, his affectionate astonishment I cannot describe."[2] Disraeli himself described the monument simply as "one of the most beautiful not only in the County of Buckingham, but in England."[3]

FIGURE 14.1. Portrait of Disraeli, Earl of Beaconsfield, K.G., by (Cornelius) Jabez Hughes (1819–1884). (Photo copyright © National Trust / Thomas Boggis)

The story of the Hughenden monument has in it many of the elements that are particular to the story of Hughenden itself. Benjamin Disraeli bought the house and its surrounding estate in 1848. Today the house is owned by the National Trust and it stands as a monument to the life the Disraelis built together, just as the hilltop memorial to Isaac D'Israeli recalls his name. Hughenden reveals the story of the Disraelis' marriage in every room: in the portraits of the friends and family that hang throughout the house, in the chairs that Mary Anne had embroidered with ornamental Bs when she was elevated to the rank of Viscountess Beaconsfield, in the compact double bed that they shared until the last

FIGURE 14.2. The drawing room at Hughenden Manor, Buckinghamshire. (Photo copyright © National Trust Images / Andreas von Einsiedel)

days of Mary Anne's life. The formal garden represents Mary Anne's great creative achievement, and like the monument it displays her delight in bold schemes, surprises, and unexpected vistas. In the magic of a monument that apparently appeared overnight, meanwhile, is something of the magic that ultimately settled over the Disraelis at Hughenden as in old age they performed the roles of a chivalrous knight and his lady against a backdrop of neo-Gothic panelling and Italianate planting. Hughenden is also part of Disraeli's political story; its role is best summed up by the epitaph Mary Anne had carved on the monument to her father-in-law: "This monument was raised in affectionate remembrance by Mary Anne, the wife of his Eldest Son the Rt Honorable Benjamin Disraeli, Lord of this Manor, Chancellor of the Exchequer 1852–8 and 9 and now for the Sixth Time Knight of his Shire." The story of how the Disraelis came to own Hughenden, however, reveals that its reputation-making solidity was hard won and that the financial foundations of Disraeli's possession of the house were shaky from the outset.

Disraeli's first constituencies in Parliament were urban seats. He was elected as the Conservative MP for Maidstone in 1837 and subsequently as the MP for Shrewsbury in 1841. As the 1840s progressed and his power within the Conservative Party increased it became clear that he would need to represent a country seat if he were ever to lead the country party. In 1847 he stood as the Conservative candidate for Buckingham, the county in which his parents rented the estate of Bradenham. He was elected unopposed and immediately started negotiations for the purchase of Hughenden. Disraeli's determination to buy Hughenden was given added impetus by the knowledge that he needed to look like a member of the landed classes, complete with a country estate, in order to exert control over his party. He had a powerful backer in his quest for a country estate of his own in the form of his parliamentary colleague Lord George Bentinck. Bentinck was the younger son of the Earl of Portland and, with Disraeli, he led the Protectionist rump of the Conservative Party in the House of Commons. In the aftermath of the repeal of the Corn Laws the Conservatives had split into Peelites and Protectionists, and the latter group knew that their parliamentary fortunes were dependent on Disraeli's rhetorical firepower. Bentinck thought it crucial to the success of the Protectionist and agricultural cause that Disraeli should become a member of the landed gentry and thus the true representative of the agricultural interest. He offered to use his own sizeable fortune to guarantee the purchase of Hughenden and thus to aid Disraeli's transformation into a country gentleman. In 1848 Disraeli inherited his father's money, and with Bentinck's backing he was able to complete the purchase and make Hughenden his. In September 1848 he wrote to Mary Anne that "it is all done—& you are the Lady of Hughenden." She responded by buying him a farmer's hat to mark the moment.[4]

In reality it took more than a hat to make Disraeli the squire of Hughenden. Three weeks after the purchase of the house was completed George Bentinck died of a heart attack. With no guarantor the shaky financing of the sale was revealed and for a period it appeared that the Disraelis would be forced to sell Hughenden before they had even moved in. In October 1848 Disraeli went to London where he spent several hours in deep conversation with Lord George's brother Henry. Henry Bentinck offered Disraeli a loan of £25,000 on behalf of his father, the Duke of Portland. Portland and Henry Bentinck shared Lord George's commitment to the agricultural cause but they were less convinced of Disraeli's trustworthiness. The loan offered by Portland was contingent on him taking a mortgage on the estate: he also insisted on receiving the rents directly. Disraeli refused to be the representative of another master in his house and on his land and threatened to retire from public life completely. To Mary Anne he reported having gone "into the state of my affairs . . . observing that it wd. be no object to them & no pleasure to me, unless I played the high game in public life; & that I cd. not do that without being on a rock."[5] The Portlands were sceptical of Disraeli's professed commitment to the Protectionist cause and feared his potential as a dangerous parliamentary opponent, so to prevent his desertion they agreed to lend him money for the purchase on the clear understanding that the loan could be recalled at any time and that Disraeli would collect the rents and pay them directly to the duke. In public he would appear to be the landed leader of the agricultural interest but in private and in practical terms he would be a tenant in his own home, who could be required to sell on the word of another man.

The provisional, chaotic nature of Disraeli's purchase of Hughenden illustrates how much the house meant to him personally and politically, since he was prepared to risk his public career as he compelled the Portlands to support him. It also illustrates that the ownership of the house and land was instrumental in the political agendas of others right from the beginning of Disraeli's occupancy. For the next fifteen years Hughenden remained a chimera of landed security, the physical embodiment of dreams just out of reach. After the election of 1858 the new Duke of Portland called in the Hughenden loan. Over the following months the loan was transferred twice between Conservative backers, before ultimately being purchased by a sympathetic lender who charged only a modest rate of interest and who also bought Disraeli's other debts (which amounted to a further £25,000). It was only in 1863, however, when Disraeli received a substantial legacy from an eccentric widow living in Torquay, that Hughenden finally became securely his. The Disraelis

marked this moment of possession by embarking on a large-scale programme of renovations in the house and garden as, freed from the financial anxiety the house represented, Disraeli fell in love with his home
anew. Constance de Rothchild recalled visiting Hughenden during this
period, when she herself was a child. "How he loved the place!" she
wrote of her host. "And how he tried to act up to the character he had
imposed upon himself, that of the country gentleman."[6]

Constance de Rothchild was far from being the only visitor to comment on the theatricality of the Disraelis at Hughenden. Disraeli himself reached for the metaphor during a period of intensive renovations,
as they prepared to receive fourteen overnight visitors in ten days. "Its
as hard work as having a playhouse—or keeping an Inn."[7] Even the fabric of the building had the qualities of a stage set. When the Disraelis
bought the house they became possessors of a mid-eighteenth-century
building with a classical stuccoed exterior, which they set about updat-
ing. They employed the architect Edward Buxton Lamb to redesign the
house in the Gothic revival style for which Lamb was noted, and he duly
added a crenelated façade and threw a scattering of Ds through the stone-
work. During their early years at Hughenden the united picture the
Disraelis presented to the world from their house was itself a façade, as
the house's emotional significance was outweighed by the danger it represented. As new owners of a country estate the Disraelis found that in
the autumns they were isolated in the countryside for weeks on end,
unable to seek refuge from mutual alienation in the company of others.
"Anything is better than Hughenden," Disraeli wrote to his sister in
November 1849. "I meditate decamping privately on Monday to town."[8]
In these years Hughenden also represented a world of country-house visiting from which the Disraelis periodically found themselves shut out.
Neither was an easy houseguest, since he did not hunt or shoot and she,
according to the testimony of aristocratic gossips, could not be relied
upon to keep her conversation respectable. She was often excluded from
invitations to the great houses of Tory grandees or, if she did visit, was
vulnerable to mockery from her hosts. At Hughenden Mary Anne was
mistress of a country house but not mistress of that which her house
represented, and stories abounded about her disputes with tradesmen

and her stingy housekeeping. All were designed to show her ill at ease in a world that was not hers and as an interloper who did not understand the codes she tried to imitate.

The severity of the criticism directed towards Mary Anne when she breached those codes was predictably and consistently more intense than that directed towards Disraeli. Seen in this context, her decision to erect a forty-foot monument on a hill in the Buckinghamshire countryside and to name Disraeli on that monument as "knight of this shire" has in it an unmistakable and characteristic note of defiance. As his public position solidified Hughenden gave Disraeli a space from which he could dispense invitations and patronage, but it was Mary Anne who bore the brunt of the difficulties of playing host and who had to win acceptance from the tenants and villagers on whose labour the house depended. Disraeli may have experienced his house as both playhouse and inn but ultimately it was Mary Anne who had to fulfil the roles of stage manager and landlady.

Hughenden was thus very much more than just a house for the Disraelis. It was the embodiment of long-cherished hopes, of Disraeli's political success, and of their ultimate integration into a social class in which they were for a long time viewed with suspicion. It was a symbol of romance, in all senses of the word, a place simultaneously fantastic and real. Yet for years it offered only the illusion of security, and it required them to confront in stark terms the fact that the refuge it appeared to offer from public and private storms was limited. Ultimately, though, Disraeli and Mary Anne were able to mould Hughenden into the house of their dreams just as surely as Mary Anne tamed her garden. In the last year of her life, when she was in desperate pain from the stomach cancer that was killing her, it was to Hughenden that Mary Anne wanted to be taken. For a few weeks, in the autumn of 1872, the Disraelis lived out their life at Hughenden as if nothing was happening: a fantasy of normality on which Mary Anne insisted and which Disraeli found intolerable. To distract them both he arranged a small house party, and one of his guests, Lord Ronald Gower, later wrote an account of a visit during which the pain Mary Anne was evidently experiencing could not be acknowledged. She talked ceaselessly, he recalled, "death written on her face." Disraeli, meanwhile, "seemed much the most distressed of the two, for she was wonderfully brisk and lively, and had her breakfast brought into the library."[9] It was raining when Gower drove away from Hughenden, which he wrote felt fitting given the sadness seeping into the house in spite of Mary Anne's enforced jollity.

Less than a month later it was raining still as villagers carried Mary Anne's coffin down from the house to the church, and as Disraeli stood, soaking and hatless, witnessing her burial in the churchyard. Hughenden would once again become a haven of peace for Disraeli but in his first weeks alone there his isolation was complete. To his secretary Montagu Corry he compared himself to "the fellow in the iron mask. . . . One has parks & gardens, & libraries & pictures . . . but the human face & voice divine are wanting."[10] To console himself he began to sort through Mary Anne's papers and found, to his astonishment, that she had kept every letter he had ever received of which she was aware. Slowly, as he worked through box after box of paper, he saw the story of his marriage revealed to him anew. "I am amazed!" he told Corry. "Nothing seems to have escaped her."[11]

Visitors to Hughenden today walk in and out of rooms that appear to breathe the stories of their most famous inhabitants. The house contains many of the Disraelis' possessions and the National Trust has used them to tell stories, so that the positioning of Disraeli's wastepaper basket in his study illuminates the speed and focus with which he worked at his desk, just as Mary Anne's desk is positioned at the window of her boudoir, from where she could oversee work in her garden as she ran her house. Disraeli's heir was his nephew Coningsby, who recognised that the house was a living testament to the life of his famous uncle and treated its contents accordingly. It is because of Mary Anne's desire to catalogue and curate her life, however, that we can reconstruct the history of the house's refashioning and the positioning and provenance of many of its objects.

It is also the case that much of the meaning inscribed in the fabric of Hughenden and its contents comes from paper rather than from objects alone. It is what the Disraelis said and wrote about their house that gives it so much narrative power today, and here the story of the monument to Isaac D'Israeli with which I began is again a case in point. In Disraeli and Mary Anne's telling the monument testifies to their attachment to surprise and romance, to their status as landowners, and, in the spectacular gesture it represented, to Mary Anne's devotion to her husband and the grand romance of their old age. There is one final part to the story, however, in which that devotion is symbolised as reciprocal. In the memorandum he compiled years after Mary Anne's death, Philip Rose confessed that Disraeli had in fact learned of the monument before he arrived at Hughenden but that on no account would he let Mary Anne suspect he knew her secret. Even to his closest friends he wrote of it as a complete surprise. The secrecy of the monument is thus itself a fantasy, but the larger story of the Disraelis at Hughenden suggests that fantasies can be based on deeper, stronger truths. At Hughenden that truth is simple: two people made a house their own, and in so doing they made a marriage of convenience into an affair of the heart.

15

H. G. Wells at Uppark

LAURA MARCUS

The West Sussex country house Uppark (or Up Park) played a significant role in the early part of H. G. Wells's life, and its influence can be
felt throughout his thought and work. In 1880 Wells's mother, Sarah,
left the family home in Bromley, Kent, to become housekeeper at
Uppark where, as a young woman, she had once been a lady's maid.
During the years of her housekeeping position (which lasted until 1893),
the young H. G. Wells spent substantial periods of time at the house. In
his autobiography, published in the 1930s, Wells suggested that the
country house was, in its seventeenth- and eighteenth-century heyday,
the foundation of "nearly all that is worth while in our civilization today."[1] A starker picture of the country house and social hierarchy is
given in his novel *Tono-Bungay* (1909), in which Uppark becomes the
country house Bladesover. The very architecture of Uppark (redesigned
by Humphrey Repton in the early nineteenth century), with its extensive underground passages, along which servants, invisible to outside observers, would wheel laden trolleys between the kitchens and the main
house, is expressive of its social and class relations, and was one possible influence on Wells's representations of upper and lower kingdoms
in his early fictions.

Uppark had, like almost all houses of its kind, been extensively
remodelled over the course of its history. When Sir Matthew Fetherstonhaugh and his wife, Sarah (née Lethuillier), bought the house from
Charles, Earl of Tankerville, in 1747, they began an ambitious programme of building and furnishing, probably employing the architect

FIGURE 15.1. Uppark exterior; the south front of the main house showing the steps to the entrance at Uppark House and Garden, West Sussex. (Photo copyright © National Trust Images / Andrew Butler)

James Paine for the majority of the work (details of the commission and alterations have not survived). The house was further developed by Sir Matthew's son Henry (Harry) Fetherstonhaugh, who employed first Humphrey Repton, one of the most highly regarded landscape designers and architects of his day, and, after Repton's death, the neo-classical architect Charles Heathcote Tatum.

Sir Harry, who inherited Uppark on his father's death in 1774, was as fashionable a figure as the architects he chose. He was for many years a close companion of the Prince Regent and a society figure. Amongst his many mistresses was the young actress and dancer Emma Hart, a blacksmith's daughter, who would later become Lady Emma Hamilton and, subsequently, the close companion of Lord Nelson; her daughter Emma Carew (born in 1782 when Emma Hart was seventeen) was fathered by Sir Harry, though he never acknowledged the relationship. When he was seventy-one, he married for the first time; his bride was twenty-one-year-old Mary Ann Bullock, dairy maid at Uppark, who had worked (and, according to household legend, sung tunefully) in the finely tiled dairy designed by Repton. Before the marriage took place, she was sent to Paris to be educated in reading, writing, and embroidery. On Sir Harry's death, she inherited Uppark; on her death in 1874 her younger sister, Frances Bullock, was given life tenure of the house (taking the name Fetherstonhaugh).

It is with Mary Ann and Frances that the Wells family entered the story. In 1850, Sarah Neal, daughter of a Chichester innkeeper, became lady's maid to Frances. She left the post in 1853 to look after her sick mother and that year married Joseph (Joe) Wells, who was for a brief period a gardener at Uppark. Joe was unable to retain a permanent position at this time, and in 1855 the couple took over a china shop in Bromley, Kent, belonging to Joe's cousin George Wells. Supplementing the sale of china with cricket goods—Joe was a passionate cricketer— the couple eked out a living in a state of increasing mutual dissatisfaction. Herbert George Wells, the third of their sons, was born in 1866; a daughter, Frances, had died two years earlier, the loss almost certainly contributing to Sarah Wells's depression and unhappiness. When the request came, in 1880, from Frances Bullock for her to return to Uppark, this time as housekeeper, it was as if, her son writes, "the heavens opened and a great light shone on Mrs. Sarah Wells."[2]

The two houses, so radically different, play a central role in Wells's account of his early life in his *Experiment in Autobiography*. Fascinated by questions of generation, evolution, and development, Wells notes that he owed his existence to the accident of his parents' meeting during their temporary employment at Uppark. "I know nothing of the earliest encounter of my father and mother," Wells writes. "It may have been in the convolutions of Hands Across and Down the Middle, Sir Roger de Coverley, Pop Goes the Weasel, or some such country dance" (51). The world occupied by his mother at this time, for which she had trained in dressmaking and hairdressing, was that "of other ladies'-maids and valets, of house stewards, housekeepers, cooks and butlers, upper servants above the level of maids and footmen, a downstairs world, but living in plentiful good air, well fed and fairly well housed in the attics, basements and interstices of great mansions" (49).

Then followed the fifteen years at Atlas House, Bromley, "a needy shabby home" (38), in which the Wells family lived "mostly downstairs and underground" (42). The backyard—half earth and half brick—"was a large part of my little world in those days. I lived mostly in it and in the scullery and underground kitchen" (41). Sarah Wells's ambitions for her son were not far-reaching, but they extended to his education at a small private school in Bromley, one of a number of educational establishments which, by contrast with the recently created National Schools, carried on "the old eighteenth-century order." It was expected of Bertie Wells that he would, at the age of thirteen, leave school to follow his older brothers into work as a draper's assistant. His mother's departure to the housekeeper's position at Uppark did not initially alter this path, but the sense of "dislocation" it produced meant that he refused to accept his intended lot as his brothers had done: "I was awakened to the significance of a start in life from the outset, as my brothers had never been" (109).

The third chapter of *Experiment in Autobiography*, "Schoolboy," is structured around a sequence of "starts in life": a series of turning points and new beginnings, all of which are attached to particular places. In "Interlude at Up Park" (1880–81), Wells describes the period in which, after the collapse of his second hated apprenticeship, he was "allowed to take refuge . . . at Up Park," during which time "I produced a daily newspaper of a facetious nature—*The Up Park Alarmist*—on what was properly kitchen paper—and gave a shadow play to the maids and others, in a miniature theatre I made in the housekeeper's room" (135). The autobiography offers an excursus on Wells's belief that it was in the country-house world "that modern civilization was begotten and nursed. . . . Within these households, behind their screen of deer park and park wall and sheltered service, men could talk, think and write at their leisure. They were free from inspection and immediate imperatives. They, at least, could go on after thirteen thinking and doing as they pleased" (135). Wells's argument is that while the culture of this intellectual and liberal enquiry "rested on a toiling class" (136), it was through "the curiosity and enterprise and free deliberate thinking of these independent gentlemen . . . that modern machinery and economic organization have developed so as to abolish at last the harsh necessity for any toiling class whatever" (136). The country-house world of the seventeenth and eighteenth centuries is thus understood by Wells to be "the experimental cellule of the coming Modern State" (136).

In intertwining the account of his boyhood experience at Uppark with the political philosophy and the scientific and rational understanding that he developed in his later writings, Wells implies a strong connection between them. In the house's library, created in part by the "freethinker" Sir Harry Fetherstonhaugh, the teenaged Wells read widely in works of the Enlightenment (Voltaire, Samuel Johnson, Tom Paine, and Jonathan Swift) and, most significantly, the adult autobiographer records, absorbed Plato's *Republic*: "Here was the amazing and heartening suggestion that the whole fabric of law, custom and worship, which seemed so invincibly established, might be cast into the melting pot and made anew" (138). Wells does not make the connection between this early reading and his later preoccupations with the nature of utopias, but his own *A Modern Utopia* (1905) contains significant discussion of the *Republic*. Wells writes that Plato, for whom there was no possibility of envisaging an age of machines, could not conceive "that a labouring class . . . will become unnecessary to the world of men," but he finds continued relevance in the "profound intuitions" concerning "that strange class of guardians which constitutes the essential substance of Plato's *Republic*."[3]

In his *Experiment in Autobiography*, Wells described a later visit to Uppark. At a Christmas dance in the Servants Hall, "in which the upper and lower servants mingled together," the young Wells meets a kitchen maid, Mary, and comes close to the sexual fulfilment of which he dreams: "afterwards in one of the underground passages towards the kitchen, where perhaps I was looking for her, she [Mary] darted out of a recess and kissed and embraced me. No lovelier thing had ever happened to me" (183). Wells makes another connection to the *Republic*: "Now under the stimulus of Plato's Utopianism and my quickening desires I began to ask my imagination what it was I desired in women. . . . In the free lives and free loves of the guardians of the *Republic* I found the encouragement I needed to give my wishes a systematic form" (184–85).

If sexual awakening occurs for Wells in the remarkable architecture of the underground passages between the kitchens and the main house at Uppark, and with the mingling of "upper and lower servants," as a temporary departure from the rigid hierarchies of country-house life, scientific fascination is aroused in another part of the house. Rummaging around in an attic "full of odd discarded things," Wells found "a box, at first quite mysterious, full of brass objects" (137). Screwing the pieces together, he "presently found a Gregorian telescope on a tripod in my hands": "I was discovered by my mother in the small hours, my bedroom window wide open, inspecting the craters of the moon" (137). In a later visit to Uppark, where Wells spent four months in 1887–88 recuperating from a consumptive condition, there was a further interlude (in between his scientific studies and teaching and his entry into authorship) of "mental opportunity," in which he read poetry and "imaginative work" (304) and realised that he must learn how to write. He describes a further month's holiday at Uppark in 1891 after a recurrence of his illness, "a period of intellectual leisureliness" (356) in which he turned to scientific writing, including an ultimately unsuccessful but, he intimates, prophetic account of "a four dimensional space-time universe." It was from these apparently unpromising beginnings—the piece was rejected by the *Fortnightly Review*—that his early scientific tales and his best-known work, the novella *The Time Machine* (1895), seem to have emerged.

The month in 1891 was to be the last of the "interludes" at Uppark, which are represented as intervals of leisure and intellectual growth punctuating the gruelling and frustrating years of first and false starts in Wells's early life. In 1893, the seventy-year-old Sarah Wells lost her position at Uppark, allegedly for gossiping about the Bullock sisters in their younger years. Wells suggests in his autobiography that his mother had from the beginning been outfaced by the demands of her post, having none of the organizational skills that would have made her a success as housekeeper. He describes Uppark as "alive and potent," despite "the insignificant ebbing trickle of upstairs life, the two elderly ladies in the parlour [Frances Fetherstonhaugh (formerly Bullock) and her companion Miss Stevenson] following their shrunken routines, by no means content with the bothered little housekeeper in the panelled room below" (137). Sarah Wells's diaries confirm that she was, certainly by the end of her employment, indeed "bothered" in her role, commanding no respect from the other servants. "What a worry this house is!!" she wrote in early 1892, noting later that year: "12 years today I came here. . . . What anxious years they have been to me. What rude insulting people I have had to live with and it is worse *now*."[4] Yet she was bewildered and distressed when, a year later, "Miss Fetherstonhaugh rebelled," as her son puts it, "against my mother's increasing deafness and inefficiency and dismissed her."[5]

When Wells came to represent the life at Uppark in his novel *Tono-Bungay*,[6] in which he calls the country house, now transposed to the county of Kent, Bladesover House and its mistress Lady Drew, he transfers the experience of disgrace and expulsion to his youthful narrator, who develops a juvenile passion for Beatrice, a young aristocratic cousin of Lady Drew's, and gets into a fight with Beatrice's brother, after which he is summarily banished. With heavy nods to Dickens's *Great Expectations* (in particular, Pip's visits to Satis House) and *David Copperfield* (including the purgatory of David's apprenticed labour and his long journey in search of shelter), *Tono-Bungay*'s narrator begins by telling "of my boyhood and my early impressions in the shadow of Bladesover House" (14).

The first chapters of *Tono-Bungay* give a detailed account of the barely fictionalised Uppark, dwelling on both its topography and its social organization. "There came a time when I realised that Bladesover House was not all it seemed, but when I was a little boy I took the place with the entirest faith as a complete authentic microcosm. I believed that the Bladesover system was a little working model—and not so very little either—of the whole world." Wells's narrator describes the "wide park" and "the great house" as appearing to him then to be "a closed and complete social system" (15). The novel articulates far more ambivalence—

edging into hostility—towards its hierarchies and rituals, ossified from its eighteenth-century heyday, than is apparent in Wells's autobiography, while continuing to make knowledge of these structures a precondition for an understanding of English society: "Bladesover is, I am convinced, the clue to almost all that is distinctively British. . . . Everybody who is not actually in the shadow of a Bladesover is as it were perpetually seeking after lost orientations" (19). Wells gives to his narrator his own experience, as depicted in the autobiography, of mind-broadening reading in the house's library (though the eighteenth-century novel here wins out over Plato's *Republic*) and, more generally, the perception that the country-house world had lastingly shaped his conceptual universe:

In a sense Bladesover has never left me; it is, as I said at the outset, one of those dominant explanatory impressions that makes the framework of my mind. Bladesover illuminates England: it has become all that is spacious, dignified, pretentious and truly conservative in English life. It is my social datum. That is why I have drawn it here on so large a scale. (54)

Size and scale are central to Wells's depictions of the country-house world in the novel and are picked up in the autobiography's references to both the "miniature theatre" with which the young Wells entertained the Uppark servants and the Gregorian telescope through which he observes the stars. In *Tono-Bungay*, the two old ladies, Lady Drew and her companion Miss Sommerville, are described as living "like dried-up kernels in the great shell of Bladesover House" (17). The library-saloon at Bladesover is

a huge, long room with many windows opening upon the park. . . . At either end of that great still place was an immense marble chimney-piece . . . Frederick, Prince of Wales, swaggered flatly over the one, twice life-size; and over the other was an equally colossal group of departed Drews as sylvan deities, scantily clad, against a storm-rent sky. (25)

And yet, despite all this magnification, Wells also achieves the effects of miniaturization:

> All these conceptions and applications of a universal precedence and much else I drank in at Bladesover, as I listened to the talk of valets, ladies'-maids, Rabbits the butler and my mother in the much cupboarded, white-painted, chintz-brightened housekeeper's room where the upper servants assembled, or of footmen and Rabbits and estate men of all sorts among the green baize and Windsor chairs of the pantry . . . or of housemaids and still-room maids in the bleak, matting-carpeted still-room, or of the cook and her kitchen maids and casual friends among the bright copper and hot glow of the kitchens.

This vertical world has, indeed, all the appearance and appurtenances of a grand doll's house, and in *Tono-Bungay* Wells refers to "the great doll's house on the nursery landing . . . that the Prince Regent had given Sir Harry Drew's first-born (who died at five) that was not an ineffectual model of Bladesover itself, and contained eighty-five dolls and had cost hundreds of pounds." On return to school, he and his friend Ewart "made a great story out of the doll's house, a story that . . . speedily grew to an island doll's city all our own. One of the dolls, I privately decided, was like Beatrice" (30–31). The allusion, in this admixture of fact and fiction, is to the famous Uppark doll's house, which is not an exact simulacrum of the house itself—few historic dolls' houses were—but was brought to it by Sarah Lethuillier, when she and Sir Matthew Fetherstonhaugh took over Uppark in the mid-eighteenth century. A replica of a Palladian house, the elaborately decorated and furnished Uppark doll's house has four bedrooms, two reception rooms, and three rooms "below stairs" as servants' quarters. The kitchen equipment includes "bright copper" pans that are significantly out of scale.

If Uppark/Bladesover is ambivalently understood as a utopian/dystopian society, Wells plays with size and scale—his boyhood reading of Swift's *Gulliver's Travels* is significant here and in relation to the "island doll's city" (31) imagined by the narrator of *Tono-Bungay*—and with the interplay between proximity and distance. This further renders the

FIGURE 15.2. Uppark doll's house. A doll's house formed as a Palladian mansion, circa 1730. (Photo copyright © National Trust Images / Nadia Mackenzie)

country house as at once monumental and miniaturized, its inhabitants possessing the appearance, and the stiffness, of wax or wooden dolls. (In the actual Uppark doll's house, the materials of the dolls' composition depended on the status of their positions within its vertical arrangement.) As novelist, Wells opens the hinged doors of his construction (or, *pace* William Thackeray's *Vanity Fair*, the box containing the puppets and dolls of a miniature theatre and the curtain behind which they perform) and reveals the furnishings and scenarios displayed in each room: the forces of habit and the rigidity of thought he ascribes to both the upper servants and their employers fix them in place and out of time. Describing the tedium of tea parties in the housekeeper's room with a group of pensioned-off women servants, the narrator depicts characters as painted dolls:

> I remember these women as immense. No doubt they were of ne-
> gotiable size, but I was only a very little chap and they have as-
> sumed nightmare proportions in my mind. They loomed, they
> bulged, they impended. Mrs Mackridge was large and dark: there
> was a marvel about her head, inasmuch as she was bald. She wore
> a dignified cap, and in front of that upon her brow hair was *painted*.
> I have never seen the like since. . . . Mrs. Booch was a smaller
> woman, brown haired, with queer little curls on either side of her
> face, large blue eyes, and a small set of stereotyped remarks that
> constituted her entire mental range. (20)

Wells's representations of such figures are echoed in the rather more
patrician Vita Sackville-West's depictions of country-house life in *The
Edwardians* (1930),[7] in which society guests are seen as "a ventriloquist's
box of puppets" (27) and as "figures of cardboard" (36). The polar ex-
plorer Leonard Anquetil observes that the country house, Chevron,
"should be transformed into a palace of Sleeping Beauty, only they should
not be touched as with a sleep of death, but should move immortal about
their immemorial activities" (47).

I referred earlier to the ways in which the architecture of Uppark
found its way not only into Wells's social satires (notably *Tono-Bungay*)
but also into his dystopian fictions, with their division of society into
upper and lower kingdoms. In *The Time Machine* (1895), the time-
travelling narrator gradually comes to realise that what he had at first
understood to be "an automatic civilisation and a decadent humanity"—
the delicate, effete Eloi—is in fact maintained by a subterranean labouring class—the Morlocks—who both control the machinery of the
society and feed off the Eloi. Wells's son Anthony West understood *The
Time Machine* to be "a violent gut reaction" to the elitism of Uppark, built
as it was on the existence of an underground world, and a book that
"makes it evident that he thought of Uppark as an ultimately self-
destroying mechanism and a threat to much more than itself. The
underground people in the book were so degraded by the life they were
forced to endure that they became agents of the brutal destruction of
the beautiful people who lived beautifully on the surface."[8]

While West perhaps overstates his father's commitment to anti-elitism (despite his socialism, Wells was a firm believer in the need for society to have, in Plato's terms, "guardians," though his own "Samurai" volunteer for their service rather than coming into it as a birthright), the experience, and the social architecture, of Uppark undoubtedly shaped his world visions, both positively and negatively. His ambivalent responses, which are perhaps more mixed than West allows, are powerfully embodied in his representations of a world—and the life of a house—at once monumental and diminutive, vital and decaying.

The Afterlife of Uppark

A few years after the publication of Virginia Woolf's novel *To the Lighthouse*, a similar force to the one Woolf describes—that of the women "who stayed the corruption and the rot" in the Ramsay family's abandoned holiday home—was working in Uppark, which was inherited at the beginning of the 1930s by Admiral Sir Herbert and Lady Margaret Meade-Fetherstonhaugh: "Being a mere woman I was sure that nothing was impossible, and that feats of restoration must be tackled without too much hesitation," the latter wrote in an account of Uppark's history, published in 1964.[9] In her 1930s diaries she had recorded the tasks of cleaning and repairing curtains and bed hangings: "October 25th 1934. Red letter day. . . . Washed the 1st saloon curtain and dried it in the Portico & then in the Stables as a gale was blowing. October 26th. Dried the white saloon curtain in the sun. It gleamed beautifully" (v).

Her retrospective account, in describing Uppark's "quality," closes with words from T. S. Eliot's *Four Quartets*: "Time past, time present, and time future." It also seems to echo Woolf's representations of time past, in many of her essays (such as "The Pastons") and in her novel-biography *Orlando*, as well as Eliot's *The Waste Land*. Margaret Meade-Fetherstonhaugh writes of the early decades in the house's history—"Within these new-built walls men heard 'Queen Anne is dead' for the first time. The only sound was the ticking of the clock on the wall, which measured time for many of them" (108)—of her own experience as "a watch-keeper" over the solitary house during the war years, when the

FIGURE 15.3. *Tono-Bungay* and the Uppark doll's house. (Illustration by R. K. R. Thornton)

men were away fighting, and of an exceptional discovery, in 1931, in a building in the garden:

> On each of these visits to the old office lurked the possibility of a voyage into the unknown; the strokes of the clock would be the only tie to the world that lay beyond the misty green outside the

moulded glass panes, while inside the office there was the curious impression of fleeting figures that belonged to olden times at Uppark. . . .

The shrubs tapped against the obscured windowpane, a mouse ran under the hearth of the fireplace; the coiled dolphins of the carved chimneypiece . . . reminded me of the turns and plunges into icy green waters they seemed still to follow. The sunshine flickering through the green light seemed to give them movement. It was all part of the dateless fairy-tale of Uppark. (111)

On the particular occasion she describes, Margaret Meade-Fetherstonhaugh chose to open the lid of a large oak chest, in which she discovers, with "a sense of excitement that I shall never forget," "the writings of scribes from the XIVth century, describing the rulings by which all the Ford and Fetherstonhaughs had lived and died, bought and sold, had married and mated, had come to man's estates, fought and fined, had hired and harassed their neighbours, and harnessed their estates." The work of restoration began on the parchments, and "by degrees the story unfolded" (111–12).

As in *Orlando*, historical change is framed in the context of a more fundamental continuity, and the country house is its embodiment. But Meade-Fetherstonhaugh was writing during a period that had recently seen the large-scale destruction of such dwellings, during a century in which over a thousand country houses—roughly one-sixth of the total number—were demolished. This reached its height in the 1950s (following World War II, during which many country houses were requisitioned—creating a break in owner occupation—and frequently damaged) and lessened only with the planning acts that were put in force at the end of the 1960s.

Uppark survived the most destructive years of the twentieth century, having been given to the National Trust in 1954. The massive threat to its fabric came, then, not from time and neglect or from the wrecking ball but from a fire that started on 30 August 1989, at the end of a year-long restoration programme. The blaze, which began in the roof, brought down the ceilings and walls of the first- and second-floor rooms of both the ground and the first floors. Working through the night, firemen, staff, and volunteers brought out furniture and paintings from the house to the grounds, though by no means all the house's contents could be saved. After nearly five days of damping down the fire, fragments from the rooms' decorative structures and from furnishings were, as far as possible, sorted and stored for the house's future restoration. This was not, at this point, guaranteed, though two months later the decision was taken to embark on a full process of reconstruction. The outside walls of Uppark were still intact, though the roof was destroyed, and the elaborate internal plaster and woodwork required almost complete reconstitution. Five years after the fire, the contents of the house that had been saved from the fire were returned. "Old and new have been carefully interwoven and recorded," the National Trust's account states, "but it is hoped that their junction is invisible and that a seamless repair has been achieved."[10] H. G. Wells's views on this turn in the life of a house that had become so intertwined, in such complex ways, with his own formation would have been interesting to hear.

Unhoused

16
The Fear of Houses

ALEXANDER MASTERS

Once, when I was working for a Street Outreach team in Cambridge, a Housing Officer told me a story.

She'd been helping a man called Mark. A familiar type of rough sleeper, Mark had appeared on the street in middle age, drank but did not take drugs, and was in surprisingly good physical shape. The Housing Team accessed every available service and found Mark a temporary home. He destroyed it. They found him another; again he broke it apart. A third time: same result.

Homeless people often fail their first attempts to return to housing. Independent accommodation can be in lonely or dangerous parts of town; B&Bs that take the homeless are frequently violent and dirty; hostels are usually filled with drugs, and if you have a dog they demand that you get rid of it. None of this applied in Mark's case: he agreed that he liked the bedsits and houses the Housing Team found for him. A few weeks later, they were in splinters. Five times they had helped Mark out; five times he'd ended up back on the streets. There comes a point when even the most noble-minded Housing Officer gets fed up. Then someone discovered why Mark had become homeless. While he had been in the kitchen one day, his wife had been murdered in the living room. He came in just as the murderer was finishing. Mark couldn't bear to live in a house with walls. Who knew what was happening on the other side?

The sixth time they tried to find Mark accommodation, the Housing Team knew what to do. They got him a caravan: there is nowhere to hide in a caravan. For the first time in almost a decade, Mark settled down.

This story had a huge effect on me. It was the first time I appreciated what a wild mix of obscurity and obviousness homelessness is. You can shake a person awake in the rain to count him when you're on Outreach Team duty, and listen to a thousand typical problems: this man is a drunk, has mental health "issues," needs a doctor, a bath, a friend. There are multiple forms to fill out for each of these cases. But the critical thing isn't part of this exhausting clatter. It's in the shadows, a sentence away: "My wife was murdered in my living room: I cannot stand internal walls." You can talk past that for years and not hear a thing.

I was in awe of the brilliance of the Housing Team. When social work is done well, it is the stuff of genius.

And I learned that houses are more than a roof and walls. I'd often heard architects blither about it: houses have a life force. They can offer solace, security, stability, pep: everything a person in the gutter misses. They can also be malevolent. For someone like Mark, being on the streets is not about a lack of housing; it is about a fear of houses.

Matthew 25 Mission is a small day centre for the homeless in East-bourne, near to where I live now. As a building, it belongs in a village: a dour Victorian schoolroom. In a hectic suburb on the south coast of England, it looks mischievous and fun. It is separated from the chaotic road by a low wall and a cherry tree. A delightful garden borders the front and one side, and contains benches and tables reached by gravel paths, and several beds of flamboyant flowers. Inside the portico entrance is a spacious dining hall, an industrial kitchen behind a serving hatch, and toilets. The mood is genial and slow paced. Most people here do not look homeless. Pass them on the street and it would never cross your mind that they spent last night on a bench. They are tidy, polite, thoughtful. The man taking a bucket out to water the sunflowers is a homeless man. The woman mending a door with a power drill is a homeless woman. The small crowd in the kitchen, helping the cook get lunch ready: not one of them has slept under a roof since Thursday.

"Whatever you did for the least of these, you did for me," says Matthew 25:40.

Even when the police arrive to arrest a hysterical, swearing rough sleeper who's burst in during lunch (as they did when I visited, last week), the handcuffs are put on him amidst murmurs of consolation from the officers and staff, and the diners return calmly to their conversations. "Life can be difficult," agrees the mood at Matthew 25, "but let's keep it restful here."

I went to Matthew 25 Mission to ask about Mark. Was Mark the only person who didn't automatically think of home as a safe, stable place to live? How many other people remain on the streets not just because they have lost their accommodation but because the bedsit, B&B, hostel room, bed in a shelter, flat, or council house that's been offered to replace it sends shivers down their spine? What was the essential quality—physical or abstract—of a place to live?

Here are replies from eight of the people I spoke to.[1]

Dave: House as Confinement

For Dave it isn't the malevolence of houses that's kept him homeless, it's their boringness. A short, energetic man, with a ginger goatee, pale face, and steady eyes, he'd been in Eastbourne for two weeks when I interviewed him. With the other people I spoke to, there was focus: we talked about their experience of homelessness and housing until the topic was finished. But Dave perched against the arm of a chair making slight dodging movements, like a jockey. I had a sense of rush. I felt I was obstructing his schedule.

> See, look at me: I'm homeless and I've got OCD. I jump in the sea all the time, wash my body all the time. Bar of soap every day, mate.

> *Where do you sleep?*

> At the bandstand on the beach. Look at me: clean as hell. Clean shirt, clean trousers.

> *Do you sleep in a tent or on a bench?*

Never slept in a tent in my life. I've got too much pride for myself. Tents don't last very good by the wind, do they? They get mouldy, smelly. I make little houses out of pallets. Like you make a tree house out of, when you're a kid. Eight pallets: four pallets as a base, build a wall round it. Blue tarpaulin: that's your roof. Tell me the next time you come down. I'll bring some pictures down and show you.

And that's comfortable?

Of course it's not comfortable sleeping on wood, is it?

Do you decorate your houses?

Don't be silly, mate. Decorate? What, paint it with a bit of purple paint?

Dave first became homeless at age eighteen when he was evicted from his one-bedroom flat in Crawley. It took him a week to get used to living on the streets.

You know the New Forest? I lived in the New Forest for sixteen months. Built myself a little house there, too. Course I did, mate.

With pallets?

No, you don't get pallets round the New Forest very often, do you? Timber decking.

The reason Dave hasn't lived in a proper house for any length of time since he was made homeless is "because of choosing not to, really." Houses made him feel cramped when he was younger. They bored him.

My nickname's called Drifter. I'm an ex-junkie, done crack, done methadone, but I've been clean six months now. I went cold turkey on the street, all by myself. Got off the heroin: took me two months; got off the crack, crack's easy to get off; and methadone: one month. My parents made me do it. They don't want a smackhead in their family, do they? God's my witness, mate, I'm getting on with my family again. This Christmas, touch wood, will be the first time I've been at my mum and dad's for Christmas. I am looking forward, yeah. Nice two weeks in a nice warm bed. TV. Nice shower. You need a new pair of shoes, mate. Those shoes you're wearing are falling apart. Look at me: I look after myself.

Dave says life on the streets "has been a laugh. Because I've got used to the street. You get used to something and you like doing it, you do it, isn't it? I go to the pound shop and buy myself a little throwaway barbecue, buy myself £5 worth of meat, cook it myself. On the seafront."

"How old are you now?" I asked.

"I'm thirty-five, mate. I'm getting old."

"If someone came along and said, 'stop being homeless, here's a permanent house' would you take it?'

"What do you think?'

"I don't know," I said.

"I'd bite their hand off, mate."

Simon: House as Virtue

Simon is a well-built, good-looking man in his thirties, with a ready smile. He wears a good-quality duffel coat, a cotton scarf in muted colours, and clean jeans. When he strides into the dining hall he waves hello, calling out messages left and right. He grew up locally, in "a dirty great manor," and went to private schools. He says that matter-of-factly, not boastfully. Until five months ago he was a 3D computer modeller, specialising in structural and steel engineering, and he became homeless after falling foul of his employer when he tried to set up his own business.

"It was low-level stuff at first. Next door to where I was living is the largest Traveller camp in the UK, and the wife of the man who ran the company I'd left was a Traveller. I started getting surrounded by Travellers when I went out, threatening me. I'd get people calling me from strange numbers, sniffing down the phone: 'How's your family?' *Sniff.* 'How's your family?' *Sniff.* Cars waited outside my house, with windows going down, going, *sniff*, 'How's your family?' It got worse. I had high-powered rifles with silencers put to my head and the trigger pulled. There was so much money involved in these construction projects. Another time I was in East London I was stabbed in the throat with a biro and was on the floor with blood pumping out of my throat."

What happened next is barely believable—the stuff of gangster novels. Simon's casual, almost louche manner disappeared as he talked about it. We moved out of the hall into the sunny garden, where there were fewer people.

> SIMON: People broke into my flat and installed cameras. They tapped my mobile, my landline, my computer. They set up fake Snapchat and Instagram accounts in my name and filmed me in my own home with women I thought were girlfriends but who were prostitutes they'd sent: sex cams of me, pornos on three different websites, obscene shit sent to all of my friends on Facebook. A lot of my friends were given pay rises and bought brand-new cars, basically to keep their mouths shut, because they knew what was happening to me. I was surrounded by tattoo-sleeved people, steroid thugs, surrounded by a tornado of hunchbacks.

The reason Simon wants to get off the streets is because he wants to prove to the Masons (who he says are, ultimately, behind the attacks on him) that "you can't keep a good man down."

"A house symbolises strength and virtue?" I asked.

"I am a good man," he agrees, growing calm and charming again, "no matter how much they tried to destroy me. I am a good person, you know. I'm not going to let them say otherwise."

Mary: House as Pause from Walking

"It was because I went into housing that I got made homeless," said the next person I interviewed. Mary had moved into a private room and "come across a little disrepair in the property: it didn't have no running hot water. It didn't have no heating."

She went to the council and told them what was wrong, they made the landlady do the work, the landlady evicted her.

"It ain't nice when people look at the people who drink and do drugs on the street, and look at you sitting there on the kerb too, and think you're all the same. You think, 'all I've done is walk around for how many days, constantly, for miles. I'll just sit down for a minute. My feet are throbbing, it's pissing down with rain.' It does become embarrassing. People look at you and think, 'Oh, sort yourself out.' Well, when you're on the streets it's quite hard to do. You've got everything, all that you own, on you. You can't leave it anywhere because people nick it. The council confiscates it: 'That's it, we're going to evict you from this bit of land as well now.' Where can we go? We're just walking. Just walking, constant. Walking. From here, go for a little walk; from there, go for a little walk.

It's not because of the embarrassment that I want to get a home. No, no, no. I don't mind about that. I'm just saying. It's that you can actually get in your bed. And you can actually wake up and put the kettle on. You can have a cup of tea and think about doing positive things instead of where are you going to walk today."

Sam: Homelessness as Honesty

Sam the songwriter does not walk. He has gout.

"I'm also not homeless," he added quickly. "I was on the streets for just six weeks, but I'm housed now." He was standing under the cherry tree smoking mechanically and fast when I approached. He has an amiable expression and twisting hands. "I'd been relatively affluent before that. I don't mean like Alan Sugar, but I'd been renting a two-bedroom holiday flat on the seafront for four years and was eating in restaurants twice a week. How long would this interview take? I'd like my name to be changed."

Sam represents a textbook case of simple homelessness. He is responsible, skilled, intelligent, eager to work, not mentally ill or an addict. "I became homeless because I was honest." His online record distributor ran off with his earnings, but instead of saying to his landlady, "I can't afford the rent, but I'm not budging," and claiming Housing Benefit, he said, "Here are your keys" and went on the streets. "I was a bit naïve."

"Why didn't you get another job?"

"Because of my gout. Some days I wake up with a swollen foot and some days I can't move my thumb. You can't tell an employer 'I might be able to come to work tomorrow, I might not,' particularly if you're fifty-five."

His landlady gave him £50 as he left the building. "For a gentleman like yourself," she said. "I don't want it back."

I asked him about his first day on the streets.

"I went to the council office and said, 'I'd like to declare myself homeless.' I filled in forms. I went to the Salvation Army and they said, 'You can have a shower whenever you want, help yourself to sausage rolls, if you want a cup of tea the first one is free and then it's 10p a cup.'"

"Then did you walk up and down looking for a place to sleep?"

"I couldn't walk up and down, because of my gout."

Tanya and Tom: House as Bed

Tanya is tall with a lively expression that's hard to fathom given what's happened to her, and half made of metal. When she was fifteen she was brutally assaulted. "He attacked four girls and I was number two. I had twenty-two broken bones, that's not including fingers, toes, and ribs." Her boyfriend, Tom, has large attentive eyes that he keeps fixed on her. He's been on the streets, on drugs, or in prison for most of his adult life, but he's been clean since meeting Tanya three years ago. She's now thirty-four and became homeless for the first time last Thursday.

> TANYA: I popped out shopping with my children for half an hour. When I came back, I couldn't get in my flat. About fifteen people I'd never seen before had taken it over.
>
> TOM: It's called cuckooing, because that's what cuckoos do, isn't it? Cuckoos push other birds out of their nest. She was only gone half an hour!

Why didn't you ring the police and get them kicked out?

TANYA: I did, but the police being the police, changed the locks, brilliant, but they'd left all the fucking windows open, excuse my language. So there's me stood at the door with my brand-new key opening the lock, and fifteen drug addicts climbing back through the windows.

The police have been back four times, but each time the same thing happens. "There's so many needles in that flat now. Everything's been smashed. My tellies, my computer, my fridge/freezer, washing machine, tumble dryer: everything worth any money has been stripped out and sold. I've had a gun held to my face, a machete."

Like many Eastbourne homeless during the warm months, Tanya and Tom sleep on the seafront. But despite the horrendous history and arbitrary suddenness of Tanya's homelessness, her needs are the clearest of the people I spoke to. She has to find a place to live indoors, fast. Her body cannot take the outdoors. She has no time to be psychologically complex about that.

TANYA: When they restarted my heart after the attack, my body went into massive shock. The way the doctors explained it is, if you imagine your body to be a computer, my body rebooted but it sort of misfires a little bit. Now I'm producing too many white blood cells, so basically my skin replaces itself ten times faster than what it should do. This morning we had to go and get a disabled radar key to get access into disabled toilets. So I walked in with Tom because I have bandages on my legs and I have to take those off to put the cream on, then put the bandages back on. It's just easier having a hand to do it. We literally shut the door, when next thing it's bang, bang, bang, banging on the door—toilet security! I'm finding it quite rough.

So what if the council comes along now and offers you a house. What would you take?

TANYA: Anything.

TOM: A room with a bed. That's all we'd need. We'd start again.

Pauline: Homelessness as Empathy

Pauline has never been homeless, but she used to work across the road in a charity shop and she liked the rough sleepers who came in to buy blankets or shoes. One day, she went to her GP, who told her she had cancer. Pauline "burst into tears. I panicked. I was hysterical." She came to Matthew 25. The homeless were the only people she could think of who would listen and know how to comfort her.

"Thank you, but I can't," she said to the staff when they asked her if she wanted some lunch, "because I'm not homeless."

"No, love, this isn't just for the homeless," they said. "This for anyone who needs it. You're welcome here."

James: House as Memory

James was pointed out to me as a person I must definitely talk to because he is conversational and industrious, a highly trained electrician who, after a brief period on the streets, has been rehoused without fuss. When I met him he was standing beside his work van, repairing an electrical fitting for the Mission. "It's a lifesaver this place, an absolute lifesaver," he said. "So I'm giving back."

> JAMES: The best time of my life, when I was married to my wife. Ginger hair, green eyes, she made me happy. She asked me to marry her in 2008 and I was honoured. I'd never been married before. Then on the twenty-seventh of February this year I woke up and she'd died in the night. So I shut off. I went to the shop, bought twenty bottles of Courvoisier, closed the curtains, locked the door, turned off the phone, and went to the Courvoisier Club. I just wanted to be in my own little world and miss my wife. I wanted to be up there with her. Then after a couple of months I opened the door and there was the bailiff's letter on the door. My bungalow's worth £360,000. I lost that. My F-type jag, £115,000. I lost that. All I do now is pray every day and think of her every night.

As with Mark, the death of his wife drove James to collapse, but unlike Mark he could not blame the house. He didn't run from it because the memory was horrible; he stayed in it because the memory was all he had. When the house was taken from him, he left.

Directly after James arrived in Eastbourne, a maintenance man offered him a contract to do the electrics on the seafront bandstand. "I just didn't want it at the time. I wasn't stable enough, because I kept crying, crying."

Three weeks ago, a landlord came to Matthew 25.

"Have you got anyone here I could house?"

"There is only one person we'd recommend immediately," said the staff.

It turns out to be a beautiful studio overlooking the sea.

"Own fitted kitchen, double and treble wardrobe, chest of drawers: 99.9 percent of people are not as lucky. There is room to swing a cat." The landlord didn't want a deposit and no rent up front. "I've never begged, borrowed, or stolen, but when I was on the streets, the generosity of the people of Eastbourne has surprised me, because they've come over: 'here you go, mate, go and get yourself a cup of tea.' A £20 note."

It's nice to end these brief interviews with James because of his excitement for the future. Of the eight I spoke to, he alone has returned to housing in the tidy and comforting way that housed people like to hear about. In addition to being a trained electrician, he turns out to be a spotter of antiques. A few years before he became homeless he found a little vase in a church sale, for £1. He sold it at auction a week later for £6,000. "They've now got six bits of early Tiffany at the Victoria and Albert Museum. One of them is my little vase."

Conclusion

The eight people at Matthew 25 Mission who were generous enough with their time to speak to me don't represent the homeless population: even for a tiny city such as Eastbourne the sample is too small, and the interviewees were only those self-confident enough to face a stranger who'd walked in one day during lunch, brandishing a voice recorder. I am, besides, an inadequate interviewer from the social science point of view: I am gossipy, ask leading questions, and get readily carried away.

But these interviews are enough to answer the question about Mark: he was an extreme case, not an atypical one. People do, often, leave houses and end up on the streets because they cannot tolerate the house rather than because they've run out of money. The comment "we are all just a pay cheque or two away from homelessness" is a cliché to comfort the housed. Even Sam, *especially* Sam with his gout, did not leave his seaside apartment because he was broke. Sam could have contacted friends; he could have looked into his situation earlier. What pushed Sam onto the streets was a rigidity of character which insisted that living in a flat should be an "honest" act.

Simon, the 3D construction modeller, left his flat because his reputation had been destroyed. Tanya, because she was pushed out by "cuckoos," who then made the place disgusting with blood splatters and God knows what else. When the police did finally manage to get the flat back for her, she couldn't face returning to it; it was "tainted." James the electrician, like Mark, fled the loss of his wife. Dave finds houses "boring." For Mary, it was trying to move up the housing ladder and rent from private landlords that sent her sliding down the snake to the street. I would have liked to ask her more about that. Does she now view houses as tricky? They have tricked her. But she had other people to meet, so our interview was cut short. Pauline explained that the homeless community can be supportive, kind, and encouraging: it is not a hateful group, as the housed imagine it to be when stepping over beggars in the street. There is something selfish and cold about the housed.

Most of the homeless (this was certainly true when I worked in Cambridge and seems also to be true in Eastbourne) are invisible, not because we ignore them but because they look exactly like the rest of us. They dress well; they take showers or bathe in the sea. They have not lost their dignity or their brains or their manners. You could walk beside a rough sleeper such as Sam, Simon, or Tanya for the entire length of a street and it would never cross your mind that they'd spent the previous night on a bench. As the story of Mark suggested, the reasons for leaving a house and ending up on the street are rarely obvious. They cover everything from restlessness to death.

17

When There Is No House to Visit

A Migrant Writer's Sites

ELLEKE BOEHMER

home is a foreign place
—Zarina Hashmi

Port Meadow, Oxford, UK

51.7717° N, 1.2851° W

In the context of 1970s Britain the incongruity of the scene would have been striking. At first glance, however, it looks as subdued, bucolic, and English as might be imagined, but that's from a distance.

It is 1976 and we are walking on Oxford's Port Meadow, a ninth-century common to the west of the city, green and tussocky, threaded through with ancient pathways, bisected by a Thames that around the next bend fans out through the waterways of the world-famous medieval city centre. We walk as so many do on a Sunday along the low, sandy banks of this river, picking our way around muddy shallows pocked with cow-hoof marks.

Upstream is the semicircular bridge called the Rainbow Bridge, well-known to generations of Oxford students who have picnicked and partied on this—for England—surprisingly open, green space. Far downstream is Iffley lock, where those same waterways reconverge in a fast-flowing gush of grey water.

FIGURE 17.1. Dambudzo Marechera in Port Meadow. (Illustration by R. K. R. Thornton)

Now imagine, somewhere between the bridge and the lock, on the banks of the river not far from that grazing herd of brown-and-white cows, just visible above the wavy curve made by their clustered backs, the triangular point of a small one-person tent, red and threadbare, its flap open.

Curious, we move closer, to see what might be going on. People sleep out on Port Meadow sometimes, but we know they generally don't camp. Skirting the cows, we come upon the unusual tableau, at least in his setting, of a thin young black man, his hair in short spirals, sitting cross-legged within the tent's open flap, his typewriter placed atop a couple of slatted wooden boxes piled in front of him. Furiously he strikes the keys with his two index fingers, his lips pursed in concentration.

It is evident that the young man doesn't want to be disturbed, that he has perhaps already been disturbed at his work by passersby like ourselves one time too many. Though we stand close he pointedly doesn't look up. If anything he types more furiously, his fingers fly at the keys. This is his writing space, his study, his retreat, he impels us to understand.

So we turn away and move off, though we see in turning—so close were we standing in our frank surprise at the scene—that the two slatted boxes that make up his desk are strawberry crates, salvaged from the nearby fruit farm. We recognise the name of the farm printed on the sides. It's where everyone picks strawberries in the early summer. And his too-small school blazer bears the crest of a high school. It is a Rhodesian high school, though this is something that we won't know till later.

We return to the city and that evening perhaps recount the unusual scene over a drink in the pub or the MCR. We then find out that a story of the writer in his tent on Port Meadow is already doing the rounds (though in his college itself it has mostly been hushed up). We hear that this young man at his typewriter is none other than the gifted Zimbabwean (then Rhodesian) scholarship student Dambudzo Marechera. The tent is in fact his current home, the only home he has. Indeed, since his rustication from New College for various misdemeanours including trying to set fire to his room, the tent will be his final Oxford dwelling.

After this period on Port Meadow writing his first book, Dambudzo (then Charles) Marechera will leave Oxford for London, for a life of living rough on park benches and in squats. He will hang out uproariously with other African writers at the Africa Centre in Covent Garden, the place that was perhaps more his British home than any other. He will soon submit to the Heinemann African Writers Series the manuscript of his collection of short stories, *The House of Hunger* (1978). He will live on—in fact drink away—small loans from his publishers, given as advances on his next book, a novel, *Black Sunlight* (1980), that doesn't ever materialise in the completed form they had hoped for, even several years later.

Wherever he will go he will create scenes and disturbances. He will always be dressed in outrageous costumes—jodhpurs with a bowler hat "like an English lord," Basuto blankets and ponchos and sometimes women's clothes from charity shops.[1] He will shout, roar, and cajole in the strange posh "Oxford English" accent that, like the short plaits, will become his trademark. Stammering and strained by turns, his voice will signal even to those who don't know him both the degree to which he wants to belong and the extent to which he never can. His misdemeanours and his outfits, too, will all be associated in one way or another with feelings of not fitting in—feelings that he channels into his fiction, at times inchoately, always forcefully.

A few years on from this point, in 1982, having exhausted the patience even of his long-suffering supporters with his constant demands for beer money, Marechera will leave Britain for independent Zimbabwe. However, before he does, he will win the Guardian First Fiction prize for that significantly titled first collection of short stories—a prize shared with the filmmaker Neil Jordan. The prizewinning stories will be the ones he wrote during his unhoused period living in the borrowed tent beside the Thames.

And so, sitting in the pub that evening, with the sounds of the young writer's tap-tapping perhaps still in our ears, we might ponder the almost intuitive associations of place, home, writing, and belonging that most of us make—that our reading of English literature (also *his* reading) has embedded in us. These are the associations that inform our experience as readers when we visit writers' rooms, tiptoe with reverence through the spaces where their imagination has been sheltered and stimulated. But what happens—this is the question Marechera's story poses—when, as with him, there is no home to visit, no fixed coordinates, not now, not then? What associations do we bring in those cases where a writer has worked hard to embed himself in the literary context to which he has long aspired yet has found resistant to his endeavours?

A migrant writer like Marechera—homeless both actually and in terms of a national tradition to call his own—invites us to look again at the interaction of creative work with place as well as with ideas of continuity and identity. His life crystallizes as if from the other side of the mirror how literary writing and its later reputation may be shaped not only by walled spaces but by shifting coordinates—by temporary dwellings and impermanent homes, the spaces that generally are occupied more by migrant than "home" authors, even now, when writers "from elsewhere" are so much more prevalent. His story presses us to consider more critically the connections we make between writing and bricks and mortar, and not only the bricks of actual houses but also of national culture.

Dambudzo Marechera was doubly unhoused. He had his literary heyday in Britain as an "out-of-country" writer, a phrase Salman Rushdie conjured many years ago. On top of that, wherever he lived, whether in Oxford or London, he was mostly homeless. Back in Harare, his itinerant life continued. Even his final years were spent living mainly in parks and the occasional spare room. More vividly than most postcolonial writers we might name, he offers a negative test case for what a writer's house signifies for the making of their work and reputation and, conversely, for what it is to a writer *not* to have a house whether domestic or national to call their own. Though Marechera died over thirty years ago now, at a tragically young age, in this age of ongoing debates over immigration, the questions his experience sparks continue to challenge our preconceptions of writers' houses across time.

Theatre Royal, Drury Lane, London
51.5129° N, 0.1204° W

Dambudzo Marechera is now counted as amongst the greatest of Zimbabwe's significant array of postindependence writers. He called himself the "doppelganger whom, until I appeared, African literature had not yet met."[2] But he hated to be labelled an African writer, or a writer with any kind of identity tag: "If you are a writer for a specific nation or a specific race," he said, "then fuck you."[3]

Experimental and stochastic in form, modernist and cosmopolitan in its influences, Marechera's multigeneric work departed radically from the social realist style of some of his close contemporaries, like Charles Mungoshi and Shimmer Chinodya. Accused in his lifetime of Europhilia and inauthenticity for cultivating the dense allusive style that got him noticed, he in turn charged his critics with mental colonization. His efforts to loosen readers' understanding of African literature as being about more than just calabashes and drumbeats are now recognised for the radical manoeuvres they were. Sophisticated, intertextual, wayward, his writing reshaped the landscapes of African literature.

Not long after the award of the Guardian First Fiction prize, Marechera's one-time fellow Rhodesian Doris Lessing spoke of him in a review as a great writer in the making. The editor Ros de Lanerolle also recognised the significance of his work. She saw the "house" of his prize-winning title for what it was, signifying both home and country, in both senses standing for a "place of madness and violence and despair." Marechera's predicament, shared with other southern African writers at the time, was to be in spiritual (if not actual) exile, suffering "the increasing loss of a context within which the writing is done," as his editor James Currey observed.[4] Yet he did not only *lose* contexts due to politics. He also actively discarded them.

At the Guardian prize ceremony at the Theatre Royal, for example, which marked the high point of his literary life, Marechera turned the celebration into a fiasco of invective. Inflamed perhaps by the ongoing UDI crisis in Rhodesia, or the, to him, crazy grandeur of the ceremony, he began to shout and throw plates at the eighteenth-century theatre's mirrors. Keeping a copy of Pound's *Cantos* under his arm even as he was being removed from the premises, Marechera railed at being called a black writer and deplored the business of collecting prizes in London while his people were being killed in Zimbabwe.[5]

Marechera was born in 1952 in the black township of Rusape, in what was then Rhodesia, now Zimbabwe, and scavenged rubbish dumps close to the white suburbs for his first books. After the death of his father in 1966, the family experienced extreme poverty and his mother was forced into prostitution. The hard times took a permanent toll on the young Marechera's psychic well-being, experiences that are refracted in *The House of Hunger*. The onset of his stammer dated from this time as did the psychotic tendencies that would pursue him for the rest of his life.

Despite these difficulties, the precocious Marechera managed to complete his secondary education at St. Augustine's School in Penahlonga on a missionary scholarship. He went on to study English literature at the University of Rhodesia in what was then Salisbury, now Harare, again on a scholarship. Halfway through his studies he received his first university rustication, for engaging in student demonstrations. However, with the support of his English tutors, he secured a Junior Common Room studentship from New College and went on to continue his studies there.

His fellow students at Oxford recall the infectious excitement that Marechera, then still called Charles, brought to his studies. He was often seen carrying around enormous piles of books, not only of his set texts but also of other classics of world literature, Goethe, Dostoevsky, Ionesco. He loved to read from these works to his friends. However, he also drank excessively and his behaviour grew more erratic. Amongst many incidents of rowdiness, he assaulted the college porters at least twice and disrupted a summer school. He was soon deep in debt, including to Blackwell's bookshop. The fire in his college room, however, may not have been deliberate. He claimed that he was burning paper in his wastepaper bin in an attempt to get warm. His move to Port Meadow followed his college rustication.

Aspects of the Port Meadow story may of course be apocryphal. There are so many colourful myths surrounding Marechera that it is difficult to separate fact from fiction. We do know that substantial parts of *The House of Hunger* were written after New College and before leaving Oxford. Moreover, the central image the myths convey of the writer-vagrant in a distant land, aspiring with his posh English accent to belong, yet repeatedly dropping out, rings true. According to his fellow student Jane Bryce, even in those early Oxford days the rake-thin Marechera always looked "insubstantial and unanchored."[6]

After Oxford, Marechera's main British homes would be a squat in Tolmers Square, those park benches, and, briefly, Cardiff gaol. He had been arrested for possession of cannabis and book theft. Heading back to Zimbabwe he tried to obtain a return ticket, to allow him back into England in the future, but his papers were in a mess and the attempt failed. In Harare he again did time in prison, for protesting against censorship. He continued to write energetically but disconnectedly. *Mindblast*, a collection of poetry and prose fragments, was published in Harare and London in 1984. It would be his last book. Other collections of his scattered work appeared posthumously, edited by friends.

Marechera died in 1987 of lung complications relating to AIDS. He was buried in Harare, in a grave plot in Warren Hills cemetery. In the decade or so following his death, disagreements erupted from time to time about his reputation and influence, because of his "Euro-modernist" inclinations and rejection of African nationalism. In the twenty-first century, however, these debates have all but died down. The quarrels that arise are mainly about the dishevelled state of his grave, which is deemed to give insufficient recognition to a writer now seen as a Zimbabwean literary hero and, importantly, a precursor of the many African writers who since the millennium have built their careers in diaspora.

Grave Plot 1237, Warren Hills Cemetery, Harare, Zimbabwe

17.8309° S, 30.9668° E

For the critic Will Stone, a writer's house, unless sensitively done up, can be something of a "plastic intervention," a "[carapace] of canonical legends."[7] In an article on visiting Coleridge's restored house in Nether Stowey, Stone expresses irritation with the stagey trip back in literary time these places invite. To him, visitors should rather rely on their imagination than "theatrical coinage" to conjure visions of the once-resident writer at work.

Stone's critique raises interesting questions for any devoted reader keen on taking a look around their favourite writer's house. For my purposes, however, it is noteworthy in particular for the unstated premise that informs his article throughout, namely, that though some writers' former dwellings may be overly done up, nonetheless they are worth visiting. It is the nature of the restoration that to him is at issue, not the attempt to preserve the house, room, or atelier in order that we may stand within that space and re-create for ourselves its occupant's literary doings.

For Marechera, as the state of his grave might suggest, no such place exists, neither in Zimbabwe, his land of birth, nor in Britain, where he wrote his major work and built his reputation. Not for Marechera the panelled study, solid desk, and heavy chair that we find, for example, at Bateman's, Rudyard Kipling's home, now a National Trust property— by any measure one of the more substantial of writers' houses open to visitors in England. Not for Marechera the artefacts brought back from the writer's travels that at Bateman's Kipling arranged around the room as familiars to goad the genie of his imagination, as he described it. Not even for Marechera the lighter stuff—portable memorabilia, boxes of letters—in fact, quite the opposite. In England, he had no significant possessions other than his typewriter and towards the end may have pawned even that. In Harare he had even less. He relied on well-wishers to give him paper to write with.

The difficulty about the idea of a house for Marechera is not just his permanent homelessness or how that seemed to underscore his wandering state. It is also that he had no country, no "national trust" to honour his name. In his lifetime, and subsequently, neither of the countries that fostered him was sufficiently invested in his work to mark any spot as in some sense imbued with his spirit. In his first country, a culture of literary consecration did not exist; in the other a migrant writer like him did not stay on long enough to be deemed worth consecrating. Hence my attempt in this essay to reclaim for him three sets of coordinates on the map, in both countries.

For most of us—it is an assumption that underpins this book—a writer has a primary affiliation to one or another nation, even when they may for political reasons reject that association. It is this that determines how the nation honours them, where they are placed in bookshops and on reading lists, how they are presented in journals and, importantly, dictionaries of biography. Countries like Britain and France make so strong a connection between national identity and literary expression that they set aside sacred spaces to house their revered literary remains—in London, Poets' Corner in Westminster Abbey; in France the Panthéon, an entire cathedral reserved for the purpose.

Peripatetic writers confuse these categories in the minds of readers, and this makes it difficult to publicise their work in the same way as for other "in country" writers. Even in relation to his "motherland," Marechera was ambiguously positioned. With his country's postcolonial history moving as rapidly as it did, he was first Rhodesian and then Zimbabwean, and his relationship with both incarnations was tempestuous.

Yet, though Marechera may be an extreme example of a writer without a roof endeavouring to build a place for himself within the precincts of English literature, he was by no means the only one. Postwar London was full of aspirant writers from the wider English-speaking world desperately eking out a living in the great metropolis while at the same time trying to get published. The image of the skinny Zimbabwean in his tent may recall, for example, V. S. Naipaul transmuting the isolation he experienced in the various seedy Earl's Court bedsits he occupied in the 1950s into the supreme disdain he then developed as a distancing device in his fiction. Marechera did not live long enough perhaps to develop such condescension. We might also recall Doris Lessing arriving in London from Rhodesia, trying to keep afloat and keep writing in various squalid communes, the kinds of places she records in her novel *The Good Terrorist*. Or J. M. Coetzee a decade or so later, fostering his literary dreams in miserable "bedsitters with curtainless windows and forty-watt bulbs"—an area New Zealand writer Janet Frame living in London in the same period called a "bleak, unfriendly no-man's-land."[8] These and many others from elsewhere found that the day-to-day reality of keeping a roof over their heads made regular writing impossible and the writing life a tenuous thing to maintain.

In comparison, British writers of the same era look incredibly settled though no doubt they also struggled. But they had parents' homes to fall back on, not to mention family networks, groups of friends, clubs, societies, contacts. How different is their situation to that of writers drawn to the motherland of English literature by nothing more substantial than romantic dreams acquired as part of their education in the distant provinces of the world. Writers like these unravel the idea of the writer's house and show it up for the fragile thing it is—fragile yet also essential for building a career and a readership.

Afterword

THE COORDINATES OF MY HANDBAG

From the time that I first heard about Dambudzo Marechera—it was the anecdote about his "setting fire" to New College—something about his story piqued my interest. Over the years it has never ceased to resonate with me.

Like Marechera, though a few years later on, I spent many hours at the Africa Centre in Covent Garden hanging out with other African-born writers talking about writing, not only African. It was around the time that Marechera died and I remember that his former friends often reminisced about him.

Impossible though he must have been to deal with, as we talked I saw that there was something about his itinerant situation to which we all related. Certainly I related to it—to that, and to his dogged persistence at his writing, even despite his drifting. But I didn't perhaps realise how much I identified till a friend at the centre one day asked why my handbag was so very large and so very heavy. I had been carrying some boxes upstairs and she had offered to bring along my bag.

I explained that my handbag contained everything I needed were I ever to be stranded anywhere—notebook, pens, raincoat, toothbrush, moisturizer, change of underwear, and so on. If I were travelling, I explained, and my suitcase got lost, I'd have backup. I would be able, say, to give the talk I'd been invited to give, to do the reading. *All* the time though? she asked, still mystified. You don't *always* need this stuff, do you? There isn't a constant danger of being stranded?

In fact, yes, I said, or thought to myself, yes, there is. I am a migrant myself, so my underlying sense is of always being somehow in transit. And so I need my heavy handbag with me, my emergency pack, in case I can't get home. As with Marechera, my mentality remains out of country. I lack coordinates to call my own.

That was many years ago, and I am now a homeowner here in Britain, in England. I have a UK passport, a family, a job, published work. Yet my handbag is no less heavy, no less large. I still carry my essential stuff with me, all the time. An itinerant mentality dies hard, as Marechera knew. At some point I hope it will go away. But for now it remains. We migrants can perhaps never quite be confident that here in Britain there is always a door to open to our key.

18
"A Place One Can Go Mad In"

Ivor Gurney, Dwelling in Shadows

KATE KENNEDY

> forget thyself and the world will willingly forget thee till thou art
> nothing but a living-dead man dwelling among shadows and falsehood.
> —John Clare (1841), poet, asylum patient

In 1922 the poet, composer, and World War I survivor Ivor Gurney was certified insane. He was committed, against his will, to Barnwood House, a private asylum in Gloucester, and moved a few months later to the large county asylum near Dartford, the City of London Mental Hospital. He died there in 1937.

Barnwood House Asylum, Gloucester

There are websites, if you know where to look, full of images compiled by anonymous people with a passion for breaking into derelict asylums and taking photographs; the creepier the better. From arty angles, usually in black and white, the decay of asylums is captured with a mix of voyeurism and ghoulish artistry. How suggestive the ripped old curtains in the main hall look, if photographed sideways, with a certain lens. And graffiti on the peeling walls speaks of the hands that shakily inscribed it. Best of all is the single slipper, forgotten by the side of a rusty institutional iron bed. Glimpses of lives lived in misery are captured with a questionable mixture of pity, horror, and gleeful fascination. It is for us to fill in the gaps, to picture the forgotten patient leaving the ward for the last time, presumably with one bare foot. And yet this strange, underground movement of asylum tourism with its fascination for the objects abandoned in these most depressing of homes has more the quality of the thrills of a ghost train. It is hard to read its images as a sincere attempt to re-create the forgotten lives whose domestic traces it rakes over.

Today, the site on which Barnwood House Asylum stood is an eerie place. All that is left of the large villa that once housed one of Gloucester's most exclusive mental health institutions is a crumbling stone wall, dividing the grounds from the modern cul-de-sacs incongruously surrounding it. Tall trees abound, many with rooks' nests and huge balls of mistletoe. It took me a long time to find it, scanning behind the bungalows for a three-storey Victorian building, tall pseudo-Elizabethan chimney stacks in clusters, large sash windows either side of an eccentrically crenelated gesture towards a castle nestled in between the tiled red roofs. It was a building unsure of its identity, unsure even of which century it was supposed to be in, a hotchpotch of borrowed architecture. It was the perfect match for its inhabitants, from bemused generals to distressed wives, poets who heard voices to an archbishop who had become increasingly difficult.

Rooks caw, as the weak winter sun sets. I check the map, wind the window down to ask pedestrians—yes, this is indeed Barnwood, and this is the road, only there's nothing there, and no one knows about an asylum. Eventually I find the site where the house once stood. Instead of the imposing Victorian edifice, there is a walled rectangle of grass, frequented only by dog-walkers. It is something between a park and a large private garden, which, I discover, has been adopted by the council and renamed an arboretum, as the asylum's trees still stand. There is a metal sign informing me of its new incarnation, an odd anomaly in the middle of the sprawling suburbs of Gloucester. A couple out for a walk turn for home, a jogger paces across the lawned space where the house once stood. How many lives had ended here in discreet confusion behind those elegant windows, draped heavily in velvet? How many had lost their way, and retreated to this elegant, leafy prison? Theirs is a double silence; not even the building remains to speak of their experiences.

Barnwood House was closed in 1968 and was subsequently destroyed in a fire. The only surviving building is the chapel, an austere, grey stone structure, half hidden by yew trees. Now light streams from its windows, and as I push open the arched double doors, I find it is being used as a gym, lit by unforgiving neon, with pounding music. A simple crucifix still adorns the bare walls, and wooden holders display the hymn numbers from the last service that took place there. Underneath hymn numbers 76, 21, and 43 ("The Lord's my shepherd; I'll not want"), muscle-bound men in tight, sweat-stained sleeveless vests grunt and strain, as weights clang to the floor.

Even without the running machines and heavy metal, the chapel would have been a comfortless, bleak place. However, Barnwood House itself was by far the best of the local provisions for the insane. It was a fraction of the size of the huge county asylums, with only 160 patients in residence.[1] This was the institution in which Ivor Gurney found himself in September 1922, having tried repeatedly to kill himself and generally been so disagreeable that he was considered impossible to live with. He had been staying with his newly married brother, who was less than sympathetic to his mental distress, and his wife was even less impressed. He would appear at their bedside in the middle of the night, peering at them by the light of a flickering candle, and covered in mud from the banks of the Severn river. He would call at the local police station in the hope that they would oblige him with a revolver so he could shoot himself, and when he wasn't trying by any underhand means to obtain whole bottles of tablets, he would sit with a cushion on his head to ward off the electrical waves. The situation was, by anyone's standards, unsustainable, and they invited a magistrate and a GP to the house to have him certified. Gurney's home was Gloucestershire, and he loved the countryside and Gloucester's cathedral with a passion that fuelled his creative work. Barnwood meant a loss of his liberty to roam the Gloucestershire meadows and hills, but it was at least in his hometown.

Barnwood was more like a genteel retirement home for sleepy generals than an asylum.[2] The interior of the house had the décor of a stifling, overfurnished, middle-class Victorian home. A great deal of energy was invested in the decoration of private asylums (which was certainly not the case in the county institutions). This was in part for the benefit of the patients but also more cynically to sanitise insanity—making the institution more palatable for sensitive and wealthy relatives. There were Turkish rugs and carpets in most rooms, with an abundance of pictures and ornaments adorning heavy oak cabinets, and Japanese wallpaper in the corridors.[3]

The sociologist Erving Goffman talks about patients' experiences of admission to asylums as akin to a "betrayal funnel."[4] A patient (and indeed his relatives) is eased into the idea of incarceration. The admissions suite in an asylum might be comfortably furnished, a deliberately home-like environment. This is no more, the patient might tell himself, than a temporary stay in a hotel. The relatives say their tearful farewells. The patient is led further and further through the rooms and procedures of the asylum, away from the plush rugs and pictures, into the whitewashed linoleum corridors. Metal doors open onto padded cells and isolation rooms, equipped with restraining devices. By now, multiple locks have been turned, and the pseudo-domesticity of the rooms in which the patient said his goodbyes both to his loved ones and to his pre-patient identity seems an age away.

So it was for Gurney. He hated Barnwood, mostly because it represented incarceration, and he'd tried (successfully) to escape, once hurling a heavy clock through a window and cutting his hands and feet very badly. But he would come to look back on his time there with something akin to nostalgia; Barnwood had been only the gentle introduction to his life as an asylum patient. The superintendent had decided that the clock-throwing must cease; Gurney was too dangerous for them to keep. On 21 December 1922 he was moved to his new home, embarking on a journey to the vast City of London Mental Hospital in Dartford, hopeful that this new asylum would be able to cure him. Flanked by attendants, he watched from the car window as the Gloucestershire hills receded into the distance. He would never again see his home county.

The City of London Mental Hospital, Dartford

He took us into a large room in which was a piano and on this
he played to us and the tragic circle of men who sat on hard
benches against the walls of the room. Hopeless and aimless

faces gazed vacantly and restless hands fumbled or hung
down lifelessly. They gave no sign or sound that they
heard the music.

—Helen Thomas, on visiting Ivor Gurney in the City
of London Mental Hospital, October 1925

Somewhere, at the end of one of many tiled corridors, a metal door slams.
The silence is punctuated by low voices, snatches of speech, sometimes
moans of patients in unseen rooms and wards.

They are called patients, but the term is almost ironic—a patient pre-
supposes a doctor treating them and a waiting, patiently perhaps, for
change or cure. There were few cures or even treatments in a lunatic
asylum in the 1920s, and at Dartford there was only one doctor for every
375 patients. In his letters, a few months into his lifelong incarceration
in the City of London Mental Hospital, Gurney took to reciting the man-
tra "I plead for release or chance of death." At Dartford, 744 men and
women moved mechanically through the anodyne routines of asylum
life. These patients, silent or unheard, were all waiting for release or
chance of death. The latter was statistically the more likely.

Footsteps echo—nearer, then further away. Then the notes of a piano,
untuned, poor quality, and a baritone voice, half singing, half mum-
bling, follows the contours of its accompaniment. Ivor Gurney, patient
number 4620, sits in his dressing gown playing his recent setting of
Edward Thomas's poem "Lights Out." He shows no sign that he is aware
of his listeners. Ranged around the bare day room, on wooden benches,
sit a number of men clad in regulation pyjamas or coarse woollen suits.
Some are eerily still, others continually moving, hands engaged in per-
petually unravelling some secret thread. Others' lips are moving, in
silent conversation with an invisible interlocutor. In moto perpetuo—
perpetual movement is one of the hallmarks of Gurney's piano accompa-
niments, an unstoppable flow of semi-quavers or quavers, falling fluidly
in crafted shapes (the contours of hills, perhaps?) under and around the
vocal line.

FIGURE 18.1. Gurney's pianos in the City of London Mental Hospital, Dartford.

I have come to the borders of sleep,
The unfathomable deep
Forest where all must lose
Their way, however straight,
Or winding, soon or late;
They cannot choose.[5]

The asylum was home to those who had lost their way. It was a death in life, a moment taken out of time, suspended between existence and non-existence. The idea of an asylum was that the lost might seek exactly that: asylum. It had been intended by the well-meaning Victorians to offer seclusion (usually rural) for the troubled of mind, to lift them from the stresses and strains of a life that was falling apart into the protection of the institution, to provide them with rest and a place of contemplation, and ideally to return them refreshed to their temporarily suspended life.

Dartford's Stone House Hospital had been designed with this intention. It had breezy verandas on which patients could sleep. Bracing fresh air, in lieu of any effective medication, might have a medicinal effect. It was a useful treatment for tubercular patients, so psychiatrists felt it was worth a try in the case of the mentally deranged. There was a farm in its grounds. If the patient could earn the trust of the doctors he or she might be allowed to work on it, as physical labour was therapeutic, as well as financially advantageous to the asylum.

Gurney had long understood the necessity for physical exercise in his fight against depression or "neurasthenia" as he termed it. He felt better as the hormones surged, stimulated by walks at breathless speed across the Cotswold hills, often with a friend struggling to keep up, or night walking, watching the constellations, Andromeda over Tewkesbury. He would drift in and out of the nocturnal communities that haunted the banks of the River Severn like Henry V before battle. He would sit in the ring of firelight with the elver fishermen who waited for the Severn's baby eels to make their nocturnal journey upstream, before he returned home to write by the light of a candle, until dawn.

The freedom to roam in his home landscape was what kept Gurney from disintegration. Experiencing Gloucestershire through his footfall, by the shapes cast by the trees in the moonlight, by the exhilaration of reaching the brow of a hill in stormy weather, provided him with the material for his poetry and much of his music. His home county was his beneficent asylum. Its hills encircled him with their maternal protection. They were, as he wrote in his poem "Strange Service,"

> not only hills, but friends of mine and kindly.
> Your tiny knolls and orchards hidden beside the river
> Muddy and strongly flowing, with shy and tiny streamlets
> Safe in its bosom.

Helen Thomas, the widow of the poet Edward Thomas, killed in 1916, stands by the great front door of Dartford Asylum, waiting to be escorted by an attendant to visit Gurney. She has never met him. She only knows that a man who loves Gloucestershire with a similar passion to her husband's is alone here, and in need of her vitality and compassion.

She is oppressed by the sights and sounds around her, just as Gurney had slipped, week by week, month by month, deeper into depression, largely as a result of the asylum itself and his separation from home. When she meets him she observes that he has the air of a man slowly drowning, just as he had once seen men he could not reach sinking in flooded shell holes on the Somme.

Walter Benjamin wrote, "Was it not noticeable at the end of the war that men returned from the battlefield grown silent—not richer but poorer in communicable experience?"[6]

How do we understand the silence of the returning soldier? As Wilfred Owen put it in the final line of his poem "Spring Offensive": "why speak they not of those who went under?" Many, of course, did speak, and published their experiences in the plethora of war memoirs that appeared in the bookshops between 1927 and 1933: *Testament of Youth, Undertones of War, Goodbye to All That*, and numerous others.[7] But these were written, after a decade of percolation, when memories might better be sublimated and laid to rest on the page. The writers hoped that the act of writing might allow them to carve out a future that was not dominated by war; might free them to bid "goodbye to all that." This presupposed that the veteran *had* a future. The asylum condemned Gurney to write his own posthumous autobiography, again and again.

Gurney's enforced domicile protected him from himself, but it also prevented him from taking his part in the literary and musical worlds, or from returning to his native landscape. At times he was forcibly given sulphonal and dial, strong drugs that prevented him from leaving his bed for weeks on end. Vaughan Williams's wife, Adeline, had been horrified at his situation when she had visited. "He is so very sane in his insanity," she mourned. Surely one day back in Gloucestershire, even if he took his own life, would be better than a lifetime in Dartford. How could he remain sane cut off from his home? "He gets no help at all for his mind from his surroundings. . . . How I longed to take him away!"[8]

Even when he was well enough to range through the grounds of the asylum, his horizons were limited to the mudflats of the Dartford estuary, with its cranes and unwieldy container ships, and expanses of brown-grey water. On the other side of the grounds was the high stone wall of the asylum boundary, delineating the artificial and much contested line between the sane world and the insane. It marked the line between society and those it had deemed unacceptable.

Gurney had returned from fifteen months of homesickness in France and Flanders, dreaming of his hills, setting to music in the trenches lines such as "I'm homesick for my hills again— / my hills again! / To see against the Severn plain / Unscabbarded against the sky, / The blue high blade of Cotswold lie!"[9] He could never reconcile himself to the realisation that the landscape he considered home had failed to protect him from incarceration. He had fought for his home; why did it not now fight for him? He never forgave Gloucestershire for betraying him but continued to reanimate the contours of the Cotswolds and the great square tower of Gloucester's St. Peter's Cathedral in his poetry and music, a landscape of his imagination.

Before she left home Helen Thomas had assembled a bundle of Edward's maps of Gloucestershire, feeling that if there was any way to connect with Gurney, it was by uniting their different griefs through a shared love of their home county.

As soon as she places the maps in Gurney's hands, he becomes animated. She helps him spread them out on the grey blanket of his bed, smoothing out the rectangular creases. Intently focused, he traces with a finger the curves and perorations of the lanes and tracks on Helen's maps.

He peers to see the tiny names of the villages that pepper the flat water meadows around the River Severn, and nestle between the daffodil fields and orchards. Helen takes off her hat (she had chosen her brightest one with flowers, in the hope that it would cheer him) and puts it on the bed so she too can bend over the maps. Tentative at first, being so close to this unpredictable, taciturn stranger, she becomes increasingly confident in their shared bond. With the suggestion on paper of river and stream, orchard and dry stone wall, she had provided Gurney with a way home. Crickley, Birdlip, Longford. The very act of naming his villages summons them into being for him.

In the trenches he had been amused to find that the names of familiar places had been transplanted into the most unlikely corners of muddy, subterranean France and Flanders. Buckingham Palace (usually the least luxurious trench) and Piccadilly Circus (for particularly busy junctions) all spoke of a peculiar amalgamation of the familiar and the alien, home and the unbroachable distance between it and the world of the trenches. Gurney found that he could summon up home in his poetry by rehearsing and repeating the names of the places he loved most. He called on them as others might call on their God—"O Crickley! O Framilode!" The place-names on an Ordinance Survey map became an incantation, each name a magic symbol for its associations. As his separation continued into the 1920s the names became increasingly resonant in his poetry. Poetic description of the places became increasingly unnecessary. He had a mental image of his home and was, in effect, talking to himself; the mere mention of a place transplanted him there. No need to take your readers with you when, writing in an asylum, you have none.

Gurney had begun to develop this shorthand for homesickness in the summer of 1916, at much the same time as he had tried to create something between a shrine and a portal to home in the less salubrious, temporary home of a dugout in Flanders. Here he took out a treasured black-and-white picture postcard of a view of the River Severn, curving round through the meadows, with the Cathedral towering above, lit by sunbeams streaming through the clouds. This was his religious icon, and he carefully wedged it in a crevice in the sandbagged wall of the dugout. It was

> a place that stands for delight with all Gloster men. It means a good tea, clean air, feminine society, a good row on a pretty stretch of river, Beauty and leisure to enjoy it; Home and all its meaning.[10]

Home, with a capital H. In the poem "Strange Service" he had imagined consecrating the sacred memories of Gloucestershire within his "deep heart."[11] Now the shrine had become literalised, and he could make his worship a communal act. But would a photograph of Gloucestershire indeed "stand for delight with all Gloster men," however homesick they might be? It seems so. His little picture postcard moved others just as much as its owner.

> I lead weary men into this commodious residence, and show them this pennyworth of poor printing. They cannot speak, or do so in such phrases as—"That hurts my cory."[12] "My God, my God!"

"What a life!" or more explosively, "How *Long* is this ******* War Going to *Last?*"[13]

Amidst the twisted wire and blasted trees of Belgium he was yearning for Gloucester *alongside* his comrades. His love of home could, for a brief period in his solitary life, link him to others, enable him to share the passion that drove him to create.

Now Gurney finishes playing. His hands rest momentarily over the keys, then he slowly, carefully, pulls down the curved lid. The patients continue to sit in the shadows. They will remain there, as they do every day, until they are taken for their meal, and then put to bed.

Asylums, like prisons, have been likened to a concrete womb, enclosing and protecting with a sinister inflexibility. But the asylum was not the mother to whom Gurney appealed for a secure attachment. Just as he had in the trenches, he looked to his landscape for his maternal security, finding it in the more fluid, buxom contours of the Gloucestershire hills, the encircling, amniotic waters of its rivers, rather than in the sterile walls of Dartford. But although his relationship with his maternal landscape was his lifeblood, it was riven with complexity and contradiction. In his 1917 sonnet "England the Mother" he wrote:

> We have done our utmost, England, terrible
> And dear taskmistress, darling Mother and stern.
> The unnoticed nations praise us, but we turn
> Firstly, only to thee—"Have we done well?

He clung to the protection his imagined mother/homeland offered him, but his relationship to her, the land that had sent him out to France to honour her, was as scarred and tortuous as the topography of the trenches themselves.

> Say, are you pleased?"—and watch your eyes that tell
> To us all secrets, eyes sea-deep that burn
> With love so long denied; with tears discern
> The scars and haggard look of all that hell.

FIGURE 18.2. Ivor Gurney in Dartford Asylum. (Illustration by R. K. R. Thornton)

Home, on which he depended for his sanity, was as treacherous a concept as the asylum's protection.

> Now these are memories only, and your skies and rushy sky-pools
> Fragile mirrors easily broken by moving airs. . . .[14]

However deeply he absorbed its image, however many poems he wrote, it would not remain static and dependable. It would not save him.

19
Safe Houses

BERNARD O'DONOGHUE

I find that I have started recently
to keep spare keys to the front door
in several pockets, such is my fear
of being locked out. Caught by the wind
the door could shut quietly behind you,
leaving you to face the outer world alone.
Once safe inside I don't put on the chain.

In guerrilla conflicts, the combatants
change their safe house at intervals
to give their hosts a rest from listening
for the thump on the door in the early hours,
as at the end of winter you escape
from cold and dark by making for
the sunnier climates to the south.

But where do we retreat to in the end
when the call to open up will not subside?
Kate in her nineties was no longer fit
to mind herself, so they took her in
to the Lee Road. When I called to see her
the nurse unlocked the door to the main room
and turned the key again behind me.

She was there with twenty other women,
all chattering and laughing like the magpies

in *Purgatorio*, not to each other
but to the unhearing outside world.
I thought of Masaccio's grieving couple,
not grasping what they've been exiled from,
some corner where the serpent cannot reach.

FIGURE 19.1. *Expulsion from Paradise*. Fresco
by Masaccio, Brancacci Chapel, Church of
Santa Maria del Carmine, Florence. (Credit:
Alinari Archives, Florence/Mary Evans)

The Afterlives
of Houses

20
"When All Is Ruin Once Again"

Thoor Ballylee

ROY FOSTER

When W. B. Yeats heard that his closest friend, Augusta Gregory, was seriously ill, in 1909, he wrote poignantly, "Friendship is all the house I have."[1] The metaphor cuts to the bone. He had grown up peripatetically, his impoverished artist father moving the family from one modest rented accommodation to another. The houses belonging to his mother's family in Sligo were the only enduring presences in his background; perhaps because of this, the poet had a longing all his life, as his friend Oliver Gogarty said, for a "household of continuance."[2] For much of his life, from the time he left home in 1895 until his marriage at the age of fifty-two in 1917, he lived in a rented apartment in Woburn Buildings, near the Euston Road (and convenient for the Irish boat train). But during the summers he had an adopted home in the Irish countryside—not in Sligo but near Gort, County Galway. This was Lady Gregory's house, Coole Park.

Coole was Yeats's "household of continuance" and he loved it with a passion—"more than all other houses," as he once said. It was substantial rather than grand, a plain Georgian house buried in its fabled woods, and full of contents which expressed its history and that of the Gregory family; as Yeats recalled, "Balzac would have given twenty pages to the stairs."[3] But he was a guest there only. The house was in fact the property of Lady Gregory's son Robert, though she was chatelaine for her lifetime, and Robert and his wife deeply resented Yeats's constant presence there. As in his friend Ottoline Morrell's house at Garsington near Oxford, which also inspired his poetry, or (towards the end of his life) Dorothy Wellesley's beautiful Sussex house Penns in the Rocks, Yeats was essentially a bird of passage. He loved houses, cared deeply about art and architecture, and was preoccupied by the way a room looked and what went into it—he had been an art student, after all. The style of his Woburn Buildings flat was remarked upon by many— tall candles in massive candlesticks, William Blake engravings, busts of poets, piles of books everywhere. But throughout his life, he lived in leasehold properties. He only ever owned one house outright: the old tower house at Ballylee near Gort, usually described as "Norman" though there is not much record of it before the sixteenth century.

Yeats had seen it on his visit to Galway in 1896, when his long association with Gregory and Coole began; built by the de Burgo clan, and at one point owned by the Gregorys, by 1916 it was transferred with other lands to the state, in the form of the Congested Districts Board. Yeats first saw it when accompanying Augusta Gregory on her folklore-collecting missions. As he recorded in 1899:

I have been lately to a little group of houses, not many enough to be called a village, in the barony of Kiltartan in County Galway, whose name, Ballylee, is known through all the west of Ireland. There is the old square castle, Ballylee, inhabited by a farmer and his wife [actually the retired Master of the Loughrea workhouse], and a cottage where their daughter and their son-in-law live, and a little mill with an old miller, and old ash trees throwing green shadows upon a little river and great stepping-stones. I went there two or three times last year to talk to the miller about Biddy Early, a wise woman that lived in Clare some years ago, and her saying "There is a cure of all evils between the two mill-wheels of Ballylee", and to find out from him or another whether she meant the moss between the running waters or some other herb. I have been there this summer and I shall be there again before it is autumn, because Mary Hynes, a beautiful woman whose name is still a wonder by the turf fires, died there sixty years ago; for our feet would linger where beauty has lived its life of sorrow to make us understand that it is not of this world.[4]

The eighteenth-century poet Antoin Raftery had celebrated Mary Hynes's beauty in verses that Lady Gregory had translated. So the tower house carried sacred associations—with poetry, with a legendary beauty who brought sorrow in her wake (Yeats was always on the lookout for a Helen of Troy), and with the folklore and history of this beautiful part of Ireland. And it was a tower. Yeats's poetic education, heavily featuring Milton, Shelley, and Keats, is full of towers, where lonely scholars (or poets) toiled by candlelight, or where tragic princesses were immured. There are other kinds of symbolism too, as Ezra Pound mischievously noted when Yeats eventually bought the tower, describing it as a "phallic symbol on the bogs—Ballyphallus or whatever he calls it with the river on the first floor."[5]

Though Yeats "long coveted it," he had very little money, at least until he started giving lecture tours in America and acquired a Royal Literary Fund pension. In 1916 he began negotiating to buy the tower, which was now roofless and with its floors fallen in, the two attached cottages (one of them in ruins), and a small piece of land across the road. He bought the freehold for £35 and by May 1917 was sharing his ideas for it in excited letters: to his father stressing that it would be made habitable "at no great expense" and would in fact be an economy (just in case the old man thought he had come into funds and started applying for some of them); and telling his friend Olivia Shakespear that the cottages would be rebuilt to give three bedrooms, sitting room, kitchen, and bathroom, before he repaired the castle; this would cost £200. He would raise the money by lecturing. But by late 1917 his position had changed. His love life went through spectacular somersaults in 1916–17, when he proposed marriage once more to the newly widowed Maud Gonne, and—after being turned down—to her daughter Iseult, before suddenly marrying the much younger Georgina or "George" Hyde-Lees in

FIGURE 20.1. Thoor Ballylee. A rare contemporary photograph of the tower, early 1920s; the children sitting on the bridge parapet are probably Anne and Michael Yeats. (Credit: Thomas Hynes / Yeats Thoor Ballylee Society)

October 1917. He would subsequently claim that he restored the tower "for his wife," but the project was conceived and begun well before this sudden step. Moreover, it was her money that enabled the restoration (over several years) to get going.

It was quite an undertaking. There were four rooms, one on each floor of the tower house, connected by a spiral stone staircase embedded in the huge wall. Each had a window overlooking the river. There was a flat roof on the top. Advised by aesthetic friends, Yeats retained the services of Professor William Scott of the National University's School of Architecture, well known for his ecclesiastical work in a Celtic Revival mode but also for being more or less permanently drunk. Scott designed fireplaces and furniture for the tower, working with local materials and craftspeople; slates and stones were bought from an abandoned mill nearby, though the envisaged roof of "sea-green" Liscannor slates didn't materialise; given the wild Atlantic storms, a flat cement roof was settled upon instead. (Yeats thought at one point of having a tarred canvas roof, as in Wagner's first theatre at Bayreuth.) The builder was a local man called Michael Rafferty whom Yeats invariably called Raftery, determined to invoke the poetic associations; furniture was made to Scott's designs by Patrick Connolly, a gifted craftsman joiner in Gort. Scott's aesthetic stressed the medieval; he wanted wicker hoods on the great fireplaces, insouciant about the fire risk. Lady Gregory oversaw much of the operations while Yeats was away—relentlessly nagged by letters from the poet. By July 1918 Yeats could write to his friend John Quinn that he had drafted a poem to be inscribed by the front door of the tower:

I the poet, William Yeats,
With common sedge and broken slates
And smithy work from Gort forge
Restored this tower for my wife George;
And on my heirs I lay a curse
If they should alter for the worse
From fashion or an empty mind
What Raftery built and Scott designed.[6]

The eventual inscription would have a more elegiac conclusion:

> I the poet William Yeats
> With old mill boards and sea-green slates
> And smithy work from the Gort forge
> Restored this tower for my wife George.
> And may these characters remain
> When all is ruin once again.

Perhaps this scaling back of the "household of continuance" to a less ambitious conclusion reflects the fact that the building project went on so long and raised so many difficulties. Yeats, George, and their baby Anne were able to spend the summer of 1919 there, though they lived mainly in the cottages as the upper rooms of the tower still were unfinished. In July Yeats wrote to his father: "I am writing in the great ground floor of the castle—pleasantest room I have yet seen, a great wide window opening over the river and a round arched door leading to the thatched hall. . . . There is a stone floor and a stone-roofed entrance hall with the door to a winding stair to left, and then a larger thatched hall, beyond which is a cottage and kitchen. On the thatched hall imagine a great copper hanging lantern (which is however not there yet but will be, I hope, next week). I am writing at a great trestle table which George keeps covered with wild flowers."[7]

The upper rooms were slowly conquered in the early 1920s; our main impression of how the tower looked, and its arts-and-crafts aesthetic, comes from photographs of the interior taken in 1926 by Thomas Hynes. The Yeatses chose roughly woven curtains, dyed strong colours such as blue and orange, and furniture of medieval inspiration; they considered installing a stained glass window by Burne-Jones, a wedding present from Charles Ricketts, but (luckily) didn't. They were also establishing their Dublin life at number 82 Merrion Square; and the Irish Free State, in whose government Yeats was a senator, was coming into existence amidst civil war. The tower was broken into on several occasions, and objects such as mirrors were stolen: one was left upright in a ditch and terrified a local drunk returning from the pub, who thought his reflection was a ghost. The building work proceeded fitfully, and dealing with the alcoholic Scott raised difficulties, compounded when he suddenly died in 1921. Yeats's Nobel Prize in 1923 eased the financial situation, though it was fairly rapidly dissipated by the demands of his sisters' Cuala Press and his Abbey Theatre colleague Lennox Robinson's disastrous advice to invest it in railway shares.

But the excitement Yeats felt at creating his own house from historic materials pulses through his letters, notably one to George in April 1924:

> I have seen Ballylee—you will have the whole Castle ready to inhabit very soon. The new room Raftery has plastered is practically ready. The room above—the top room—is the great surprise. It is magnificent—very high and even with one window—Raftery has for the moment filled up the others—sufficiently light. . . . There has been no flood since the day we left & the house looks perfectly dry and habitable. The little enclosed garden seems all right. It looked a pleasant friendly house.[8]

Though Yeats calls it "the Castle" he was determined to avoid the term as formally applied to the house because of its associations with "deer-parks and modern Gothic": he chose "Thoor," an anglicisation of the Irish "Túr" (tower), instead. There are other implications in this letter too. The house is not yet finished—only four years before they would give up going there. And there is a constant threat of floods. This would in fact make the tower and cottages uninhabitable outside the summer. On several occasions the Yeatses had to retreat up the winding stair clutching their possessions or evacuate to Coole. Their small children loved the place but they also remembered the sweeping of accumulated mud and worms out of the lower rooms as a ritual of arrival. Sanitation was elementary: one lavatory in one of the cottages, accessible only through the children's bedroom. Supplies had to be ordered from Gort (though a garage was built to house a Ford car, the vehicle never materialised). George loved the place and devoted much time to embellishing it, painting the wooden ceilings in vivid colours with symbolic and occult significance—though it was Yeats who decreed that the window frames be bright red, to Lady Gregory's disapproval. (George wanted bright blue.)

With Yeats's serious illness in 1927–28, the family moved for some time to Rapallo in Italy, which signalled the end of their summers in Ballylee. In 1930, Lennox Robinson approached George on behalf of a possible tenant (Pamela Travers, author of *Mary Poppins*, a rather unexpected addition to the Irish literary set in the 1930s). George sent Robinson a characteristically frank outline of its disadvantages:

*A. no indoor "accommodation" except one earth closet
B. all water for bath or washing up has to be taken from the river by bucket. There is a large galvanized iron water carrier on wheels which we get filled every day.
C. Drinking water has to be fetched either half a mile or a mile according to flood or drought.
D. The nearest shops are 4 1/2 miles away; this would not matter if the tenants had a car.
E. The garden will not produce much in the way of vegetables, unless there is a man to cope with sowing and weeding one or two days a week.
There are four bedrooms (six beds), two sitting-rooms, one kitchen, one garage (with boiler to produce hot bath water). The kitchen has a small range with copper boiler for hot water; the range works well.
When floods arise they generally subside within 24 hours. When there is a flood there is one sitting-room and one bedroom, 2 beds in the tower into which one may retreat. The two cottages and the dining room (tower) and garage flood roughly 12–18 inches.
*indoor "accommodation" is in the far room of the back cottage and is reached either from the garden door or through two back bedrooms.
In wet weather the limestone "weeps" so that you have to keep turf fires or oil stoves (there are two) going, otherwise there is an awful dampness. In July, August, Sept: everything is as a rule dry.

Against all the above I will add that there has not been a flood
for twentythree months in spite of last winter and summer's
rains. I just want to make sure you know the worst.[9]

The year 1928 was the last time Yeats and George were there together
(though George and the children occasionally visited). By then the tower
had served its purpose.

That purpose was artistic as well as domestic. Living in a tower not
only put Yeats in line with poetic heroes such as Shelley's Prince Atha-
nase, Milton's "Il Penseroso," and Villiers de l'Isle-Adam's "Axël"; it also
linked him to Irish history, with its successions of invasions and settlements. His 1921 collection *Michael Robartes and the Dancer* ended with
the poem "to be carved on a stone at Thoor Ballylee," and much of that
collection reflects the tower. Most dramatically, "A Prayer for My
Daughter" opens with an invocation of the house where his infant sleeps.

Once more the storm is howling, and half hid
Under this cradle-hood and coverlid
My child sleeps on. There is no obstacle
But Gregory's wood and one bare hill
Whereby the haystack- and roof-levelling wind,
Bred on the Atlantic, can be stayed;
And for an hour I have walked and prayed
Because of the great gloom that is in my mind.
I have walked and prayed for this young child an hour
And heard the sea-wind scream upon the tower,
And under the arches of the bridge, and scream
In the elms above the flooded stream;
Imagining in excited reverie
That the future years had come,
Dancing to a frenzied drum,
Out of the murderous innocence of the sea.

But his next collection, in 1928, took as its central theme and principle the building of the tower—which supplied the title poem of the

book, as well as the wonderful cover illustration by Sturge Moore. The
title poem is an interrogation of old age and philosophy, and again the
tower house is sharply evoked; the poet paces on his battlemented roof,
staring at the countryside around and remembering the associations, stories, and traditions it evokes (including, of course, the legendary beauty
Mary Hynes). The poem also resurrects the tower's previous inhabitants
("Rough men-at-arms, cross-gartered to the knees") and interrogates
Yeats's own memories of his life. The final section, cast in the form of
a testament, invokes jackdaws building nests in the loophole windows
of the tower. Above all, the great sequence "Meditations in Time of Civil
War," started at Coole in early June 1922 and continued at Ballylee,
stands as the tower's monument. It begins with the marvellous stanzas
of "Ancestral Houses," where he takes the theme of houses like Garsington and Coole to suggest ominously that violence and bitterness are
an inescapable part of building a civilization, which will decline as those
qualities mutate into gentleness. The next section of the sequence, called
simply "My House," is an utterly concrete evocation of his own tower,
subtly following through that theme of bitterness and violence:

> An ancient bridge, and a more ancient tower,
> A farmhouse that is sheltered by its wall,
> An acre of stony ground,
> Where the symbolic rose can break in flower,
> Old ragged elms, old thorns innumerable,
> The sound of the rain or sound
> Of every wind that blows;
> The stilted water-hen
> Crossing stream again
> Scared by the splashing of a dozen cows;
>
> A winding stair, a chamber arched with stone,
> A grey stone fireplace with an open hearth,
> A candle and written page.
> *Il Penseroso*'s Platonist toiled on
> In some like chamber, shadowing forth
> How the daemonic rage

Imagined everything.
Benighted travellers
From markets and from fairs
Have seen his midnight candle glimmering.

Two men have founded here. A man-at-arms
Gathered a score of horse and spent his days
In this tumultuous spot,
Where through long wars and sudden night alarms
His dwindling score and he seemed castaways
Forgetting and forgot;
And I, that after me
My bodily heirs may find,
To exalt a lonely mind,
Befitting emblems of adversity.

The sequence continues to interrogate themes of descent, inheritance, the bearing of children, and the possible futures of "this laborious stair and this stark tower," which he has chosen for an old neighbour's friendship and decked and altered "for a girl's love":

And know whatever flourish and decline
These stones remain their monument and mine.

The sequence records his life in the tower as civil war rumbles all round him. He recalled this in his speech accepting the Nobel Prize:

I was in my Galway house during the first months of the civil war, the railway bridges blown up and the roads blocked with stones and trees. For the first week there were no newspapers, no reliable news, we did not know who had won nor who had lost, and even after news-papers came, one never knew what was happening on the other side of the hill or of the line of trees. Ford cars passed the house from time to time with coffins standing upon and between the seats, and sometimes at night we heard an explosion, and once by day saw the smoke made by the burning of a great neighboring house. Men must have lived so through many tumultuous

FIGURE 20.2. Thomas Sturge Moore's beautiful cover for Yeats's *The Tower*, an accurate depiction of Ballylee mirrored in the River Cloon. (Private Collection)

centuries. One felt an overmastering desire not to grow unhappy or embittered, not to lose all sense of the beauty of nature. A stare (our West of Ireland name for a starling) had built in a hole beside my window and I made these verses out of the feeling of the moment:

The bees build in the crevices
Of loosening masonry, and there
The mother birds bring grubs and flies.

My wall is loosening; honey-bees,
Come build in the empty house of the stare.

We are closed in, and the key is turned
On our uncertainty; somewhere
A man is killed, or a house burned.
Yet no clear fact to be discerned:
Come build in the empty house of the stare.

A barricade of stone or of wood;
Some fourteen days of civil war:
Last night they trundled down the road
That dead young soldier in his blood:
Come build in the empty house of the stare.

We had fed the heart on fantasies,
The heart's grown brutal from the fare,
More substance in our enmities
Than in our love; O honey-bees,
Come build in the empty house of the stare.[10]

The sequence ends as it began, with a complex meditation on the inheritance of violence, the infection of bitterness, the visions of the clanging wings and terrible vengeance of the Furies—as seen from— yet again—the broken stone battlements of his roof. The tower also dominates Yeats's next collection in 1933, as indicated by the title: *The Winding Stair*. In "Blood and the Moon," written in the wake of Kevin O'Higgins's assassination, Yeats issues a celebrated manifesto:

I declare this tower is my symbol; I declare
This winding, gyring, spiring treadmill of a stair is my
    ancestral stair;
That Goldsmith and the Dean, Berkeley and Burke have
    travelled there.

Thus his tower enabled him to link his own life and achievements with those eighteenth-century thinkers whom he was adopting more and more closely. This volume also includes his beautiful elegy for Augusta

Gregory, written before her death in 1932, which links their two houses by the image of the underground river that connects Ballylee to Coole.

But by the time *The Winding Stair* was published, the Yeatses had given up the tower; the poet's uncertain health, the death of Augusta Gregory in 1932, and the impracticality of the house made it inevitable. It had served its purpose: not only had it supplied a powerful governing focus for the new married life begun in 1917 (which was also a new journey into spiritual and occult discoveries); it also inspired some of Yeats's greatest poems and supplied the organizing principle whereby he explored his own relation to the violent past and the unknown future. It is, therefore, a literary monument of the first importance.

When the American poet Robinson Jeffers visited the shuttered-up Thoor Ballylee in 1929 (which inspired him to build his own tower on the Californian coast), it was already effectively abandoned.[11] Throughout the 1930s it gradually began to decay back towards its original state. The stone with Yeats's dedicatory poem was erected there by the Board of the Abbey Theatre in his memory, nine years after his death, in 1948. Four years later the Yeats scholar Virginia Moore visited it and found it inhabited by cattle and crows; furniture, rose garden, and bridge were all gone. (When she reported this to George Yeats, she received the crisp reply, "That's the way we found it; it's come full cycle.")[12] Nine years later, in 1961, Mary Hanley founded the Kiltartan Society to develop interest in the extraordinary literary history of the area and to restore Ballylee—which was impressively achieved, with local enthusiasm and the help of the Tourist Board, Bord Fáilte. The Yeats family made over the property to a trust to ensure its maintenance and the building was declared a National Monument. The roofs were repaired, original furniture was hunted down or reproduced, and the interiors were restored as closely as possible. George was able to advise on this, as she lived on until 1968.

The tower was opened in 1965; visitors over the next thirty years could absorb its atmosphere and climb the winding stair to the flat roof where Yeats stared out from his battlements (and on one occasion, sat reading an early copy of *Ulysses* until driven inside by horseflies). Those visitors included other poets—such as Sylvia Plath and Ted Hughes, brought there by Richard Murphy in 1962. But even the future of a National Monument is not secure. In 2002 an American Yeatsian, Linda

Satchwell, contacted me to tell me that planning permission had been given by Galway County Council for a new bungalow close to the tower, opening the way for others to follow; objections from Galway West Tourism had availed nothing (and the Irish heritage organization Dúchas refused to protest as they said there was no "archaeological significance" attached to the site). With Linda Satchwell and the architect Paul Keogh, and supported by the Irish Georgian Society and An Taisce, I contested the planning permission, appealing to the central planning board, and in a hearing at Galway, we won our case. That unique and inspirational landscape can still—for the moment—be seen as Ireland's greatest poet had seen it. But the tower continues to suffer the vagaries of weather and uncertain funding; by 2009 it was badly in need of further restoration and was inundated during the freak floods that winter. Given the state of national finances, there were few resources to repair it; but the Thoor Ballylee Society and the generosity of the American Yeats scholar Joseph Hassett enabled a reopening on Yeats's 150th anniversary in June 2015. Cruelly, during the ensuing winter disastrous floods invaded the tower once more, but it has recently reopened again, as atmospheric as ever.

Buildings carry a certain historical baggage in Ireland, though finally the great architectural heritage of the eighteenth and nineteenth centuries has been accepted as the national treasure it is rather than merely the evidence of colonial domination. Impressive work has been done in adapting military institutions designed as barracks or prisons for new purposes. Thoor Ballylee, as Yeats wrote, itself possesses a history reflecting violence and domination—but it was readapted, in his custodianship and through his poetry, into what Seamus Heaney called it, "a sacramental site."[13] Poetic prescience enabled Yeats to predict the tower's future vicissitudes, as well as to invoke its chequered past, but it has avoided the ruination he accurately prophesied for Coole. For all the comedy and inconveniences attendant upon his attempts to live in a symbol, his instinct that Ballylee was essential to him was triumphantly vindicated. Those stones remain his monument in more ways than one.

21

W. H. Auden in Austria

"Publicly Private" and Globally Local

SANDRA MAYER

It is one of those inconspicuous, lazy scribblings that are so easily over-looked, while the scholar's eye, in no mood for detours and distractions, impatiently flits across the handwritten page looking for clues and references that could be important. I am skimming Stephen Spender's notes on W. B. Yeats and T. S. Eliot and am just about to reach back into the cardboard box to retrieve the next item when the black-and-white marbled journal, almost pristine and left blank save for a few densely covered pages, falls open to reveal five lines of Spender's handwriting:

Kirchstetten
Westbahn
Winterholz 6
N. Ö.
Austria[1]

Scrawled across the page, they are randomly cut loose from any explanatory context, and yet these lines trigger a smile of recognition. The pleasure of decoding the significance of a casually scribbled string of words is heightened by a more visceral sense of connection as the letters translate into the imagined sound of my native language. Though these words are deterritorialised, in the timeless archival limbo zone, they point to a distinct space, and one that for me is close to home, literally and metaphorically. They form part of an address I instantly

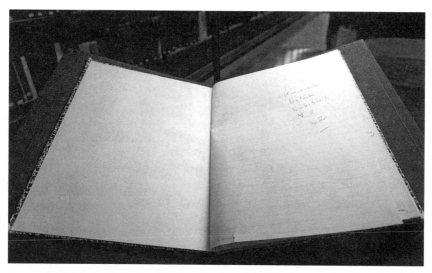

FIGURE 21.1. Undated notebook by Stephen Spender. (Photo copyright © Sandra Mayer, reproduced by permission of the Curtis Brown Group Ltd. on behalf of the Stephen Spender Estate and the Bodleian Libraries, University of Oxford)

recognise—even if it contains a spelling mistake and tantalisingly withholds the name of the individual who once made his home there. I am experiencing one of those epiphanies when everything connects—a moment not uncommon in the archive, where absence and presence, public and private converge; where the real meets the imaginary, the documented the creatively reconstructed; and where ghostly afterlives come into being through the enduring footprints of materiality and the varied responses they provoke.

A few days later, I have left the archive behind and am back on my home turf, pursuing those ghostly footprints and hoping for signs of their lingering imprint on geographical space. A friend and I have taken the "Westbahn," the train line cutting right through the genteel western suburbs of Vienna and scenic vistas of the Vienna Woods into the Lower Austrian "Mostviertel" ("Must Quarter"). After a forty-five-minute journey, we get off the train and make our way up the narrow country

FIGURE 21.2. The W. H. Auden Memorial, Kirchstetten, Lower Austria. (Photo copyright © Wolfgang Woessner, reproduced by permission of the Documentation Centre for Literature in Lower Austria)

lane steeply winding towards the address noted down in Spender's journal. It is the same hillside path Spender climbed up and down forty-five years earlier, almost exactly to the day. Many years later, he would write a poem, revisiting the sensual impressions and the emotions of that day. As in that poem, there is a "white October sun" in the sky as we walk past gardens "with colours of chrysanthemums" where "bronze and golden under wiry boughs, / A few last apples gleam like jewels."[2] Nestled against a stretch of fierily autumn-leafed woodland, a small-windowed farmhouse comes into view, quaint, red-tiled, and brightly painted in yellow and green. As I approach the gate that guards the neat grounds that surround the house, I glance up at the wooden balcony and discover a life-sized image of the former lord of the manor fixed at exactly the same spot where the photograph was originally taken in the mid-1960s. It produces an odd, uncanny impression of the famous po-et's ghostly presence, coolly looking down on the curious visitor with an air of imperious nonchalance. His distinctive weathered face is "like a map of physical geography, criss-crossed and river-run and creased with lines";[3] his gaze is guarded, reserved, and private, yet bold, defi-ant, and transgressive.

In the "cross-questioning glance" of this "ghost of a ghost"[4] there is also an expression of proud ownership, softened by a barely perceptible ironic smirk. I cannot help wondering whether it is because he is aware of, and delights in, the strangeness of finding a home in postwar pro-vincial Austria. It is indeed no less than a "quasi-humorous perversity"[5] that he, the world-famous cosmopolitan poet, should have ended up a curiously outlandish "transplant / from overseas,"[6] ardently (but selec-tively) embracing domestic and community life in an environment that must have seemed both mind-bogglingly alien and alienating. And yet, the house that I am about to enter was, and still is, a liminal space of resolved paradoxes: where he could be "publicly private,"[7] known and yet obscure, at home and yet absent, distanced.

~~~

It is one of the quirkier turns in literary history that one of the most influential English poets of the twentieth century should have acquired the only home he ever owned, which became his most permanent base, in the sleepy Lower Austrian village of Kirchstetten. W. H. Auden (1907–73), feted literary celebrity, notorious émigré, and, by then, Oxford Professor of Poetry (1956–61), had bought the farmhouse cheaply in 1958 with some of the proceeds from the Feltrinelli Prize for Literature and, together with his partner Chester Kallman, would spend the last fifteen summers of his life there. The roaring motorway, cutting through the rolling agricultural landscape, would conveniently take him into Vienna in just under an hour, allowing him to enjoy the quiet steady comforts of village life while having easy access to the ame-nities and manifold attractions (intellectual and otherwise) of the nearby metropolis. According to Stephen Spender, the ownership of

Auden's Kirchstetten house occasionally brought on "tears of gratitude and surprise."[8] The gratitude, perhaps, was for having found, at last, some respite from the heavy toll of a wildly accelerated life by moving to a place where he could cultivate a whole range of theatrical personae, including lionised celebrity poet, "autocrat of the cocktail hour," venerated "Herr Professor," and droll factotum.[9] The surprise, shared with the speaker in his poem "Thanksgiving for a Habitat," might have come from the fact that "I . . . at last am dominant / over three acres and a blooming / conurbation of country lives, few of whom / I shall ever meet, and with fewer / converse."[10] His sense of pride, comfort, and relief over the vague possibility of having found a home was muted by an acute awareness of unalterable outsiderdom: of remaining a curiously eyed foreigner, no matter how faithfully church- and tavern-going.

An exile and foreigner for most of his life, hardly forgiven in his native country for his "defection" to the United States on the eve of World War II, Auden, from 1948, divided his time between New York City and his rented summer home on the island of Ischia. The rising influx of tourists in the 1950s and, as a consequence, the sharply increased costs of living seem to have figured prominently in Auden's decision to bring his Italian intermezzo to an end and move north after winning the Feltrinelli Prize in 1957. Biographers argue that the choice of possible host countries was narrowed down by Auden's wish to settle in a German-speaking environment, preferably within easy reach of a renowned opera house and affordable quantities of good-quality wine.[11] These were good enough practical reasons, but his decision to move his continental summer home also had an important emotional component. Reading Brecht and Toller as an undergraduate and counting Rilke and Kafka amongst his poetic influences, Auden felt a close affinity for German literature and culture. He had a strong connection with the German language, which he spoke reasonably well, having left Britain in 1928 to live in Berlin for nine months. In the mid-1920s, his travels had taken him to the Tyrol and the home of Hedwig Petzold, widow of the Austrian poet Alfons Petzold, with whom he had a brief affair and subsequently stayed in touch. It was Petzold's daughter, Christa, who found the advert for the Kirchstetten farmhouse in a Viennese newspaper after Auden had mobilised his Austrian friends in his house-hunting mission.[12]

It seems that everything about Wystan Auden's life in Kirchstetten, this rural enclave at the heart of Europe, halfway between north and south, geopolitically wedged between East and West, is about the global subject's playful transgression of boundaries. Neither public nor private, neither famous nor obscure, Auden in Austria defied categorisation and took full advantage of the liberating potential of his cultural, social, linguistic, and sexual outsiderdom, which freed him from any pressures to fit in and observe the stifling rules and conventions of village life. Paradoxically, the small scale and the provincial provided him with a considerable degree of licence that condoned the foibles of the eccentric foreigner and his "housekeeper." He could take part in Kirchstetten life as a respected member of the local community, regularly attending Catholic Sunday mass and joining in the annual Corpus Christi procession. Meanwhile he could count on the villagers (hardly known for their sexual liberatedness) to turn a blind eye to the more unorthodox aspects of his and Kallman's lifestyle, which included regular visits from Greek boyfriends, Viennese rent boys, and petty criminals. Kirchstetten, as one commentator so aptly puts it, "may not have been home exactly, but it was as close as [Auden] would ever come to home, and probably ever wanted to come."[13] This central ambivalence is captured in "Thanksgiving for a Habitat": "what I dared not hope or fight for / is, in my fifties, mine: a toft-and-croft / where I needn't, ever, be at home *to* / those I am not at home *with*."[14]

While local dignitaries were clearly proud of their internationally famous resident, it is fair to say that in 1960s Kirchstetten Auden was "famous for being famous elsewhere."[15] But just as there was only a vague sense of the full dimensions of Auden's foreign fame in his adopted home, his move to an obscure Austrian village, heralding a new style in his writing, raised eyebrows amongst critics and commentators who knew and admired Auden as one of the prime political poets of the 1930s. A 1965 *Sunday Times Magazine* feature by TV producer Christopher Burstall, who visited Auden in Kirchstetten for his BBC1 documentary *W. H. Auden: Poet of Disenchantment*, starts off musing, "Where does Auden stand today?"—a question easily answered, it seems, as Burstall proceeds to give an atmospheric account of the poet's Kirchstetten life, punctuated by religiously observed domestic routines. The image created of Auden is that of a rapidly aging eccentric of quirky and compulsive habits, whizzing through the "heavy, rich, unspectacular countryside" in his Volkswagen Beetle and shuffling about the house in "broken-down woolly carpet slippers." It is that of a poet who has lost his biting, sociocritical edge and whose writing, too, has become "modest, Horatian, slippered."[16]

Yet Auden's Austrian summers amount to more than just a random aberration. Still underrated and underresearched in Auden scholarship, the "Austrian years" marked a phase of renewed creativity and artistic exploration that saw a departure from the overtly political and a revaluation of the ordinary, intimate, and potentially trivial. Like earlier changes of scene in his life, this one "coincided with fundamental changes in his work and outlook,"[17] which critics often reduced to an apotheosis of the domestic, the small scale, and the insular in the wake of a disillusioned break with the radicalism of his youth. Dense, opaque, and seemingly parochial, peppered with obscure local references and untranslated turns of phrase, some of his later poetry is not easily accessible for readers unfamiliar with Austrian village life. Poems like "Whitsunday in Kirchstetten" are firmly anchored within the cultural and linguistic context of Auden's new home, but they also transcend the local and ostensibly banal, the sphere of private musing and self-indulgent introspection.

> . . . When Mass is over,
> although obedient to Canterbury,
> I shall be well-gruss-gotted, asked to contribute
> to *Caritas*, though a metic come home
> to lunch on my own land: no doubt, if the Allies had not
> conquered the Ost-Mark, if the dollar fell,
> the *Gemütlichkeit* would be less, but when was peace
> or its concomitant smile the worse
> for being undeserved?[18]

The private, peaceful act of the "metic," the foreign resident, attending Catholic mass less than a hundred miles from the Iron Curtain is intricately entangled with the weighty implications of world history and its contingencies. Austria in the 1960s was a country largely in denial of its guilty complicity with National Socialism while pragmatically subscribing to a "zero hour" mentality and presenting itself to the world as the first victim of Hitlerite aggression. A half-truth at best, Austria's victim status had been confirmed by the Allies in the Moscow Declaration of 1943, providing a convenient pretext for the country to disavow its shared responsibility for decades to come. Auden's poem thus brings together public and private, local and global, homecoming and uprootedness, community life and world politics, and highlights their inextricable interdependence.

The same is true of the work most intimately associated with Auden's Kirchstetten years: *Thanksgiving for a Habitat*, the sequence of poems included in his 1965 collection *About the House*. Each poem focusses on a specific room in the house, from the writer's study to the privy. The sequence thus charts the life and topography of the house itself, but it also reflects the importance of space for the artist's creative process and sense of personal and social belonging. The poems address the way in which houses "are projections of personalities"[19] and their identities. Through their dedications to friends and companions, both the living and the dead, they emphasise the function of houses as meeting points of social networks, literary influences, and intellectual inspirations. *Thanksgiving for a Habitat* might initially appear as a straightforward tribute to the process of arrival, homecoming, and home-making, but the cycle more complexly develops what has been described as a "subjective poetic anthropology of being at home while remaining a stranger."[20] Home appears as a safe in-between space that serves as a fitting abode for an in-between subject who has cut himself loose from geographical, linguistic, and cultural boundaries.

~)

As I climb up the narrow and perilously steep outside wooden staircase that leads up into this space where nothing seems fixed, where even "silence / is turned into objects,"[21] it strikes me how in Auden's life the intricacies, the fault lines, and the beauties of the transnational life commingle. Such in-between lives as Auden's, transgressive in every way, not only transcend national borders and cultural environments but also profoundly challenge the rigid categories by which literary historiography and biographical traditions often remain tethered to the frameworks of the nation-state. The house Hinterholz 6 is therefore not a grand memorial to the "transformation of Anglo-American into Austrian Auden"[22] but more a site of, and a material testimony to, all these different lives connecting, aligning, and intersecting. These days, the Community of Kirchstetten owns the house, and while parts of it are still lived in, the building's first-floor rooms have been converted into a writer's house museum, set up in the mid-1990s in collaboration with the Documentation Centre for Literature in Lower Austria, which also holds a significant collection of Auden's and Kallman's literary papers. Situated in a locale not widely associated with the author's life and work, and faced with the challenge of addressing both well-read pilgrims from afar and visitors popping in by chance, the museum resists any institutional agenda of affirming narratives of national identity and cultural memory. Instead, the Kirchstetten W. H. Auden Memorial and its permanent exhibition display, revised in 2014 under the auspices of literary curator Helmut Neundlinger and exhibition designer Peter Karlhuber and called "A Transplant from Overseas," does justice to the interconnectedness of life stories and life journeys.

As soon as the wooden door creaks open and I step into the low-ceilinged shadowy room, I am swallowed up whole and at once by Auden's inner sanctum, his "Cave of Making." Taking in the dark-panelled writer's study, secluded, dim, intimate, and indeed cave-like, I cannot help feeling that I am a trespasser in this space "More private than a / bedroom even, for neither lovers nor / maids are welcome."[23] The atmosphere is heavy with afterlife, suggested by the metonymic objects standing in for the act of creation. On the writing desk just by the window, there is the portable typewriter, complete with a half-written typescript page of "The Cave of Making," the "house poem" dedicated to Louis MacNeice. If it was not for the protective glass case, the onlooker might think that the writer has just finished his day's work and gone downstairs to pour himself an aperitif before dinner. Auden had a strict domestic timetable of set times for work, meals, and cocktails, as well as a routine of weekly trips to Vienna for his rendezvous with "Hugerl," whose loyalty as a long-standing "bed-visitor" is celebrated in Auden's 1965 poem "Glad." There is, therefore, no historical accuracy in the three wine glasses that stood on the desk next to Auden's typewriter. They look like props meant to flesh out the display with a touch of quirky detail, in a playful engagement with the subject's reputation, thus balancing, as museum spaces do, the "documented and the imaginary."[24] The image of Auden that emerges from the memoirs of friends and visitors and from the typed timetable pinned to the wall in his study is that of a painstakingly diligent writer, one "who knew, none better, how nice it is to sit sipping a cool drink in the shade of a tree, looking with contentment at his flowers and asparagus beds. He did this only after he had worked steadily from 9 a.m. until lunchtime and then again throughout the afternoon."[25]

Writers' house museums invite visitors to relate the imaginary world of their reading experience to the historical and biographical framework of the text's creation. This "hospitality," anchored in the literary work itself,[26] becomes particularly pronounced when the work so self-consciously engages with the myriad functions of the house and their significance to the writer, as in Auden's *Thanksgiving for a Habitat*. It is tempting for visitors who are familiar with Auden's "house poems" to try to align intra- and extratextual worlds. They cannot help looking out for the "Olivetti Portable" in the room where "all is subordinate / . . . to function, designed to discourage day-dreams."[27] Auden's study in the Kirchstetten house has indeed been only moderately interfered with. The public and private dimensions of his work have been pointed up through the integration of the existing library in the new display, which emphasises the major intellectual influences on Auden's writing and thinking. While the study-cum-library has largely retained its original appearance and features, the remaining attic space has been transformed to give visitors an overview of Auden's life and work, his networks of friends and collaborators, via the skilful use of multimedia

FIGURE 21.3. Auden's study in the W. H. Auden Memorial. (Photo copyright © Sandra Mayer, reproduced by permission of the Documentation Centre for Literature in Lower Austria)

material, including text, photographs, film clips, audio documents, and samples from his musical collaborations with Britten, Stravinsky, and Henze, as well as objects and artwork. First editions of Auden's poetry collections and extracts from his work both in the original and German translation are interspersed with photographs and home video footage offering an intimate glimpse into Auden's Kirchstetten life. There is Auden having a chat with the woman at the counter of the local post office; there is Auden putting on a solemn face while attending a First Communion service; and there are Auden and Christopher Isherwood engaging in boisterous horseplay in the garden of Hinterholz 6.

At the room's far end there is a precarious-looking pile of books and objects that strikes me as a fittingly tongue-in-cheek engagement with Auden's iconic status in the cultural imagination. Peter Karlhuber's art installation stacks up books of Auden criticism and primary works, paper

FIGURE 21.4. Display by Peter Karlhuber in the W. H. Auden Memorial, Kirchstetten. (Photo copyright © Sandra Mayer, reproduced by permission of the Documentation Centre for Literature in Lower Austria)

files, envelopes, an ashtray, a coffee cup, and a cognac glass into a wobbly construction, ineffectually supported by an empty Cinzano bottle and a pair of old slippers.

The display case next to it contains a mix of objects and documents. There is a letter in German written to the Austrian tax authorities, which is really a veiled theory of poetry and reveals Auden's sharp intellect and brittle humour. There is a matchbox model of a yellow Volkswagen Beetle, the kind in which Auden cruised the Lower Austrian landscape and which infamously served as a getaway car in a series of robberies committed by Auden's long-time lover Hugerl. An inconspicuous-looking scrap of paper catches my eye. It turns out to be a handwritten bill, issued by the Kirchstetten brass band, for 3,000 Austrian schillings to pay for the "music on the occasion of Professor Auden's funeral on 4 October 1973." Just above the display, on a small screen, I can see them in action: part of the bizarre *pompe funèbre* that is so essential to Austrian funerary culture, they spearhead the cortege with the heavy, wreath-laden oak coffin and the train of mourners. They are a motley crew. Members of the British intelligentsia, including Stephen Spender, Sonia Orwell, and Charles Monteith, are paired with representatives of the Viennese underworld; delegations of English and Austrian governmental and cultural institutions walk side by side with groups from the local voluntary fire brigade, the veterans' association, and the gamekeepers. What I cannot hear is their jaunty tune, jarring with the "Down-crashing drums and cymbals cataclysmic"[28] of Siegfried's funeral march in *Götterdämmerung* that Auden's friends and family listened to just before joining the funeral procession. The footage cuts to a close-up of a grief-stricken Chester Kallman, supported by Stephen Spender and Auden's brother, John, as the coffin is lowered into the grave. That grave in the local churchyard is marked by a simple iron cross and a plaque reading "W. H. Auden 21.2.1907–28.9.1973 Poet and Man of Letters." It is still a place of pilgrimage, where visitors might come close to grasping that "the imaginings / Of the dead makers are their lives," now that "Word [is] freed from world."[29]

All visits to sites of literary heritage are more than just one-way practices of passive absorption. They are performances of cultural values and desires, and at the same time they actively shape individual and collective, social and political identities. Nowhere does this become more obvious than in the visitors' book, which, like the archive, the museum, and the memorial, makes visible the interconnectedness of human lives. I flick through the lined pages of neat, sprawling, or cramped handwriting that attest to a surprisingly international visitor base stretching from Texas to St. Petersburg. What brought them here, I wonder, as I step out of the dimness of Auden's "Cave of Making" and back into the sharp October light. Whatever it was, they must have left, like me, under a deep impression of unanticipated intimacy—not born of false expectations of authenticity but stillness, smallness, ordinariness; the absence of spectacle and commodification.

Not long afterwards, I am back in the archive, and one of Stephen Spender's notebooks again lies open in front of me. The page contains a handwritten draft version of a poem commemorating, almost a decade later, that sunny October day in Kirchstetten in 1973, when Spender was amongst the group of people who "cast a clod of earth from those heaped there / Down on the great brass-handled coffin" of his friend. It is a poem that clearly grapples with the tension created by the haunting presence of bodily, textual, material, and spiritual remains: "Gone from our feast, your life enters your poems / Like music heard transformed into notes seen. / Your funeral dwindles to its photograph / In black and white, of friends around your grave." The pencil inscription on the autograph page reads "Columbia, South Carolina," where Spender taught in 1981.[30] In a few weeks' time I will be looking at more of Spender's materials at the Harry Ransom Center in Austin, Texas, and will be reading about his own funeral in 1995. Both Spender and Auden powerfully illustrate how literary lives, and the ways in which they are told and remembered through texts and material culture, are essentially transnational. So too is the scholar's journey following their trail.

22
John Soane and House Autobiography

GILLIAN DARLEY

The more I consider John Soane's house-museum, the more the nature of the project, the dogged presentation of the architect's life work and preoccupations within four walls, begs its own questions. When I wrote his biography, I described it as Soane's autobiography. Yet, I now feel that there is something incomplete and somewhat facile in that view because Soane, despite his grasp of the past, and his taste for illusion, entirely failed to account for an unforeseeable future. While Soane's reputation rests on the judgement of passing generations, the house itself could not adjust—at least until it had been freed from the strictures that he had laid upon it.

To stay with the metaphor of autobiography, the house itself can be seen as a book, even down to the living index, an extraordinary archive. Chapter by chapter, room after room, it winds on, until at one moment a room literally turns to pages, with the unfolding hinged panels in the Picture Room displaying, amongst much else, Hogarth's *Rake's Progress* series. Abraham Booth was one of the earliest guidebook writers to feature what he called the "Soanean Museum."[1] He calculated that the double-sided "pages" in that confined space, each measuring just under 14 by 12 and a half feet, in aggregate would be a gallery measuring 45 by 20 feet. Modern room stewards extract maximum theatre in front of astonished visitors as they peel back the laden shutters on their gleaming brass hinges.

FIGURE 22.1. *Perspective of the Dome*, c. 1813, by J. M. Gandy. (Copyright © Sir John Soane's Museum, London)

Soane lived to see his house secured for the nation by private Act of Parliament in 1833, the year that he turned eighty, and his case argued by the Radical MP Joseph Hume. Opposition came from William Cobbett, who voiced the claims of the enraged, estranged George, Soane's surviving, and younger, son. That was not the end of the matter, but on Soane's death the museum irrevocably came into being. George Bailey, who had been in his office for many years, became the curator while its trustees were nominated by learned societies and appropriate institutions including, from 1844 to 1856, the Royal Society of Arts whose candidate was the Prince Consort. With the museum comfortably endowed, its form and contents frozen, Soane had earlier told students at the Royal Academy that he was establishing an academy for architectural education. In his last years, knowing that the Act was securely on the statute book, Soane made numerous further expensive purchases and altered the fabric, such as glazing the open loggias on the Lincoln's Inn Fields front. He also moved his bust by Sir Francis Chantrey from an alcove to a considerably more prominent position, centre stage under the Dome.

Long before, in the unhappy years leading up to his wife's early death, he had toyed with making the house his burial place. His old friend Richard Holland remembered "some hints"[2] that Soane considered following the example of Noel Desanfans and Francis Bourgeois, whose mausoleum he was designing at that time alongside their collection at Dulwich Picture Gallery. Whatever the potential the house might promise as an Academy of Architecture, it was to be, supremely, a monument to himself.

On paper, Soane tended to leave matters unfinished. The extraordinary ramblings, compounded from family frustrations, professional slights, and misunderstandings of every tint, that make up *Crude Hints* (1812) were unpublishable. He meandered between his house as reality (and reminder) and as imagined in the form of an emblematic ruin. But as Helen Dorey points out in her introduction to the text, as he wrote his house was, in fact, a building site and hence a ruin on the way to transformation.[3] Having disposed of his handsome country villa in Ealing, Pitzhanger, envisaged briefly as a theatre for an imaginary Soane

FIGURE 22.2. "Sir John Soane's Museum in Lincoln's-Inn-Fields: The Sarcophagus Room,"
Illustrated London News, 25 June 1864. (Copyright © the British Library Board P.P.7611)

architectural dynasty, he laboured on, now perpetually enraged by the inadequacies of his sons. The house-museum was becoming a casket for his growing collections as well as his reputation, a permanent gallery of his architectural achievements (again, juxtaposing both dreams and reality). His work was glowingly rendered in large, exhibition-quality watercolours by Joseph Gandy and distributed throughout the house. Perhaps Gandy's most remarkable evocations were of the house-museum itself. Of the domestic aspects of the house, there was little sign.

As Soane finalised the work on the museum in 1834–35, he was also engrossed in penning his furious (privately printed) *Memoirs of the Professional Life of an Architect* and, more fruitfully, in perfecting the ultimate *Description of the House*, with a preface by the poet Barbara Hofland, which was to be his last word on the subject, superseding several earlier editions with slightly different titles. As a fellow writer, Anna Jameson, put it, Mrs. Hofland had been induced to "say for him what he could not well say himself, though by no means scrupulous in self-love and self-lauding."[4] Once the *Description* was in print, he scattered it liberally.

In 1836 Isaac D'Israeli, father of the future prime minister (and himself a novelist), wrote effusively to thank him for a copy. As he put it, "Some in Poems have raised fine architectural Edifices, but most rare have been those who have discovered . . . that they had built a Poem."[5] This testimonial was not, perhaps, entirely unsolicited. Disraeli's wife was born Maria Basevi and her nephew George, who would be the architect of the Fitzwilliam Museum in Cambridge, had worked in Soane's office from 1810 to 1816. He found himself one of the unhappy few who attended Eliza Soane's funeral in 1815. Tellingly, Arthur Bolton, curator from 1917 and who compiled the first biography of Soane, based on his correspondence, dedicated his book "to those who are, and all who will be, wives of architects."

Those who succeeded in gaining entry in the years immediately after Soane's death cannot have known what to expect. Booth's guide had described a "suite" of four rooms while Mrs. Jameson's *Handbook* found no less than twenty-four rooms. Peter Conrad evoked the literary freedom of the Victorian romantics, following no rules or genres and essentially formless. In parallel, he argued, "architects, like painters, become narrators, novelists."[6] Soane's pre-Victorian compilation offers something of that, an uneven treasure house (or a mixture of gold heavily weighted by dross as most visitors of that period found it to be), displayed, figuratively framed and glazed, within an architectural setting. Early visitors could read the Soane Museum as they might a Walter Scott novel, placing their emphasis at will.

Many questioned its appeal and, on occasion, were downright critical. Soane's well-publicised unrelenting feud with George, a considerable literary figure in his own right, if a cruel spendthrift, had severely damaged his reputation and exacerbated the impression of the 1833 Act being an act of hubris. The repetitive, often plagiarising guides to London of these years presented antipathy to the man rather than admiration for the architect. Even his professional peers saw him, by the 1830s, as a difficult old man, former Professor of Architecture at the Royal Academy but whose recent work had led into a cul-de-sac. The house-museum as inspiration to a nation of young architects was dead in the water.

The museum was free but a little catalogue was available for one shilling, as Anna Jameson explained to the general public. It was "for the solace and improvement of the people" and prompts a "thousand thoughts, remembrances and associations." But for the German art historian Dr. G. F. Waagen it was all "a feverish dream"—very far, Augustus Hare considered, later, from the example of "artistic and instructive purposes to which it is possible to devote an English private residence."[7]

Steadfast George Bailey, nearing fifty, became curator in 1837 (remaining in post until 1860) but was in no position to moderate or influence the publicity around the museum. Anna Jameson had written a remarkably frank, and unflattering, account of Soane's character, detailing the tensions with George, and even turned architectural critic, considering the frontage to demonstrate Soane's "perverted predilection for misplaced ornament, the want of simplicity," which, she or an anonymous informant (even George himself?) suggests, were "the besetting sins of Sir John Soane as an architect." Indoors, the "alloy of vanity, of selfish feeling, of an impetuous temper long irritated, mingled with the public spirit which dictated this magnificent bequest." He had, she pointed out acutely, placed the "objects of his life . . . beyond the caprices of individual feeling, of chance, and of change."[8]

Yet Anna Jameson was happy to promote the quirky charms of the house-museum, the physical complexities of which, she wrote, reminded one overseas visitor of the bifurcations of a mineral mine, with treasures at the end of each tunnel rather than ore. "I am told that on some days the visitors have amounted to between five and six hundred." That level of interest, if maintained, would be highly damaging: she judged that "promiscuous, unlimited admission to this Lilliputian Museum . . . would be impossible." However, the complexities of gaining entry and the low level of interest in Soane's work at the time, together with the jaded displays, ensured that this was not to be a problem.[9]

In town, Charlotte Brontë tracked down the Foundling Hospital and the Bethlem Hospital but was not drawn south to Lincoln's Inn Fields or through the door of number 13. Had she done so she might have benefitted from Tuesday openings from February to the end of August for "foreigners, artists and persons making but a short stay on London" in addition to the midweek, high-summer openings. Arranging a visit was a cumbersome business requiring the deposit of a card and address after which an admission card would appear in the post. The initial endowment was shrinking as costs grew and visitor numbers were paltry. New approaches were required. A nearly full-page feature in the *Illustrated London News* on 25 June 1864 made much of the "self-help" that had seen Soane ascend from a background of poverty to "a position of opulence and celebrity." Meanwhile, Joseph Bonomi, Egyptologist and architect, became Bailey's successor as curator.

By the 1880s, 13 Lincoln's Inn Fields had become a place of intriguing obscurity. Henry James's *A London Life*[10] is a novella, first published in the United States in *Scribner's Magazine* in 1888. Laura Wing, a serious young American in London, is growing familiar with the city, having cultivated her mind over the previous year by visiting "the curiosities, the antiquities, the monuments." Guided by John Timbs, whose innumerable titles included *Curiosities of London* and *Walks and Talks about London*, she had tracked down the surviving "old corners of history" and "houses in which great men had lived and died." Over dinner one evening, Mr. Wendover, a sympathetic young compatriot with "worthy eyes," offered to accompany her to somewhere unusual in London, of her own choice; after dinner she came up with an idea, "a place to which she was afraid to go alone and where she should be grateful for a protector." Later that week they took the "mysterious underground railway" to the Temple, investigated the gardens of the Inns of Court and the crusader tombs in the church, while discussing Johnson and Goldsmith and how "London opened one's eyes to Dickens." After a visit to the disappointingly colourless St. Paul's they took a hansom cab to Lincoln's Inn Fields to visit the charming place that Laura had in mind, "one of the most curious things in London and one of the least known."

The stage is set. On arrival, where menacing storm clouds hang over the square, James slips into what was, surely, his own memory of a visit. Inside "the place gives one the impression of a sort of Saturday afternoon of one's youth—a long, rummaging visit, under indulgent care, to some eccentric and rather alarming old travelled person." As Wendover continues, "it would be a very good place to find a thing you couldn't find anywhere else—it illustrated the prudent virtue of keeping." Going room to room, the pair find everything displayed odd or even unsettling, "and some few objects interesting." As ever, there is no reference to the architect donor of this curious labyrinth, or to his work, but as they stand by the open upstairs windows and breathe in the scent of rain freshly falling on the dry streets, they realise half an hour has gone by. As the storm reaches a crescendo, they are directed by a "keeper" to head downstairs to the basement, against a thunderous percussion and into the darkness. Faced with the dim vaults, encrusted walls, and little passages and nooks, everywhere encumbered with "strange vague things . . . some of which had a wicked, startling look . . . like a cave of idols," Laura grows frightened. Suddenly a flash of lightning illuminates one, then two figures in the shadows, accompanied by a shriek. It is her married sister Selina, on an illicit assignment with her lover, in a place as empty and obscure as they could have found anywhere in the city. On the page Soane's house has been transformed into a theatre for Gothic horror—readied for a script by George Soane.

In 1878 James Wild was the first curator to be challenged on his appointment. Frederick Soane, George's sixty-three-year-old son, wrote asking to be considered for the role. This ghostly family claim was easily dismissed in law, but it must have disturbed the dusty equilibrium on Lincoln's Inn Fields. Perhaps it was this, and the knowledge that the lease on number 12 would soon fall in, that made Wild decide to instigate a programme of transformative works. However, most of his plans, including major structural changes, came to nothing, as his distinguished successor Sir John Summerson wrote in *Georgian London*, his "ruthless project" to modernise the museum was deemed illegal.

By the late 1930s, the difficult access, the lack of information, and the ever-more shabby state of the house and its contents, still overseen by the aged Arthur Bolton, became a matter for parliamentary concern. The Sudeley Committee, which sat from 1923 until 1946, was responsible for the promotion of museums and the encouragement of their wider use by the general public. On 14 July 1938 Commander Marsden raised the committee's concerns regarding 13 Lincoln's Inn Fields in the House, including changes to "make the contents of the Sir John Museum . . . available at hours convenient to the public and appoint a committee of museum experts to rearrange the contents so that they can be better seen, as improvements of this nature have, during the past 20 years, been frequently but unsuccessfully suggested to the trustees of the museum." This full-frontal assault was immediately parried by Captain Wallace, Sir Edwin Lutyens's son-in-law, who countered that the museum was private and so the government would not be asking Parliament to intervene in its management.

Now the trustees were under siege by a phalanx of heavyweight art historians, eminent scholars, and museum directors ranging from Fritz Saxl of the Warburg Institute to Kenneth Clark of the National Gallery. In the face of their criticism, it was pointed out to them, very reasonably, that "the great value of the House and its interest to the Public lay in its presentation in its original state as a private House and Collection arranged and lived in by the Collector Owner himself." There were insufficient funds for more open days or hours, or for refreshing the labels. The curator's position, and salary, had been originally designed to assist visiting students. And things had changed, at least regarding the

Victorian curator's privileges, Arthur Bolton pointed out. "Wyatt Papworth used to sit in the front room and if any visitor failed to remove his hat, he would go up to him and say 'Sir, I beg to point out that this is a private house.' George Birch always lunched in the Breakfast Room and closed it accordingly around midday."[11]

The trustees were seemingly much more exercised by what to call the house. The curator suggested "Sir John Soane's House and Museum," although he thought it might well become, in general usage, "Sir John Soane's House." In his memorandum Bolton pointed out that it was "not intended to be a Museum in the modern sense of the word" and advocated dropping "museum" (while "library" had already disappeared of its own accord). As he put it, the analogy with the "Ashmolean, Fitzwilliam . . . and other museums not possessing the essential residential character gives a wrong impression." John Summerson referred to the "Parnassian ring" that came with the idea of a Soane *Museum* although in that instance he was referring to Soane's effort to make Pitzhanger "the ideal environment for a classic breed of architects."[12]

In mounting desperation Lord Harewood, the chairman of the Sudeley Committee, took to *The Times* letters page. First in July 1938, and then a year later, he described his committee's continued exasperation with the intransigence of the trustees, who "further state that no explanatory talks beyond those which are now given by special arrangement seem to be required." Nor had there been any movement towards extending days of opening or rearranging the exhibits. As always, the museum pleaded the restrictions of the Act and the shortage of funds (although it had, by then, received a generous grant from the Pilgrim Trust). Reginald Blomfield, the arch-conservative architect and chairman of the Soane Trustees, made his rebuttal through the means of *The Times* letters column in August 1939, claiming that the dispute was based upon a fundamental misunderstanding of the nature of Soane's museum, which is not "supported by the taxpayer but a private museum established and maintained by a specific Bequest." And there it rested.

Eventually modifications to the constitution in the shape of the Charities (Sir John Soane's Museum) Order of 1969 and further amendments in 1996 and 2003 modernised and improved the rules of engagement. Over the past thirty years substantial funds, imaginative directors, and ambitious but careful plans have come together to transform and complete the presentation of the three houses to the public as well as provide ancillary space for exhibitions, conservation, and other administrative purposes. It now includes the entirety of number 14, for many years leased out.

The afterlife of such a cultural monument, fixed in the moment of donation like an elaborate fly in amber, is bound to be less perceptibly, but crucially, determined by the continuous reevaluation of the subject matter. In the twentieth century Soane's architectural career was of interest once more. In the 1920s his greatest public work, the Bank of England, on which he had worked from 1788 until 1833, was torn down. One of the most eloquent protests came from a young John Summerson, whose long term as director (with Dorothy Stroud as inspectress) began in 1945.

Interestingly, in *Georgian London* Summerson argued that Soane's house was, by definition, itself now a public building. Inexorably, the wheel was beginning to turn in Soane's direction. Dorothy Stroud embarked upon an ambitious count of surviving Soane buildings, eventually the material for her 1984 monograph. In Norfolk in 1952 she was helped by the aerial observations of a young man flying a Meteor bomber out of Horsham St. Faith, Ian Nairn.[13]

In 1966, Ian Nairn wrote the most eloquent introduction to the Soane Museum of all. "After a visit here, four walls and a ceiling can never look quite the same," he wrote in a scintillating two-page entry in the incomparable *Nairn's London*.[14] His words took me to 13 Lincoln's Inn Fields and introduced my generation to Soane. In the late decades of the twentieth century his star rose as no one could have predicted. Soon, an astonishing range of international architects began to discuss and respond to Soane's work. Arch-priest of the idiosyncratic in architecture, his arguments lie, for those with the eyes to see them, within that tall thin house-museum which has, quite remarkably, tolerated the buffeting of time and opinion and continues to stimulate and inspire. Thank you, John Soane.

23
Ainola

Music and Silence

JULIAN BARNES

There are two famous silences in the history of classical music: those of
Rossini and Sibelius. Rossini's, which lasted nearly forty years, was a
worldly, cosmopolitan silence, much of it spent in Paris, during which
time he co-invented *tournedos Rossini*. Sibelius's, which lasted nearly
thirty years, was more austere, self-punishing, and site-specific; and
whereas the Italian finally yielded again to music, writing those late
works he referred to as "the sins of my old age," Sibelius was implacable. He fell silent, and remained silent.

I first got to know his music almost half a century ago in recordings by
Anthony Collins and the London Symphony Orchestra. The record sleeves
of those old Ace of Clubs LPs featured black-and-white photos of appropriately Nordic scenes: snowscapes, fjords, towering pine trees, and so
on. I think these images were mixed up with my early appreciation: there
was a cool yet turbulent melancholy to them that I also found in the music
and that seemed to harmonise with my unrestful late-adolescent soul.
But the music has stayed with me all my life, and though generally unin-
terested in the lives of composers, I made an exception for Sibelius. I admire his mixture of puckish humour and obdurate high principle. During
a conducting tour of England, he said in one post-concert speech, "I have
plenty of friends here, and, naturally, I hope, enemies." He consoled a
young colleague for a bad review with the words: "Always remember,
there is no city in the world which has erected a statue to a critic." And

during his final, silent years—he died at the age of ninety-one—he noted at one point in his diary: "Cheer up! Death is round the corner." So for years I have wanted to visit the composer's house, forty kilometres north of Helsinki, a region of lakes and pine forests and towering silver birches. For me it has always been a place with a dual, divided reputation: for both creation and destruction, for both music and silence.

Most artists' houses have had previous and subsequent owners; in some you feel only a vestige of the artist's presence; others have had their spirit crushed by museumification, by curatorial intervention and the accretion of study centres. The Sibelius house is one of those rare places where no other presence interferes with the genius loci: it is a house of, for, by, with, and about Sibelius. The composer bought a one-acre plot at Järvenpää near Lake Tuusula in 1903. There was already an artists' colony here; but Sibelius was as much attracted by the empty landscape in which he loved to walk, by the swans and geese passing overhead. In September 1904 he moved his family into the still unfinished house, which he named Ainola (the suffix "-la" meaning "place of") after his wife, Aino. Here they brought up their five daughters (a sixth died in infancy). Here Sibelius composed most of his major works, from the violin concerto of 1905 to the last five of his seven symphonies; and here he spent three decades not publishing a single note. When, in 1957, death's long round-the-corner wait ended, he was buried in the grounds. Aino lived on here for another twelve years; their joint tomb, a six-foot-square low bronze slab—which has the monumental inevitability of the later symphonies—was designed by their architect son-in-law Aulis Blomstedt. The five daughters, old themselves by the time of Aino's death at the age of ninety-seven, sold the house and contents to the Finnish state in 1972; it opened as a museum in 1974.

The house was designed (for free) by an architect friend, Lars Sonck, in the "National Romantic" style. It is essentially a grand log villa built on a heavy stone base and clad with weatherboard; in the grounds Aino designed a sauna house (with laundry room), laid out vegetable and flower gardens, and planted fruit trees, some of which still survive. Inside, the main rooms have heavy pine beams and those typically Scandinavian high stoves finished in glazed brick or tile. There is the feel of solid, continuous living to the place. Even the Sibelius's two housemaids were solid and continuous: both lasted nearly sixty years. Almost nothing has changed (though Sibelius's original manuscripts have been removed to national archives); and the place that once held Sibelius and his music still holds them both. The composer's white summer suit rests on a hanger in his study; his broad-brimmed Borsalino and stick are on a nearby table. Here is the Steinway grand he was given on his fiftieth birthday (though he composed in his head, not on a piano); there is a run of the *National Geographic Magazine* covering the last five years of his life. On the Russian oak desk at which he worked from the time of his marriage in 1892 lies the wooden ruler Aino carved for him, with which he ruled his scores; also, an empty box of Corona cigars, and an elegant Tiffany photo frame, containing a portrait of Aino, through which the light streams. Open on the desk is a facsimile score of his greatest symphony, the Fourth. But the homely is never far away: in the kitchen, screwed to the wall, is an apple-coring machine Sibelius brought back from one of his trips to America. Made of black cast-iron, it is a Heath Robinsony contraption of prongs, screws, and blades that will peel, core, and slice your apple at the turn of a handle. From the same trip he also brought his wife a Tiffany diamond; but it is the apple-corer that sticks in the mind.

Reminders of his fame are everywhere, from an enormous laurel wreath (now much dried) that once encircled him on a notable birthday to the multiple commemorative images made of him. Every time a plaster medallion of Finland's greatest artist was cast, he was given a personal copy, and most seem to have ended up on his walls. But genius had to coexist with family life, and it was not always easy. "Our souls are worn down through continuous contact with one another," Sibelius wrote in his diary. And: "I am building a studio for myself—at least one. Next to me are all the children whose babbling and pranks ruin everything." But he never did build himself a studio; instead, he relocated his study upstairs and forbade the noise of any instrument while he was in the house. The children had to wait until he had gone for his daily walk to do their music practice.

The house, though comfortable and practical, is by no means grand. The average visitor to Ainola might reasonably conclude this was just

Sibelius's summer home, used by the composer to get away from the city. Not a bit of it. For most of his life he was in serious debt. At first these were young man's debts, caused by his taste for high living: he was a committed drinker who would often go missing for days (but could always be located in "the best restaurant serving oysters and champagne"). And though the drinking was lifelong, and his tastes remained luxurious—that white suit came from Paris, his shoes and shirts were made for him in Berlin—this was not the reason why Aino kept chickens, laid out a vegetable garden, planted fruit trees, and schooled her own children. Sibelius took on a huge debt when he built Ainola and wasn't able to clear it for more than two decades. The Sibelius website (www.sibelius.fi) contains a terrifying graph of the composer's indebtedness for the period 1892–1926: it peaks at the equivalent today of 300,000 euros.

But, you will say, he was a world-famous composer. His music was constantly played; he was feted everywhere, not least in Britain—"the land without chauvinism," as he called it (we are to presume he was only talking musically). Constant Lambert, in his 1934 study *Music Ho!*, extravagantly called him "the most important writer [of symphonies] since Beethoven." Yale gave him a doctorate in 1914. How could such a man not afford to pay off the debts on his house? How come he was only saved from bankruptcy in 1910 by the intervention of generous patrons? The answer lies mainly in history and the curious laws of copyright. When Sibelius started composing, Finland was part of the Russian Empire, and Russia was not a signatory to international copyright treaties. So—apart from performing fees (and he often conducted)—Sibelius's income came from selling his work outright to music publishers. In 1905, for instance, he signed an agreement with Robert Lienau in Berlin to supply "four major works" in the coming year, the first of which went to pay for the sauna house Aino designed. Finland gained independence from Russia in 1919 but didn't sign the Berne Convention on Copyright until 1928— by which time Sibelius had entered into his silence.

And in any case, you couldn't retrospectively claim copyright on what you had previously sold outright. To take the most egregious example: Sibelius composed his famous *Valse Triste* as part of the incidental music to *Kuolema* (1903). The following year he made two arrangements of the piece, each of which he sold outright for 100 marks (a little less than 3,000 euros in modern money). This may have seemed canny at the time. But *Valse Triste* was to become the best-known piece of music Sibelius ever composed; in the 1930s it was estimated to be the world's second most-played tune after *White Christmas*—yet from all the recordings and playings and sheet music Sibelius didn't receive a cent. He survived with the help of donations, national collections, and a government pension; in 1912, he even thought of emigrating, whereupon the government raised his stipend and there were relieved newspaper headlines reading "Jean Sibelius Remains in Finland." He finally became solvent at the age of sixty-two, in 1927, and was eventually to die a fairly rich man. But it is an instructive story at a time when copyright is once again an issue, music piracy rife, and "Don't-be-evil" Google has illegally digitalised hundreds of thousands of books still in copyright.

There is something heroic about those writers and artists who choose silence when it would be easier to supply profitable titbits to an adoring audience. Sibelius struggled with his Eighth Symphony for many years. He was constantly badgered about its progress; conductors and concert impresarios begged a foretaste. He always refused. Some believe that in the decades he worked on it he had finished only one movement. Sibelius himself claimed that he had "completed" the Eighth "many times"—though perhaps only in his head. In any event, at some point in the early 1940s, Sibelius piled the manuscript sketches of the Eighth plus a large quantity of other unfinished or (in his view) inadequate works into a big laundry basket, took them to the dining room, and, with Aino's initial help, began to feed them into the stove. After a while, Aino no longer had the strength to watch and left the room, so she was unable to confirm exactly what had gone into the flames. But she reported that afterwards, "My husband became calmer and his attitude was more optimistic. It was a happy time."

The stove, made at the local brickworks, is chunky and rustic, with a glistening green finish (Sibelius saw colours as keys: green was F major, yellow D major). I bent down and tried to open the small steel doors, to see exactly where all that potential music had turned to ash. But they were screwed shut—not, it transpired, out of any piety, rather because in the years of Aino's widowhood the stove had been converted to electricity. Electricity also powered the library's shiny walnut-cased Philips radiogram that the head of Philips gave the composer in the early 1950s. This was the last of a series of such instruments on which, all through the three decades of his personal silence, music had come into Ainola from Berlin, London, Paris, and New York. Or from just forty kilometres away. At the exact time Sibelius lay dying, on 20 September 1957, the Helsinki City Orchestra was playing his Fifth Symphony under Sir Malcolm Sargent. Naturally, the concert was being broadcast on Finnish radio, and Aino later recalled that she had been tempted to turn on the radiogram, in the hope that her husband's music might bring him back to consciousness; but in the end, she decided not to.

In his last year, Sibelius wrote in his diary about the wildlife of the local region:

> The swans are always on my mind, and they lend magnificence to
> life.
> It is strange to note that nothing in the whole world, not in art,
> literature or music, has such an effect on me as these swans and
> cranes
> and bean geese. Their calls and their appearance.

If you stand in the grounds of Ainola today you are more likely to hear the steady thrum of traffic from a nearby road than the honk and wail of any passing wildlife. But the place retains its magic as a meeting point of high art and practical living, of musical fame and apple-peeling machines, of conjured sounds and final silence.

Acknowledgements

The editors would like to thank the following for their help, advice, and support in the making of this book: Dr. Katharine Collins; Professor Elleke Boehmer, FRSL; Dr. Sandra Mayer; Sumaya Partner; Professor Kelsey Thornton; Wolfson College for its support of the Life-Writing Centre; and, at Wolfson, Louise Gordon and Phil Nixon for help with the "Lives of Houses" Conference.

The editors and publisher are grateful to all the institutions and individuals for permission to reproduce the materials in which they hold copyright. Every effort has been made to trace the copyright holders; apologies are offered for any omission.

Contributors

SIMON ARMITAGE is a poet, playwright, novelist, librettist, broadcaster, documentary-maker, and teacher of writing. He was Professor of Poetry at Oxford (2015–19) and is now Poet Laureate and Professor of Poetry at Leeds University. He holds numerous honours and awards, is a Fellow of the Royal Society of Literature, and in 2010 was made a CBE for services to poetry. His first poetry collection was *Zoom!* (1989); his most recent poetry collections are *Paper Aeroplanes* (2014), *The Unaccompanied* (2017), *Flit* (2018), *Sandetti Light Vessel Automatic* (2018), and his translations of *Pearl* (2017) and *Sir Gawain and the Green Knight* (2007, revised 2018).

JULIAN BARNES is a novelist who also writes nonfiction, essays (often on art and on French literature), and reviews. He has written thirteen novels, from *Metroland* in 1980 to *The Only Story* in 2018. His novel *The Sense of an Ending* won the Man Booker Prize in 2011. He has written three books of short stories, four collections of essays, and four books of nonfiction, including *Nothing to Be Frightened Of* and *Levels of Life*, and, most recently, *The Man in the Red Coat*. In 2017 he was awarded the Légion d'honneur.

ELLEKE BOEHMER is a novelist, short-story writer, and critic. She is Professor of World Literature in English at the University of Oxford. Her novels include *Screens Against the Sky* (1990), *Bloodlines* (1997), and *The Shouting in the Dark* (2015). Her latest volume of short stories is *To the Volcano* (2019). Among her academic books are *Colonial and Postcolonial Literature* (1995, 2005), *Nelson Mandela: A Very Short Introduction* (2008), *Indian Arrivals, 1870–1915* (2015), *Postcolonial Poetics* (2018), and her edition of Baden-Powell's *Scouting for Boys* (2004, reissued 2018). She has received numerous awards, including the ESSE Prize (2016) and the Olive Schreiner Prize (2018), and is a Fellow of the Royal Society of Literature.

REBECCA BULLARD is Associate Professor of English at the University of Reading. She works on seventeenth- and eighteenth-century literature and culture, gender, genres, and book history. She has written on authors such as Margaret Cavendish, Aphra Behn, Defoe, Swift, and Eliza Haywood. Her books include *The Politics of Disclosure, 1674–1725: Secret History Narratives* (2009) and, coedited, *The Secret History in Literature, 1660–1820* (2017) and *The Plays and Poems of Nicholas Rowe, Volume 1* (2017).

DAVID CANNADINE is Dodge Professor of History at Princeton University, visiting Professor of History at Oxford University, general editor of the Oxford Dictionary of National Biography, and president of the British Academy. His many books on British history include *The Decline and Fall of the British Aristocracy* (1990), *Ornamentalism: How the British Saw Their Empire* (2001), *Making History Now and Then* (2008), *The Undivided Past: Humanity Beyond Our Differences* (2013), *Victorious Century: The United Kingdom, 1800–1906* (2017), and *Churchill: The Statesman as Artist* (2018). He holds many honours and Fellowships and was knighted for services to scholarship in 2009.

GILLIAN DARLEY is a writer, broadcaster, and architectural journalist. She was awarded an OBE in 2015 for services to the built environment and conservation and is currently president of the Twentieth Century Society. Her books include a study of British planned and utopian settlements, *Villages of Vision* (1975, revised 2007), a cultural history of Vesuvius (2011), *Ian Nairn: Words in Place* (with David McKie, 2013), and *Excellent Essex* (2019). She has written three biographies: *Octavia Hill* (1990, revised 2010), *John Evelyn* (2006), and *John Soane: An Accidental Romantic* (1999).

MAURA DOOLEY is Professor of Creative Writing at Goldsmiths, University of London. Before that she was a director at the Arvon Foundation at Lumb Bank and director of the Literature Programme at the

Southbank Centre in London, and has also worked in theatre, in film for Jim Henson, and freelance for a variety of arts organisations. Her poetry collections include *Explaining Magnetism* (1991), *Kissing a Bone* (1996), *Life Under Water* (2008), *The Silvering* (2016), and *Negative of a Group Photograph* (2018), recipient of a PEN Translation Award, versions of work by the Iranian poet Azita Ghahreman. She is a Fellow of the Royal Society of Literature.

ROBERT DOUGLAS-FAIRHURST is a writer, teacher, reviewer, and broadcaster, specialising in nineteenth-century literature. He is Professor of English at Oxford University and a Fellow of the Royal Society of Literature. His books include *Victorian Afterlives* (2002), *Becoming Dickens: The Invention of a Novelist* (2011, winner of the 2012 Duff Cooper Prize), and *The Story of Alice: Lewis Carroll and the Secret History of Wonderland* (2015).

ROY FOSTER is Professor of Irish History and Literature at Queen Mary College, University of London, and before that was the Carroll Professor of Irish History at Oxford University from 1991 to 2016. His many books on Irish history, culture, politics, and literature include *Modern Ireland, 1600–1972* (1988), *Paddy & Mr. Punch* (1995), his two-volume biography of Yeats (1997, 2003), *The Irish Story* (2001), *Luck and the Irish* (2008), and *Vivid Faces: The Revolutionary Generation in Ireland, 1890–1923* (2014, winner of the British Academy Medal and the Frokosch Prize from the American Historical Association). He is a Fellow of the British Academy, the Royal Society of Literature, and the Royal Historical Society, and an Honorary Fellow of the Royal Irish Academy.

ALEXANDRA HARRIS is a writer, teacher, and reviewer, and is Professorial Fellow at the University of Birmingham. Before that she was Professor of English at the University of Liverpool, where she worked from 2007 to 2017. She is the author of *Romantic Moderns* (2010, winner of the Guardian First Book Award), *Virginia Woolf* (2011), and *Weatherland: Writers and Artists under English Skies* (2015). She is currently working on a history of landscape and local feeling centred on West

Sussex, as well as a project about the cultural history of the year. She is a Fellow of the Royal Society of Literature.

DAISY HAY is Associate Professor of English Literature and Life Writing at the University of Exeter. She works on late eighteenth- and early nineteenth-century British Literature. She is the author of *Young Romantics: The Shelleys, Byron and Other Tangled Lives* (2010, winner of the British Academy Rose Mary Crawshay prize), *Mr. & Mrs. Disraeli: A Strange Romance* (2016, winner of a Somerset Maugham Award), and *The Making of Mary Shelley's Frankenstein* (2018). She has been awarded a Philip Leverhulme Prize and is a Fellow of the Royal Society of Literature. She is working on *Dinner with Joseph Johnson*, a cultural history of English Romanticism.

FELICITY JAMES is Associate Professor in eighteenth- and nineteenth-century English literature at the University of Leicester. She is currently editing the children's writing of Charles and Mary Lamb for the new Oxford *Collected Works*, and her books include *Charles Lamb, Coleridge and Wordsworth: Reading Friendship in the 1790s* (2008) and the coedited *Religious Dissent and the Aikin-Barbauld Circle, 1740–1860* (2011) and *Writing Lives Together: Romantic and Victorian Auto/biography* (2017).

KATE KENNEDY is a writer, BBC Radio 3 broadcaster, and Associate Director of the Oxford Centre for Life-Writing. She has held Research Fellowships at Cambridge University (2010–15) and is the Research Fellow in Life-Writing at Wolfson College, Oxford. Her biographical documentaries for the BBC were selected for Pick of the Year 2018, and she is the recipient of Oxford's Vice Chancellor's Prize for Public Engagement with Research (2018). She is author of libretto *Out of the Ruins* (Royal Opera House, 2015), editor of *The First World War: Music, Literature, Memory* (2013), *The Silent Morning: Culture, Memory and the Armistice 1918* (2014), and *Literary Britten* (2017). Her biography *Dweller in Shadows: Ivor Gurney— Poet, Composer* will be published by Princeton University Press in 2021.

HERMIONE LEE is a biographer whose work includes lives of Virginia Woolf, Edith Wharton, and Penelope Fitzgerald (winner of the 2014

James Tait Black Prize). Her biography of Tom Stoppard will be published in 2020. She was Goldsmiths' Professor of English at Oxford from 1998 to 2008, and from 2008 to 2017 president of Wolfson College, Oxford. She is a Fellow of the British Academy and the Royal Society of Literature and in 2013 was made a DBE for services to literature.

MARGARET MACMILLAN is a historian and broadcaster who specialises in modern international and British imperial history. Her books include *Women of the Raj* (1988), *Paris 1919: Six Months That Changed the World* (2007), *The War That Ended Peace* (2013), and *History's People* (2015). In 2018 she gave the BBC's Reith Lectures, on war; the book from the lectures, *The Mark of Cain: War and the Human Condition*, will be published in 2020. She has taught at Ryerson, Toronto, and Oxford universities and from 2007 to 2017 was the Warden of St. Antony's College, Oxford. She is an Honorary Fellow of the British Academy, a Companion of Honour, and a Companion of the Order of Canada.

LAURA MARCUS is Goldsmiths' Professor of English Literature at Oxford University; before that she held posts at Birkbeck College, Sussex, and Edinburgh. Her interests include life-writing, modernism, Virginia Woolf, contemporary fiction, and literature and film. Her books include *Auto/biographical Discourses: Theory, Criticism, Practice* (1994), *Virginia Woolf: Writers and Their Work* (1997, reissued 2004), *The Tenth Muse: Writing about Cinema in the Modernist Period* (2007), and, as coeditor, *The Cambridge History of Twentieth-Century English Literature* (2004). She is currently working on the concept of "rhythm" in the modernist period and on editions of Woolf and Dorothy Richardson. She is a Fellow of the British Academy.

ALEXANDER MASTERS is a writer (and illustrator) of books and screenplays. He took degrees in maths and physics before writing *Stuart: A Life Backwards* (2005), which won the Guardian First Book Award and the Hawthornden Prize and which he has since adapted for BBC TV. He has also written *The Genius in My Basement* (2011), a life of the mathematician Simon Norton, and *A Life Discarded* (2016), the story of diaries found in a skip in Cambridge. He works with the homeless.

SANDRA MAYER is the Hertha Firnberg Research Fellow in English Literature at the University of Vienna and at the Oxford Centre for Life-Writing at Wolfson College. She has also taught at the University of Zurich. She works on celebrity, life-writing, literary networks, and the reception of Oscar Wilde. Her first book, *Oscar Wilde in Vienna*, was published in 2018, and in 2019 she guest-edited an issue titled "Life Writing and Celebrity" for the journal *Life Writing*. Her current book project explores the intersections of literary celebrity and political activism in autobiographical life-writing.

BERNARD O'DONOGHUE is a poet and scholar who was Fellow and Tutor at Wadham College, Oxford from 1995 to 2011, where he taught old and medieval literature and modern Irish literature. His first poetry collection, *Razorblades and Pencils*, was published in 1984. Other collections include *Gunpowder* (1995, winner of the Whitbread Prize), *Here nor There* (1999), *Outliving* (2003), *Farmers Cross* (2011), *The Seasons of Cullen Church* (2016), and a verse translation of *Sir Gawain and the Green Knight* (2006). His academic work includes editions of Hoccleve and Chaucer, *Seamus Heaney and the Language of Poetry* (1995), the *Cambridge Companion to Seamus Heaney* (2008), and *Poetry: A Very Short Introduction* (2019). He is currently translating Piers Plowman and editing the poems of Seamus Heaney.

SEAMUS PERRY is Professor of English at Oxford University, coeditor of *Essays in Criticism*, and general editor of *21st Century Oxford Authors*. He is writing a life of Auden, and his work includes many essays on Hughes, Hill, Eliot, Coleridge, Arnold, and others, a guide to *The Waste Land* (2018), *Alfred Tennyson* (2005), *Coleridge* (2003), and *Coleridge and the Uses of Division* (1999).

JENNY UGLOW is a biographer and historian, broadcaster and reviewer, and writer on art. For many years she was editorial director of Chatto & Windus. Her books include *Elizabeth Gaskell: A Habit of Stories* (1993), *Hogarth: A Life and a World* (1997), *The Lunar Men* (2002, winner of the James Tait Black Prize), *Nature's Engraver: A Life of Thomas Bewick* (2006),

The Pinecone: The Story of Sarah Losh (2012), *In These Times: Living in Britain through Napoleon's Wars, 1793–1815* (2014), and *Mr. Lear: A Life of Art and Nonsense* (2017, winner of the Hawthornden Prize). Among many honours and appointments, she was Chair of the Royal Society of Literature (2014–16), is a trustee of the Wordsworth Trust, and was made an OBE in 2008.

LUCY WALKER is Director of Public Programming and Learning at the Britten-Pears Foundation. She has worked intensively on Britten's life and work, researching his juvenilia, his correspondence, and his life at the Red House. She is the author of *Britten in Pictures* (2012) and editor of *Benjamin Britten: New Perspectives on His Life and Work* (2009).

SUSAN WALKER is an honorary curator of the Ashmolean Museum, where she was Sackler Keeper of Antiquities from 2004 to 2014. Before that she was Assistant then Deputy Keeper of Greek and Roman Antiquities at the British Museum, where she curated major exhibitions, including *Ancient Faces: Mummy Portraits from Roman Egypt*. She specialises in the art and archaeology of the Roman Empire, with interests and publications ranging from Britain to North Africa. She is a Fellow of the Society of Antiquaries of London.

Notes

Preface

1. Readers interested in following up academic studies on these areas might like to consult recent key books such as: Alison Booth, *Homes & Haunts: Touring Writers' Shrines and Countries* (Oxford: Oxford University Press, 2016); Diana Fuss, *The Sense of an Interior: Four Writers and the Rooms That Shaped Them* (London: Routledge, 2004); Kate Hill, *Museums & Biographies: Stories, Objects, Identities* (Woodbridge: Boydell & Brewer, 2012); Nicola Watson, *The Literary Tourist: Readers and Places in Romantic and Victorian Britain* (London: Palgrave, 2006); Nicola Watson, ed., *Literary Tourism and Nineteenth Century Culture* (London: Palgrave, 2009); Andrea Zemgulys, *Modernism and the Locations of Literary Heritage* (Cambridge: Cambridge University Press, 2018).

1. Moving House

1. Charles Lamb to Thomas Manning, 29 March 1809, in *The Letters of Charles and Mary Lamb*, ed. E. V. Lucas, 3 vols. (London: Dent, 1935), 2:69.

2. William Cowper to Walter Bagot, 17 November 1786, in *The Letters and Prose Writings of William Cowper*, ed. James King and Charles Ryskamp, 5 vols. (Oxford: Clarendon Press, 1979–86), 2:596.

3. House-moving has seldom been examined in literary and cultural criticism, but Louise DeSalvo gives the subject book-length consideration in *On Moving: A Writer's Meditation on New Houses, Old Haunts, and Finding Home Again* (New York: Bloomsbury, 2009). She reflects on her own experiences in relation to a rich gathering of modern writers "who elevated the act of moving . . . from the merely humdrum to one of the most significant acts . . . they would undertake." DeSalvo finds her chosen writers "invariably passionate" about matters of interior decoration and readily articulate about their house-moves. I remain intrigued by the degree to which moving has gone unrecorded. It has never become a popular subject for painting; there is no great literary tradition of removal writing. Few have used art to think through its chaos or to bestow some order. It remains one of the least examined of life events.

4. Robert Chambers, *The Book of Days*, 2 vols. (London: Chambers, 1863), 1:679.

5. *Jacob et Abel Grimmer: Catalogue Raisonné*, ed. Reine de Bertier de Sauvigny (Brussels: La Reanissance du Livre, 1991), 199.

6. Thomas Hardy, *Tess of the D'Urbervilles* (1891), ed. Tim Dolin (London: Penguin, 2003), chap. 51, p. 351.

7. Ford Madox Ford, *The Heart of the Country* (London: Alston Rivers, 1906), 60.

8. On furniture removal and hire, see Margaret Ponsonby, *Stories from Home: English Domestic Interiors, 1750–1850* (Aldershot: Ashgate, 2007), 57–59.

9. Museo Civico Ala Ponzone, Cremona.

10. William Cowper to John Newton, 17 November 1786, in *Letters*, 2:597.

11. Walter Scott to Lady Alvanley, 25 May 1812, in *Letters of Sir Walter Scott*, ed. H. J. C. Grierson, 10 vols. (London: Constable, 1932), 3:122.

12. Walter Scott to Daniel Terry, 9 June 1812, in *Letters*, 3:128.

13. Charles Lamb to Thomas Manning, 28 March 1809, in *Letters*, 2:69.

14. Charles Lamb to Thomas Hood, 18 September 1827, in *Letters*, 3:131. With thanks to Felicity James.

15. Lamb to Hood, 18 September 1827, in *Letters*, 3:131.

16. John Clare to John Taylor, 7 March 1831, in *The Letters of John Clare*, ed. Mark Storey (Oxford: Clarendon Press, 1985), 537.

17. John Clare to John Taylor, unsent, January 1832, in *Letters*, 561.

18. Clare to Taylor, unsent, January 1832, in *Letters*, 561.

19. John Clare to John Taylor, October 1831, in *Letters*, 549.

20. John Clare, "Reminiscences," in *Selected Poems*, ed. Jonathan Bate (London: Faber, 2003), 132–34.

21. John Clare, "To the Snipe," in *Selected Poems*, 207, discussed as one of Clare's "most searching poems about home and homelessness," by Mina Gorji in *John Clare and the Place of Poetry* (Liverpool: Liverpool University Press, 2008), 97–121, and as a pivotal poem of the move to Northborough by Jonathan Bate, *John Clare* (London: Picador, 2003), 390.

22. "The Flitting," in *John Clare: Major Works*, ed. Eric Robinson (Oxford: Oxford University Press, 2004), 250–56.

23. William Cowper to John Newton, 17 November 1786, in *Letters*, 2:597.

24. William Cowper, 3 May 1780, in *Letters*, 3:336.

25. William Cowper, "To my dearest cousin on her removal of us from Silver End to Weston," in *Poems*, 3:6.

26. William Cowper to John Newton, 16 December 1786, in *Letters*, 2:618–19.

27. Laurence Scott, *Picnic Comma Lightning* (London: William Heinemann, 2018), 245.

2. Built on Memory: Notes on the Later Life of a Roman House at the Edge of Empire

1. This chapter draws on two more detailed studies by the author: "La Maison de Vénus: Une residence de l'antiquité tardive?" in *Volubilis après Rome*, ed. Elizabeth Fentress and Hassan Limane, Les fouilles UCL/INSAP, 2000–2005 (Leiden: Brill, 2019), 38–50, and "Memories of Mauretania: A Late Antique Installation in the House of Venus, Volubilis," in *Beyond "Art Collections": Owning and Accumulating Objects from Greek Antiquity to the Early Modern Period*, ed. Gianfranco Adornato, Gabriella Cirucci, and Walter Cupper (Berlin: de Gruyter, 2019).

2. The excavation was published by Raymond Thouvenot, *Maisons de Volubilis: Le Palais dit de Gordien et la Maison à la mosaïque de Vénus* (Rabat: Publications de la Service d'Antiquités Marocaine, Fasc. 12, 1958).

3. This and the other bronzes from the House of Venus were studied by Christiane Boube-Piccot, *Les bronzes antiques du Maroc, I: Le Statuaire*, Études et travaux d'archéologie Marocaine IV (Rabat: Royaume du Maroc. Ministère d'État chargé des affaires culturelles et de l'enseignement original. Direction des monuments historiques et des antiquités, 1969); *II: Le Mobilier*, Études et travaux d'archéologie Marocaine V (Rabat: Royaume du Maroc. Ministère d'État chargé des affaires culturelles et de l'enseignement original. Direction des monuments historiques et des antiquités, 1975); *III: Les Chars at l'Attelage*, Études et travaux d'archéologie Marocaine VIII (Rabat: Royaume du Maroc. Ministère d'État chargé des affaires culturelles et de l'enseignement original. Direction des monuments historiques et des antiquités, 1980).

4. Raymond Thouvenot, "La Mosaique du 'Navigium veneris' à Volubilis (Maroc)," *Revue Archéologique* (1977): 37–52.

5. Roger Hanoune, "Trois pavements de la Maison de la Course de Chars à Carthage," *Mélanges de l'École française de Rome. Antiquités* 81 (1969): 219–56; Adeline Pichot, *Les monuments de spectacle dans les Maurétanies romaines*, Archéologie et Histoire Romaine, 22 (Montagnac: Éditions Monique Mergoil, 2012).

6. Jean Aymard, "A propos de la mosaïque au chat de Volubilis," *Latomus* 10 (1961): 52–71.

7. I am grateful to Ruth Pelling and Lisa Fentress for this observation, made during very recent work at Volubilis.

8. David Parrish, *The Season Mosaics of North Africa* (Rome: Giorgio Bretschneider, 1984), 234–236, no. 65, plates 86–87a.

9. Useful plans showing room functions appear in Martina Risse, ed., *Volubilis: Eine römische Stadt in Marokko von der Frühzeit bis in die islamische Periode* (Mainz: Philip von Zabern, 2001).

10. Yvon Thébert, "Private Life and Domestic Architecture in Roman Africa," in *A History of Private Life from Pagan Rome to Byzantium*, ed. Paul Veyne (Cambridge, MA: Belknap Press of Harvard University Press, 1987), 313–410. See also Kimberley Bowes, *Houses and Society in the Later Roman Empire* (London: Duckworth, 2010).

11. Jean-Pierre Darmon, *Nympharum Domus: Les pavements de la Maison des Nymphes à Néapolis (Nabeul, Tunisie) et leur lecture* (Leiden: Brill, 1980), unnumbered inserted plan.

12. Janine Lancha, *Mosaïque et culture dans l'occident romain, I–IV siècle* (Rome: L'Erma di Bretschneider, 1997), 164–68, no. 82, with plates LXXI–III.

13. Rita Paris, "Il pannello con Hylas e le Ninfe della Basilica di Giunio Basso," *Bollettino d'Archeologia* 1–2 (1990): 194–202; Katherine Dunbabin, *Mosaics of the Greek and Roman World* (Cambridge: Cambridge University Press, 1999), 264, plate 38. The villa mosaic of Hylas is displayed in Amphipolis Museum.

14. Philippe Leveau, "Les maisons nobles de Caesarea de Maurétanie," *Antiquités Africaines* 18 (1982): 109–65. For portraits of Juba II, see pp. 115 (La Maison des Iulii), 116 (La Maison de Domitia Lucilla), and 132 (La Maison de la mosaïque des travaux champêtres). On late antique collections of sculpture, see Lea M.

Stirling, *The Learned Collector: Mythological Statuettes and Classical Taste in Late Antique Gaul* (Ann Arbor: University of Michigan Press, 2005), esp. 188–89.

15. Duane W. Roller, *Cleopatra's Daughter: And Other Royal Women of the Augustan Era* (New York: Oxford University Press, 2018).

16. Michel Ponsich, "Techniques de la dégage, repose et restauration des mosaïques romaines," *Mélanges de l'École française de Rome. Antiquités* 72 (1960): 243–52.

17. Plutarch, *Life of Mark Antony* 28, 2.

18. Extracted from C. P. Cavafy, "Waiting for the Barbarians," in *C.P. Cavafy: Collected Poems*, trans. Edmund Keeley and Philip Sherrard (Princeton: Princeton University Press, 1975).

19. E. Fentress, "Un tremblement de terre?" in *Volubilis après Rome: Les fouilles UCL/INSAP 2000–2005*, ed. Elizabeth Fentress and Hassan Limane (Leiden: Brill, 2018), 57–59.

3. A House of Air

I am grateful for helpful advice for this essay from John Barnard, Alexandra Harris, Bernard and Heather O'Donoghue, and Jenny Uglow.

1. Penelope Fitzgerald, *Edward Burne-Jones* (1975) (London: Hamish Hamilton, 1989), 116–17; "Life at The Grange" (1998), in *A House of Air: Penelope Fitzgerald Selected Writings* (London: Flamingo, 2003), 133–42.

2. Penelope Fitzgerald, *Edward Burne-Jones*, 65; Virginia Woolf, "Sketch of the Past," in *Moments of Being* (1976) (London: Pimlico, 2002), 97–98.

3. Thomas Hood, "I Remember, I Remember" (1826); Alfred Tennyson, *In Memoriam A.H.H.* (1850).

4. Elizabeth Bowen, "Out of a Book," 1946, in *The Mulberry Tree: Writings of Elizabeth Bowen*, ed. Hermione Lee (1986) (London: Vintage, 1999), 50.

5. Woolf, "Sketch of the Past," 78–79.

6. John Keats, "This mortal body of a thousand days," *John Keats: The Complete Poems*, ed. John Barnard (Harmondsworth: Penguin, 1975), 263; Keats to J. H. Reynolds, 11 July 1818, *John Keats: Selected Letters*, ed. John Barnard (London: Penguin, 2014), 197; John Barnard, "Keats, Burns and Scotland: 'Blind in Mist'" (unpublished lecture, John Keats and Romantic Scotland Conference, University of St. Andrew's, 11–12 May 2018); Paul Strohm, *The Poet's Tale: Chaucer and the Year That Made the Canterbury Tales* (London: Profile Books, 2014).

7. Richard Holmes, *Footsteps: Adventures of a Romantic Biographer* (Harmondsworth: Penguin, 1986), 27.

8. "The Fulness of Life" (1893), Edith Wharton, *Collected Stories* (New York: Library of America, 2001), 2:14.

9. Hermione Lee, *Edith Wharton* (London: Chatto & Windus, 2007), 755.

10. Hermione Lee, *Virginia Woolf* (1996) (London: Vintage, 1997), 771, 318; "A Haunted House," 1921, in Virginia Woolf, *Selected Short Stories* (Harmondsworth: Penguin, 1993), 3–4, 107.

11. Penelope Fitzgerald to Tina Dooley, n.d., in Hermione Lee, *Penelope Fitzgerald: A Life* (London: Chatto & Windus, 2013), 427.

12. Penelope Fitzgerald, *Offshore* (1979) (London: Fourth Estate, 2013), 7, 18.

13. Elizabeth Bowen, *Bowen's Court and Seven Winters* (1942) (London: Virago, 1984), 459, introduction by Hermione Lee, xii; "The Big House," in *The Mulberry Tree: Writings of Elizabeth Bowen*, ed. Hermione Lee (1986) (London: Vintage, 1999), 28; https://farrelljane.wordpress.com/2014/10/16/what-remains-of-bowens-court.

6. Romantic Home

1. Samuel Taylor Coleridge, "Frost at Midnight," in *Coleridge's Poetry and Prose*, ed. Nicholas Halmi, Paul Magnuson, and Raimonda Modiano (New York: W. W. Norton, 2004), 121.

2. Samuel Taylor Coleridge, "Effusion XXXV, Composed August 20th, 1795, at Clevedon, Somersetshire" ["The Eolian Harp"], in *Coleridge's Poetry and Prose*, 17.

3. Samuel Taylor Coleridge, *The Friend: A Literary, Moral, and Political Weekly Paper* 11, 26 October 1809 (Penrith), 161.

4. William Cowper, *The Task* 4.88–89, in *The Task and Other Poems*, ed. James Sambrook (London: Longman, 1994), 144.

5. William Cowper to the Rev. William Unwin, 8 June 1783, in *The Letters and Prose Writings of William Cowper*, ed. James King and Charles Ryskamp, 5 vols. (Oxford: Clarendon Press, 1979–86), 2:139.

6. Samuel Taylor Coleridge, "Reflections on Having Left a Place of Retirement," in *Coleridge's Poetry and Prose*, 52–54.

7. Samuel Taylor Coleridge to Thomas Poole, November 1796, in *Collected Letters of Samuel Taylor Coleridge*, ed. Earl Leslie Griggs (Oxford: Clarendon Press, 1956), 1:275.

8. Samuel Taylor Coleridge to John Thelwall, 6 February 1797, in *Letters*, 1:308.

9. William Wordsworth, "Lines Written a Few Miles above Tintern Abbey," in *The Major Works*, ed. Stephen Gill (Oxford: Oxford University Press, 2008), 135.

10. See Coleridge's letter to Wordsworth, describing the project of *The Recluse*, in *Letters*, ed. Griggs, 1:527.

11. William Wordsworth, "Home at Grasmere," in *Major Works*, 175. Hereafter, page numbers in the text.

12. Dorothy Wordsworth to Jane Pollard, 2 September 1795, in *The Letters of William and Dorothy Wordsworth, Vol. 1: The Early Years: 1787–1805*, ed. Ernest De Selincourt and Chester L. Shaver (Oxford: Clarendon Press, 1967), 146.

13. Stopford A. Brooke, *Dove Cottage: Wordsworth's Home from 1800–1808* (London: Macmillan, 1895), 64.

14. William Wordsworth to Samuel Taylor Coleridge, 24 December 1799, in *Letters*, 1:274–75.

15. Thomas De Quincey, *Recollections of the Lakes and the Lake Poets: Coleridge, Wordsworth, and Southey* (1868; Cambridge: Cambridge University Press, reprinted 2013), 132.

16. Brooke, *Dove Cottage*, 12, 60.

17. https://wordsworth.org.uk/.

18. William to Dorothy Wordsworth, late 1800 [fragment], *Letters*, 1:282.

19. Hartley Coleridge, "A Lonely Wanderer upon Earth Am I," in *The Complete Poetical Works of Hartley Coleridge*, ed. Ramsay Colles (London: George Routledge and Sons, 1908), 114.

20. See the excellent discussion of Wordsworthian pilgrimage in *Dove Cottage*, by Stephen Hebron (Grasmere: Wordsworth Trust, 2009).

21. William Wordsworth, "I Wandered Lonely as a Cloud," in *The Golden Treasury* by Francis T. Palgrave (London: Macmillan, 1903), 291.

7. At Home with Tennyson

1. [F. G. Kitton], "Celebrities of the Day—Lord Tennyson, Poet Laureate," *The Graphic*, 22 March 1884, n.p.

2. All quotations from Tennyson's poetry are taken from Christopher Ricks, ed., *The Poems of Tennyson*, 3 vols. (Harlow: Longman, 1987).

3. Grant Allen, "Tennyson's Homes at Aldworth and Farringford," *English Illustrated Magazine* 10 (December 1892).

4. Charlotte Boyce, "At Home with Tennyson: Virtual Literary Tourism and the Commodification of Celebrity in the Periodical Press," in Charlotte Boyce, Páraic Finnerty, and Anne-Marie Millim, *Victorian Celebrity Culture and Tennyson's Circle* (Basingstoke: Palgrave Macmillan, 2013), 20.

5. See Nicola J. Watson, ed., *Literary Tourism and Nineteenth-Century Culture* (Basingstoke: Palgrave Macmillan, 2009).

6. Hallam Tennyson, *Alfred, Lord Tennyson: A Memoir by His Son*, 2 vols. (London: Macmillan, 1897), 2:25, 47.

7. Allison Lockwood, *Passionate Pilgrims: The American Traveller in Great Britain, 1800–1914* (New York: Cornwall Books, 1981), 350.

8. Norman Page, ed., *Tennyson: Interviews and Recollections* (Basingstoke: Palgrave Macmillan, 1983), 31, 60.

9. J. W. Croker, review of Tennyson's *Poems* (1832), *Quarterly Review* (April 1833): 92.

10. Herbert F. Tucker, "House Arrest: The Domestication of English Poetry in the 1820s," *New Literary History* 25, no. 3 (Summer 1994): 593.

11. Croker, review, 95.

8. Chartwell: Winston Churchill's Dream House

1. S. Buczacki, *Churchill & Chartwell: The Untold Story of Churchill's Houses and Gardens* (London: Frances Lincoln, 2007), 104.

2. W. S. Churchill, *Thoughts and Adventures: Churchill Reflects on Spies, Cartoons, Flying, and the Future* (London: Thornton Butterworth, 1932), 154–213.

3. Buczacki, *Churchill & Chartwell*, 67–76, 83–88.

4. A. Roberts, *Churchill: Walking with Destiny* (London: Allen Lane, 2018), 280.

5. M. Soames, ed., *Speaking for Themselves: The Personal Letters of Winston and Clementine Churchill* (London: Doubleday, 1999), 224.

6. Buczacki, *Churchill & Chartwell*, 115.

7. Roberts, *Churchill*, 298–301.

8. M. Soames, *Clementine Churchill: The Biography of a Marriage* (Boston: Houghton Mifflin, 1979), 284–88; S. Purnell, *First Lady: The Life and Wars of Clementine Churchill* (London: Aurum Press, 2015), 171.

9. D. Lough, *No More Champagne: Churchill and His Money* (London: Picador, 2015), 194–200, 239–65; D. Cannadine, *Aspects of Aristocracy: Grandeur and Decline in Modern Britain* (New Haven: Yale University Press, 1994), 146.

10. W. S. Churchill, *My Early Life: A Roving Commission* (New York: Charles Scribner's Sons, 1930), 5; Roberts, *Churchill*, 23–24.

11. Churchill, *My Early Life*, 72–73; Roberts, *Churchill*, 15–16, 21, 24, 74.

12. R. S. Churchill, *Winston S. Churchill*, vol. 1, *Youth, 1874–1900* (London: Heinemann, 1966), 196–98.

13. W. S. Churchill, *Marlborough: His Life and Times*, 2 vols. (Chicago: University of Chicago Press, 2002), 1:33.

14. V. Bonham Carter, *Winston Churchill as I Knew Him* (London: Eyre and Spottiswoode, 1965), 27.

15. Churchill, *My Early Life*, 62.

16. Roberts, *Churchill*, 81; Cannadine, *Aspects of Aristocracy*, 137–38.

17. Churchill, *Thoughts and Adventures*, 31–32; R. F. Foster, *Lord Randolph Churchill: A Political Life* (Oxford: Oxford University Press, 1981), 382–403.

18. P. Johnson, *Churchill* (New York: Viking, 2009), 26.

19. M. Gilbert, *Winston S. Churchill*, vol. 5, *1922–1939* (London: Heinemann, 1976), 59; D. Cannadine, *Heroic Chancellor: Winston Churchill and the University of Bristol, 1929–65* (London: Institute of Historical Research, 2016), 20.

20. R. Jenkins, *Churchill* (London: Macmillan, 2001), 10.

21. Lough, *No More Champagne*, 298–347, 322–33, 381–82.

22. Buczacki, *Churchill & Chartwell*, 258–59.

23. Soames, *Clementine Churchill*, 562–63, 621–22; I. Berlin, *Mr. Churchill in 1940* (London: John Murray, [1949]), 39.

24. Lough, *No More Champagne*, 341–42, 357–58.

25. Roberts, *Churchill*, 904–6; M. Gilbert, *Winston S. Churchill*, vol. 8, *"Never Despair," 1945–1965* (London: Heinemann, 1988), 364–72 for the full text.

26. Roberts, *Churchill*, 906, 936; J. R. Colville, *The Fringes of Power: 10 Downing Street Diaries, 1939–1955* (London: Hodder, 1986), 661.

27. Soames, *Clementine Churchill*, 660–62, 671–72; Lough, *No More Champagne*, 407.

9. The Quangle Wangle's Hat: Edward Lear in the Villa Emily, San Remo

1. "a stone terrace." Edward Lear to Thomas Woolner, 1 May 1870, in *Selected Letters of Edward Lear*, ed. Vivien Noakes (Oxford: Clarendon Press, 1988), 216.

2. "if you are absolutely alone." E. L. to Chichester Fortescue, 1 May 1859, in *Letters of Edward Lear to Chichester Fortescue* . . . , ed. Lady Strachey (London: T. Fisher Unwin, 1907), 136.

3. "there is great charm," Edward Lear Diaries, 21 February 1871 (London: T. Fisher Unwin, 1907).

4. "singularly good," Lear Diaries, 1858–1888 (MS Eng 797.3), 10 February 1872.

5. "worked hard," diary, 20 April 1870.

6. "my only remaining fig tree." E. L. to Lady Wyatt, 11 December 1870, Morgan Library, MA 6421, *Selected Letters*, 225.

7. "working like slaves." E. L. to Lady Wyatt, in *Selected Letters*, 226.

8. "so, exactly a year," diary, 26 March 1871.

9. "Rose at 6.30," diary, 31 March 1871.

10. "I never before had." E. L. to Lady Waldegrave, 22 January 1871, in *Later Letters of Edward Lear*, ed. Lady Strachey (London: T. Fisher Unwin, 1911), 133.

11. "for we are all." E. L. to Fortescue, 28 February 1872, in *Later Letters* 145.

12. "Many little birds," diary, 8 April 1871.

13. "Going up & down stairs." E. L. to Fortescue, 25 December 1871, in *Later Letters*, 121.

14. "Too late," diary, 8 December 1875; "Jobiska," diary, 30 April 1876; "Quangle Wangle Quee," diary, 9 November 1875.

15. Vivien Noakes notes that Lear made a copy of "Mr and Mrs Discobbolos" on 24 December 1871. See Vivien Noakes, ed., *Edward Lear: The Complete Verse and other Nonsense* (London: Penguin Books, 2001), 521.

16. "parble massage." E. L. to Lady Wyatt, 11 December 1870, in *Selected Letters*, 226.

17. "The Quangle Wangle's Hat," written for Arthur Buchanan, 26–27 May 1872, copied for Gertrude Lushington, 8 June 1872.

18. "After which I quite," diary, 24 August 1876.

19. "Wrote to F. Lushington," diary, 27 August 1876.

20. "altogether I should be." E. L. to Chichester Fortescue, 28 October 1878, in *Later Letters*, 211.

21. "unless the Fishes." E. L. to Emily Tennyson, 16 February 1880, Tennyson Research Centre, Lincoln, TRC/Letters 5538.

22. "*the walls*," diary, 26 February 1880.

10. Benjamin Britten in Aldeburgh

1. Benjamin Britten, "Freedom of Borough of Aldeburgh," draft of a speech given on 22 October 1962, reproduced in Paul Kildea, *Britten on Music* (Oxford: Oxford University Press, 2008), 217.

2. In July 1964 Britten was the recipient of the inaugural Robert O. Anderson Aspen Award in the Humanities. His speech upon receiving the award is reproduced in Kildea, *Britten on Music* and in Peter Wiegold and Ghislaine Kenyon, eds., *Beyond Britten: The Composer and the Community* (Suffolk: Boydell, 2015).

3. Quotes from *Letters from a Life: Selected Letters and Diaries of Benjamin Britten*, vol. 2: 1939–1945, ed. Donald Mitchell and Philip Reed (London: Faber and Faber, 1991), 707, 708, 690.

4. For an account of this household, see Sherill Tippins, *February House: The Story of W. H. Auden, Carson McCullers, Jane and Paul Bowles, Benjamin Britten, and Gypsy Rose Lee, Under One Roof in Brooklyn* (New York: Simon & Schuster, 2005).

5. Benjamin Britten to Piers Dunkerley, 23 December 1948, reproduced in *Letters from a Life: Selected Letters and Diaries of Benjamin Britten*, vol. 3: *1946–1951*, ed. Donald Mitchell, Philip Reed, and Mervyn Cooke (London: Faber and Faber, 2004), 470.

6. *The Composer Speaks*, BBC radio, 7 July 1957, reproduced in Kildea, *Britten on Music*, 146.

7. Acceptance speech, given on 28 July 1951, reproduced in Kildea, *Britten on Music*, 108.

8. See the Britten-Pears Foundation film *Work of the Week 38: Peter Grimes*, https://brittenpears.org/explore/benjamin-britten/music/work-of-the-week/38-peter-grimes/.

9. George Crabbe, *The Borough* (Kindle edition, 2011), 210.

10. Benjamin Britten to Ralph Hawkes, 9 September 1947, reproduced in *Letters from a Life*, 3:324.

11. Benjamin Britten to Elizabeth Mayer, 4 February 1948, reproduced in *Letters from a Life*, 3:357.

12. Britten to Mayer, 4 November 1948, reproduced in *Letters from a Life*, 3:455. Emphasis added.

13. Note to letter 777 in *Letters from a Life: The Selected Letters of Benjamin Britten*, vol. 4: *1952–1957*, ed. Philip Reed, Mervyn Cooke, and Donald Mitchell (Suffolk: Boydell, 2008), 179.

14. Note to letter 590 in *Letters from a Life*, 3:423.

15. From an interview in Tony Palmer's television documentary *A Time There Was* (London Weekend Television, 1980).

16. *Imogen Holst: A Life in Music*, ed. Christopher Grogan (Suffolk: Boydell, 2007), 197.

17. Benjamin Britten to Elizabeth Mayer, 14 November 1957, reproduced in *Letters from a Life*, 4:577.

18. Colin Graham, "Staging First Productions 3," in *The Operas of Benjamin Britten*, ed. David Herbert (London: Hamish Hamilton, 1979), 44.

19. Kildea, *Britten on Music*, 135. These evocative "night pieces" include *Nocturne* (1958), *A Midsummer Night's Dream* (1960), *Nocturnal* (1963), and *Notturno, or Night Piece* (1963).

20. Benjamin Britten, "A New Britten Opera," originally published in the *Observer*, 5 June 1960, reproduced in Kildea, *Britten on Music*, 189.

21. W. H. Auden to Britten, 31 January 1942, reproduced in *Letters from a Life*, 2:1016.

22. Pears to Britten, 16 February 1959, reproduced in *My Beloved Man*, 240.

23. Britten to Pears, 28 October 1948, reproduced in *My Beloved Man*, 120.

24. Britten, "Freedom of Borough of Aldeburgh," 217.

11. 77 St. Mark's Place

1. Auden had spent the summer in Germany, part of the U.S. Strategic Bombing Survey. He took the Seventh Avenue property in the autumn of 1951. Humphrey Carpenter, *W. H. Auden: A Biography* (London: Allen and Unwin, 1981), 373

2. To Alan Collins, 23 February 1967, Carpenter, *W. H. Auden*, 376.

3. "I count myself a man of letters / Who writes, or hopes to, for his betters": "Doggerel by a Senior Citizen."

4. W. H. Auden, *Prose*, ed. Edward Mendelson, 6 vols. (Princeton: Princeton University Press, 1996–2015), vol. iv, 451.

5. Charles H. Miller, *Auden: An American Friendship* (New York: Paragon House, 1989), 99.

6. Stephen Spender, *World Within World* (London: Hamish Hamilton, 1951), 298.

7. Margaret Gardiner, "Auden: A Memoir," *New Review* 3, no. 28 (July 1976): 15.

8. Tom Driberg's confident claim that the house had been lived in by Henry James appears quite without foundation: *Ruling Passions* (London: Jonathan Cape, 1977), 58.

9. Carpenter, *W. H. Auden*, 376; Miller, *Auden*, 107.

10. Miller, *Auden* 100–101.

11. "The indispensable presence," in *W. H. Auden: A Tribute*, ed. Stephen Spender (London: Weidenfeld and Nicolson, 1975), 124.

12. Robert Craft, *Stravinsky: Chronicle of a Friendship, 1948–1971* (London: Gollancz, 1972), 39–40. The remark is also recorded in Edmund Wilson, *The Fifties: From the Notebooks and Diaries of the Period* (London: Macmillan, 1986), 292.

13. Larry Rivers, with Arnold Weinstein, *What Did I Do? The Unauthorized Autobiography* (New York: Aaron Asher Books, 1992), 110.

14. W. H. Auden, *Collected Poems*, ed. Edward Mendelson (London: Faber, 1991), 340.

15. V. S. Yanovsky, "W. H. Auden," *Antæus* 19 (Autumn 1975): 127.

16. Louis Kronenberger, "A friendship revisited": *Tribute*, 157.

17. Carpenter, *W. H. Auden*, 303–6.

18. In interview: *Paris Review* 57 (Spring 1974).

19. Yanovsky, "W. H. Auden," 110.

20. The recollection of Peter Komadina: Dorothy J. Farnan, *Auden in Love* (New York: Simon and Schuster, 1984), 203. The schedule is reported differently by different authorities. Auden himself told another young admirer that work stopped ordinarily at 5:30: Howard Griffin, *Conversations with Auden*, ed. Donald Allen (San Francisco: Grey Fox Press, 1981), 107.

21. Orlan Fox, "Friday nights": *Tribute*, 179.

22. Fox, "Friday nights," 173.

23. Yanovsky, "W. H. Auden," 120.

24. Craft, "The poet and the rake," 155.

25. Chester Kallman, "From the Alexandrians": *For W. H. Auden: February 21, 1972*, ed. Peter H. Salus and Paul B. Taylor (New York: Random House, 1972), 49.

26. Carpenter, *W. H. Auden*, 12.

27. Fox, "Friday nights," 179.

28. Craft, "The poet and the rake": *Tribute*, 155.
29. Carpenter, *W. H. Auden*, 408.
30. Yanovsky, "W. H. Auden," 120.
31. Gardiner, "Auden: A Memoir," 19.
32. Hannah Arendt, "Remembering W. H. Auden": *Tribute*, 182.
33. "As I walked out one evening": *Collected Poems*, 135.
34. Arendt, "Remembering W. H. Auden," 182–83.
35. Wilson, *The Fifties*, 294.
36. Auden, *Prose*, iv.503.
37. "Plains": *Complete Poems*, 565.
38. Wilson, *The Fifties*, 292.

12. Samuel Johnson's Houses

1. Max Beerbohn, "In the Shades" [inscription on cartoon of Johnson and Boswell at Gough Square], 1915. See also James Boswell, *Life of Johnson*, ed. R. W. Chapman and Pat Rogers (Oxford: Oxford World's Classics, 2008), 1279.
2. John Milton, *The Major Works*, ed. Stephen Orgel and Jonathan Goldsberg (Oxford: Oxford University Press, 1991), 240.
3. Samuel Johnson, *The Lives of the Most Eminent English Poets*, ed. Roger Londsdale, 4 vols. (Oxford: Clarendon Press, 2006), 1:262.
4. Johnson, *Lives*, 1:249.
5. Samuel Johnson, *The Rambler* 60 (13 October 1750), in *The Yale Edition of the Works of Samuel Johnson*, vol. 3, ed. W. J. Bate and Albrecht B. Strauss (New Haven: Yale University Press, 1969), 321.
6. Johnson, *The Rambler*, 322.
7. Hester Lynch Piozzi, *Anecdotes of the Late Samuel Johnson, LL.D. during the Last Twenty Years of His Life*, ed. Arthur Sherbo (London: Oxford University Press, 1974), 59.
8. Piozzi, *Anecdotes*, 102.
9. Piozzi, *Anecdotes*, 89.
10. Piozzi, *Anecdotes*, 131.
11. Piozzi, *Anecdotes*, 156.
12. Piozzi, *Anecdotes*, 101.
13. Piozzi, *Anecdotes*, 156.
14. Piozzi, *Anecdotes*, 140.
15. Johnson, *Lives*, 4:55.
16. Johnson, *Lives*, 4:59
17. Piozzi, *Anecdotes*, 140–41.
18. Boswell, *Life of Johnson*, 1333.
19. Boswell, *Life of Johnson*, 81.
20. Boswell, *Life of Johnson*, 1006–7.
21. Boswell, *Life of Johnson*, 308–9.
22. Johnson, *Lives*, 1:274.

14. At Home with the Disraelis

1. Philip Rose Memorandum, Dep. Hughenden 312/3, fol. 128, Bodleian Library, University of Oxford (National Trust).

2. Mary Anne Disraeli to Philip Rose, 12 August 1862, Dep. Hughenden 271/2, fols. 269–70.

3. Benjamin Disraeli to Sarah Brydges Willyams, 21 August 1862 in *The Letters of Benjamin Disraeli*, ed. M. G. Wiebe et al., 10 vols. (Toronto: University of Toronto Press, 1982–2014), 8:202–3.

4. Benjamin Disraeli to Mary Anne Disraeli, 6 September 1848, in *Letters of Benjamin Disraeli*, 5:81.

5. Benjamin Disraeli to Mary Anne Disraeli, 18 October1848, in *Letters of Benjamin Disraeli*, 5:95.

6. Constance Battersea, *Reminiscences* (London: Macmillan, 1922), 234–35.

7. Benjamin Disraeli to Sarah Brydges Willyams, 15 September 1863, in *Letters of Benjamin Disraeli*, 8:207–8.

8. Benjamin Disraeli to Sarah Disraeli, 4 November 1849, in *Letters of Benjamin Disraeli*, 5:248–49.

9. Ronald Gower, *My Reminiscences* (London: Kegan Paul, 1885), 298.

10. Benjamin Disraeli to Montagu Corry, 14 September 1873, Dep. Hughenden 95/3, fols. 60–62.

11. Disraeli to Corry, 14 September 1873.

15. H. G. Wells at Uppark

1. H. G. Wells, *Experiment in Autobiography*, vol. 1 (London: Gollancz, 1934), 136.

2. Wells, *Experiment*, 109.

3. H. G. Wells, *A Modern Utopia* (London: Collins, 1905), 71, 180.

4. Quoted in Pamela Sambrook, *Keeping Their Place: Domestic Service in the Country House, 1700–1920* (Thrupp: Sutton Publishing, 2005), 186.

5. Wells, *Experiment*, 365.

6. H. G. Wells, *Tono-Bungay* (London: Literary Press, 1909), 14.

7. Vita Sackville-West, *The Edwardians* (London: Vintage, 2016).

8. Anthony West, "My Father's Debts of Love," *Observer*, 11 January 1976, 17.

9. Margaret Meade-Fetherstonhaugh and Oliver Warner, *Uppark and Its People* (1964; London: National Trust, 1995), 108.

10. Meade-Fetherstonhaugh and Warner, *Uppark and Its People*, 6.

16. The Fear of Houses

1. Each has been edited down from a recorded interview. When possible (i.e., if the person hasn't in the meantime disappeared from Eastbourne or stopped using the day centre) the resulting copy has been shown to the interviewee for approval.

17. When There Is No House to Visit:
A Migrant Writer's Sites

1.   Flora Veit-Wild, ed., *Dambudzo Marechera: A Sourcebook on His Life and World*, 2nd ed. (Trenton, NJ: Africa World Press, 2002), 247.
2.   Veit-Wild, *Dambudzo Marechera*, 221.
3.   Julie Cairnie and Dobrota Pucherova, eds., *Moving Spirit: The Legacy of Dambudzo Marechera in the 21st Century* (Zurich: Lit Verlag, 2012), 32, 69.
4.   James Currey, *Africa Writes Back* (Oxford: James Currey, 2008), 292.
5.   Currey, *Africa Writes Back*, 279–95.
6.   Cairnie and Pucherova, *Moving Spirit*, 29.
7.   Will Stone, "Dress Up as a Georgian!" *TLS*, 23 March 2018, 17.
8.   J. M. Coetzee, *Youth* (London: Secker, 2002), 63; Janet Frame, *Towards Another Summer* (London: Virago, 2008), 23.

18. "A Place One Can Go Mad In":
Ivor Gurney, Dwelling in Shadows

1.   Including around eight voluntary boarders. The alternatives, the nearby Old County and City Lunatic Asylum at Wotton, held up to 1,200 patients.
2.   See Peter Barham, *Forgotten Lunatics of the Great War* (New Haven: Yale University Press, 2007), 223, 256.
3.   Barnwood was visited by the superintendent of York's forward-looking asylum The Retreat in 1896, and he recorded his impression of its décor.
4.   Erving Goffman, *Asylums: Essays on the Condition of the Social Situation of Mental Patients and Other Inmates* (New York: Anchor Books, 1961), 128.
5.   Edward Thomas, "Lights Out," first published in *Poems* (London: Selwyn and Blount, 1917), 59.
6.   Walter Benjamin, "The Storyteller," in *Illuminations*, ed. Hannah Arendt, trans. Harry Zohn (New York: Schocken, 1969), 84.
7.   By Vera Brittain, Edmund Blunden, and Robert Graves, respectively.
8.   Adeline Vaughan Williams to Marion Scott, quoted in Michael Hurd, *The Ordeal of Ivor Gurney* (London: Faber and Faber, 2011), original letter written on a Wednesday, [March] 1927, http://vaughanwilliams.uk/letter/vwl3251.
9.   The opening lines of "In Flanders," F. W. Harvey, first published in trench journal *The Fifth Gloucester Gazette*, then in *A Gloucestershire Lad at Home* (London: Sidgwick and Jackson, 1916), xv.
10. 1 August 1916, Gurney Archive, ref: G.41.33, also in *Ivor Gurney: Collected Letters*, ed. R. K. R. Thornton (Manchester: Carcanet Press, 1990), 126.
11. "In my deep heart for ever goes on your daily being / And uses consecrate" (lines 15–16 of "Strange Service," 1916), first published in Gurney's first poetry collection, *Severn and Somme* (London: Sidgwick and Jackson, 1917).

12. "Cory" was Gloucestershire dialect for heart, or core, perhaps deriving from the French "coeur." "Cory" is either trench French or joke Latin for "heart."

13. 1 August 1916, Gurney Archive, ref: G.41.33, also in *Ivor Gurney: Collected Letters*, ed. R. K. R. Thornton (Manchester: Carcanet Press, 1990), 126.

14. "Strange Service," lines 13–14.

20. "When All Is Ruin Once Again": Thoor Ballylee

1. W. B. Yeats, *Autobiographies* (London: Macmillan, 1955), 478.

2. A letter from Oliver Gogarty to Horace Reynolds, 15 June 1936 (Harvard), refers to Yeats's "jealousy of the 'household of continuance'": see my *W. B. Yeats: A Life*, vol. 1, *The Apprentice Mage, 1865–1914* (Oxford: Oxford University Press, 1997), 168.

3. Yeats, *Autobiographies*, 389, 391.

4. "Dust Hath Closed Helen's Eye," first printed in *The Dome*, October 1899, and included in *The Celtic Twilight* (rev. ed., 1902). See W. B. Yeats, *Mythologies*, ed. Warwick Gould and Deirdre Toomey (London: Macmillan, 2005), 14.

5. See my *W. B. Yeats: A Life*, vol. 2, *The Arch-Poet, 1915–1939* (Oxford: Oxford University Press, 2003), 84.

6. W. B. Yeats to John Quinn, 23 July 1918, in *The Letters of W. B. Yeats*, ed. Allan Wade (London: Macmillan, 1954), 651.

7. W. B. Yeats to John Butler Yeats, 16 July 1919, John Butler Yeats Collection, Boston College.

8. W. B. Yeats to George Yeats, 8 April 1924, in *W. B. Yeats and George Yeats: The Letters*, ed. Ann Saddlemyer (Oxford: Oxford University Press, 2011), 120–21.

9. Ann Saddlemyer, *Becoming George: The Life of Mrs. W. B. Yeats* (Oxford: Oxford University Press, 2002), 407.

10. Yeats, *Autobiographies*, 579–80.

11. See Theodore Ziolkowski, *The View from the Tower: Origins of an Anti-modernist Image* (Princeton: Princeton University Press, 1993), chap. 3.

12. Virginia Moore, *The Unicorn: W. B. Yeats's Search for Reality* (London: Macmillan, 1954), 282, quoted in Mary Hanley and Liam Miller, *Thoor Ballylee: Home of William Butler Yeats* (Dublin: Dolmen Press, 1977), 26.

13. Seamus Heaney, *Finders Keepers: Selected Prose, 1971–2001* (London: Faber and Faber, 2002), 234.

21. W. H. Auden in Austria: "Publicly Private" and Globally Local

1. Papers of Stephen Spender, MS. Spender 174, undated notebook, Bodleian Library, University of Oxford, copyright © Stephen Spender. Material from the Spender Archive reproduced by permission of the Curtis Brown Group Ltd. on behalf of the Stephen Spender Estate and the Bodleian Libraries

2. Stephen Spender, "Auden's Funeral," in *New Collected Poems*, ed. Michael Brett (London: Faber and Faber, 2004), 325.

3. Stephen Spender, "Valediction," in *W. H. Auden: A Tribute*, ed. Stephen Spender (London: Weidenfeld & Nicolson, 1975), 245.

4. Spender, "Auden's Funeral," 326.

5. Peter Edgerly Firchow, *W. H. Auden: Contexts for Poetry* (Newark: University of Delaware Press, 2002), 210.

6. W. H. Auden, "Thanksgiving for a Habitat," in *Collected Poems*, ed. Edward Mendelson (London: Faber and Faber, 1994), 689.

7. Spender, "Valediction," 245.

8. Stephen Spender, "Wystan Hugh Auden, 1907–1973," *Harvard Advocate* 108, no. 2–3 (1973): 60.

9. Firchow, *W. H. Auden*, 214.

10. Auden, "Thanksgiving for a Habitat," 689.

11. See, for instance, Firchow, *W. H. Auden*, 212–13; Edward Mendelson, *Later Auden* (London: Faber and Faber, 1999), 417.

12. See Humphrey Carpenter, *W. H. Auden: A Biography* (London: Unwin, 1983), 41; Helmut Neundlinger, "'Reinventing Himself as a European': Auden, das Haus und die Welt," in *Thanksgiving for a Habitat: W. H. Auden in Kirchstetten*, ed. Helmut Neundlinger (St. Pölten: Literaturedition Niederösterreich, 2018), 115–16.

13. Firchow, *W. H. Auden*, 215.

14. Auden, "Thanksgiving for a Habitat," 690–91.

15. Timo Frühwirth, "An Austrian Auden: A Media Construction Story," *Life Writing* 16, no. 2 (2019): 161.

16. Christopher Burstall, "Portrait Gallery," *Sunday Times Magazine*, 21 November 1965, 22, 24.

17. Mendelson, *Later Auden*, xviii.

18. W. H. Auden, "Whitsunday in Kirchstetten," in *Collected Poems*, ed. Edward Mendelson (London: Faber and Faber, 1994), 744.

19. Edward Mendelson, "The European Auden," in *The Cambridge Companion to W. H. Auden*, ed. Stan Smith (Cambridge: Cambridge University Press, 2005), 64.

20. Neundlinger, "'Reinventing Himself as a European,'" 119 (my translation).

21. W. H. Auden, "The Cave of Making," in *Collected Poems*, ed. Edward Mendelson (London: Faber and Faber, 1994), 691.

22. Firchow, *W. H. Auden*, 229.

23. Auden, "The Cave of Making," 691.

24. Alison Booth, *Homes and Haunts: Touring Writers' Shrines and Countries* (Oxford: Oxford University Press, 2016), 54.

25. Stella Musulin, "Auden in Kirchstetten," in *W. H. Auden: "In Solitude, for Company"—W. H. Auden after 1940, Unpublished Prose and Recent Criticism*, ed. Katherine Bucknell and Nicholas Jenkins (Oxford: Clarendon Press, 1995), 212. See also Thekla Clark, *Wystan and Chester: A Personal Memoir of W. H. Auden and Chester Kallman* (London: Faber and Faber, 1995).

26. See Booth, *Homes and Haunts*, 1.

27. Auden, "The Cave of Making," 691.

28. Spender, "Auden's Funeral," 327.

29. Spender, "Auden's Funeral," 325, 327.

30. Spender, "Auden's Funeral," 325, 327; Papers of Stephen Spender, MS. Spender 105.

22. John Soane and House Autobiography

1. Abraham Booth, *The Stranger's Intellectual Guide to London for 1839–40* (London: Hooper, 1838).

2. Arthur T. Bolton, ed., *The Portrait of Sir John Soane, R.A.* (London: Sir John Soane's Museum Publication, 1927), 174–75.

3. Helen Dorey, introduction to *Crude Hints towards an History of My House in Lincoln's Inn Fields* (Oxford: Archaeopress, 2015), 5; see also Gillian Darley, *John Soane: An Accidental Romantic* (New Haven: Yale University Press, 1999), 215.

4. Anna Jameson, *Handbook to the Public Galleries of Art in and near London* (London: John Murray, 1842), 2:549.

5. Bolton, *The Portrait of Sir John Soane, R.A.,* 529 (Disraeli's letter dated 14 August 1836).

6. Peter Conrad, *The Victorian Treasure-house* (London: Collins, 1973), 11.

7. Jameson, *Handbook to the Public Galleries of Art*, 2:545; G. F. Waagen, *Works of Art and Artists in England* (London: John Murray, 1838), 2:181; Augustus Hare, *Walks in London* (London: Daldy, Isbister, 1878) 1:87.

8. Jameson, *Handbook to the Public Galleries of Art*, 2:548.

9. Jameson, *Handbook to the Public Galleries of Art*, 2:549.

10. All the quotes from the Henry James novella fall within section VIII, pp. 79–89, of Project Gutenberg EBook, including *A London Life*; *The Patagonia*; *The Liar*; *Mrs. Temperly* released in 2008.

11. Transcription of curator's report, kindly supplied by Susan Palmer, archivist.

12. John Summerson, *Sir John Soane* (London: Art and Technics, 1952), 43.

13. Gillian Darley and David McKie, *Ian Nairn: Words in Place* (Nottingham: Five Leaves Publications, 2013), 18–20.

14. Ian Nairn, *Nairn's London* (London: Penguin, 1966; reissued 2014), 110–11.

23. Ainola: Music and Silence

This essay is printed by kind permission of United Agents LLP on behalf of Julian Barnes.

Index